# WORDS IN THE WIND

Further Zen Ramblings from the Internet

# SCOTT SHAW

Buddha Rose Publications

Words in the Wind
Copyright ©2014
By Scott Shaw
All Rights Reserved
www.scottshaw.com

No part of this manuscript may be reproduced in any manner without the expressed written permission of the author or the publishing company.

Rear cover photograph of Scott Shaw by Hae Won Shin.
Copyright © 2014

First Edition 2014

ISBN: 1-877792-78-0
ISBN 13: 9781877792786

Library of Congress Control Number: 2014913313

Printed in the United States of America

10 9 8 7 6 5 4 3 2 1

# WORDS IN THE WIND

# Intro.

Well, here it is, *The Scott Shaw Zen Blog 3.5,* originally written for your reading pleasure on the World Wide Web. All of the writings presented in this book were written between March and July of 2014.

As was the case with the previously two published volumes based upon *The Scott Shaw Zen Blog;* entitled: *Scribbles on the Restroom Wall* and *The Chronicles: Zen Ramblings from the Internet,* this volume is presented exactly as it was viewed on scottshaw.com, with no rewriting, punctuation, or typo corrections. From this, we hope you will receive the original reading experience.

What is different with this volume, compared to the previous two books based upon, *The Scott Shaw Zen Blog,* is that the date and time is listed as to when the blog was originally posted. Also, the blog is presented from end to beginning as opposed to the previous two blog-based books that were presented from beginning to end. With this, we hope to present a transcendence back through time as opposed to an evolving evolution. In addition, we left out the traditional *Table of Contents* and the manuscript is presented in an unpaginated format. Thus, hopefully, leaving this volume as a much more free-flowing reading experience.

Okay, there's the information and the definitions. Read on... We hope you enjoy it. And, sooner or later, we are sure, when he is inspired to do so, Scott Shaw will again enter the realm of the blogosphere and a new *Scott Shaw Zen Blog* will be born and presented upon the World Wide Web.

# THE SCOTT SHAW ZEN BLOG 3.5

# When the Words Are Written

18/Jul/2014 09:08 AM

I believe that it is very interesting to place the context of, when the words were written, into the life of an author when looking at their written creations. For, we are each defined by what we are going through in life, when we are going through it.

Some people have called me a voracious reader. I don't know about that. But, I do know that I have read a lot. I have witnessed how some writers; both spiritual and literary, stay the same throughout their career, while others evolve though time. Though certain authors evolve, one can see how they remain true to their essence – though their style may change to whatever degree.

Recently, I was looking at the first full-blown book I ever wrote. It was on the more metaphysical aspects of yoga. Actually, the first book I ever began to write was the book that became, *Essence: The Zen of Everything.* This book is made up of an ongoing collection of aphorisms. But, that book was created over many years. The book on Yoga was the first one I created cover-to-cover. I wrote it when I was about nineteen.

As I slimmed through it, I read the words with a certain amount of amusement; as it is not very good. I do see that though I have certainly evolved throughout these many years, the sourcepoint of my system of understanding was already in place. Though it was a bit more exaggerated at that point in time.

When you read something like a writer's blog, one gets to peer into the immediacy of the writer's life. For in a blog, the author talks about and discusses what is going in their life at that moment.

Some believe a blog to be a bit too revealing, as there are a lot of psychos out there. And, I would agree with them. Yet, periodically I take to the blogosphere. I do, until I can do it no more, then I take a break.

When I look back at the *Scott Shaw Zen Blog 1.0* and the *Scott Shaw Zen Blog 2.0* I see the changes as to what I was going through then (compared to now) and how it affected my writing. As in all of our lives we go through very happy times and then we go through times when we are dealing with and/or are being engulfed by the bullshit of others. To a more than a certain degree I believe that has been the case with this blog, the *Scott Shaw Blog Zen 3.5.* Hopefully, that will change… But, as all bloggers do, I have used it as in inspiration to create some of the blogs, in this blog.

It is kind of funny when you look back in life… Think back to other times, both good and bad. Think about the times when you were really happy, had a lot of money, and were doing what you wanted to do. Think about what you would have written then. On the flip side of the coin, think about times when you were pissed off at someone or at life in general. Think about what you would be saying then.

In an autobiography the author tells you the story of their life. But, they tell it through the realization(s) of time – of looking back. If a person keeps a personal journal, those are, no doubt, the most intimate of personal story telling and immediate realizations. But, those are writings that others will, most likely, never read. And, it should be that way. A blog is somewhere in between. For if the blogger is honest; they keep it real, they detail their life and the way they view life as they are seeing it and as they are living it. Good or bad, it is a way to peer into the soul of another person and perhaps a method to gain some personal realizations about human existence through the eyes of another.

# I'm Sorry

18/Jul/2014 09:08 AM

I forever find it interesting when somebody does something that messes with you or messes with your life and then they say, *"I'm sorry."* I always question, what does that mean?

People go through life doing what they do. They know what they are doing. If they don't know what they are doing then, shame on them, because they should know what they are doing.

We are all in control of our own life. In life, we interact with other people. This is nothing new to us. This has been going on since the day we are born. So, we know the ramifications of our behavior. If we act in a certain way, certain things will happen. If we do certain things, certain things will occur.

We know! Because we know, when someone says they're sorry, what they are really saying is, *"I chose to do something and I didn't care if it negatively affected you."*

Why they change their mind about what they did is anybody's guess. Yes, some people actually have a conscience. Things bother them. But, mostly, people say they are sorry because they want something more from you and if you are mad at them you will not give it to them. Or, they are afraid that by not saying, *"I'm sorry,"* some negative repercussion will come their way.

So, what does, *"I'm sorry,"* really mean?

If someone has wronged you, they have robbed a portion of your life; they have taken away the next step of your evolution. At the least, they have damaged your Life-Time. So, when someone says they are sorry, and if they really mean it, instead of simply speaking meaningless words, they should really set about on a course to fix what they have broken, repair what they have done. That is, *"I'm sorry."*

# Rude

18/Jul/2014 09:00 AM

We have all encountered rude people in our lives. People that smoke around us, people that carrying on a conversation or text on their cell phone in the row in front of us at a movie theater, people who cut us off or smash into our car because they are not paying attention while they are driving, people who talk way too loudly in the presence of others with no concern for the affect they are having, and the list goes on. Are you one of these people?

The number one fact about rude people, and why they are rude in the first place is; they are too self-involved. They only care about their own space and do not take the time to care about the affect they are having on others. Rude people think first about themselves and then instead of thinking about others, again, think only about themselves. And, this is a major character flaw.

There is nothing right, righteous, good, holy, or forgivable in a rude person. Because they do what they do without thinking about others. Thus, no forgiveness is called for.

Making a mistake, that is not being rude. Doing something you didn't mean to do, like bumping into a person as you pass by or something like that, that is not rude; that is simply the interactions of life. Rude is an ongoing deviant behavior pattern. Rude is when a person is doing something, and whatever it is they are doing, they do without thought or care about anyone else.

I think we all can agree; rude is wrong.

What *karma* does the individual who is rude in an ongoing manner think they are incurring?

The main truth of life is that you have no right to be rude. You have no right to do anything if that thing negatively affects another person, no matter what your self-involved ideology may believe.

Rudeness equals a person's distaste towards you. One person equals two and two equals three; the numbers continue to grow. How do you think that will affect your life?

Don't be rude. If you are rude, stop being rude.

## Why Didn't You Tell Me?

17/Jul/2014 10:23 AM

*"Why didn't you tell me?"*
*"Because I shouldn't have to tell you."*

Life is an interactive process. We all interact with people at every juncture. Where we live, where we work, where we shop, where we drive, where we vacation, and everywhere in between, we interact with people. Most encounters are so minimal that we do not even take notice. A person passes by but we cannot describe them. Maybe if we find a person truly beautiful or exhibiting some noticeable quality our eyes will fixate for a moment but then that person is gone, out of our life forever.

The only time we actually interact with people is when that interaction is brought to us. Perhaps we are introduced to a person, maybe we work with them, or they live near us, so we see them all the time. Maybe they work where shop or eat and we must speak with them or ask them a question. Here, the dynamics of life changes. It goes from the abstract to the real. Once contact is made, by whatever means, then that individual becomes a part of our life, even if it is only for a moment.

In life, we rate our interactions. We meet people. We define them in our minds by their gender, their age, their style, and their attitude. This is simply the process of life – adding a person to a category in our mind; placing them into the realms of where they can be understood.

Some people are quickly understood. They are immediately pretty, nice, angry, rude, or ugly. Though this is the initial definition we may come to, this is not the end-point for many people end up being not as they initially appear: both good and bad. This is where life gets complicated.

People are at their source, that which they truly are. But, this root source, this place, this essence, is not necessarily what they present to the world. In this place, and we each have it, we are truly who we are.

Some people are very honest and clear about who and what they are. Others are not. They present a false sense of self to the world. Their true self is left only known by themselves and those who encounter the hidden, negative elements of that self.

Some people like their inner self; whether it is true and good or bad and evil. They embrace who they are. Others hide and run from their true inner self or simply disguise it to purist whatever it is they choose to pursuit. It is these people who project a false sense of self to the outer world and those are the ones we must be careful of.

Though good people occasionally do bad things, this is not their intention. When they do something wrong, they do all they can to alter their patterns, seek forgiveness, and remedy and pay recompense for what they have done. The latter of the personalities is not like this, however. They are self-involved and perhaps on a pathway of intended destruction.

In life we are going to come into interaction with each of these breeds. In my life, recently, one of these people, who finally realized that they were unleashing behavior that was negatively affecting my existence, questioned, *"Why didn't you tell me?"* My answer was, *"Because I shouldn't have to tell you."*

This is the point. If you are doing something wrong you should know. No one should have to tell you.

Destructive people live in a space of self. This is a very low-level place of existence where a lot of damage and destruction emanates from. Giving people live in a space of caring about others. They are conscious of their every action and from this, their negative impact on the world is minimal, whereas their positive impact on the world is immense.

Who are you? Do you care? Do you give? Or, do you care not? Do you fix? Do you repair? Or, do you break?

Life is based upon interaction. It is very evident who the good people of the world truly are; those who interact with great love and kindness: not hurting, not damage, and not destroying.

## Is Your Dream Destroying You?

16/Jul/2014 09:06 AM

For me, who has been involved in the film game for a lot of years, I always find it interesting to meet new people and have some interaction with them, even if it is only for a moment at a casting session.

Let me add a precursor here. ...Me, who has been walking the crazy place known as the, *"Spiritual Path,"* for much longer than I have been in the film game...

Okay, with that said... I always find it interesting how people perceive reality. For example, on the Spiritual Path people are always about doing good, making things better, doing *karma yoga,* and helping the greater whole as opposed to only helping themselves. In the film game, everyone is about the concept of, *"Me, me, me,"* not, *"We, we, we."* For someone with my background, I forever find it a curious space to dwell in, that place of, *"Me."* For only thinking about, *"Me,"* equals a very limited reality. It equals a very limited ability to do any good for the greater whole. In fact, I so commonly realize that the people who dance in the film game are so locked into, *"Self,"* that they have no concern about the greater good. All they want is success and admiration for themselves.

Now, I am not saying that all people who walk upon the Spiritual Path are good and holy. No, many use it as a tool to gain the self-esteem that is lacking in their life. Some use it as a means of getting over and being, *"Something."* Where true spirituality is based around the understating of being, *"No Thing."* But, I believe most who are consciously on the Spiritual Path are not on it for, *"Me."* They are on it to make the, *"All,"* better.

There is an illusion in and of, *"Hollywood."* A promise that is told but is never kept. Over the years I have watched so many people move here from across the States and around the World hoping to live the dream but virtually none of them have made it. They come, think of only, *"Self,"* and do all that they do to make that, *"Self,"* more. But, what is, *"Self,"* if it is not giving to the greater whole? What is, *"Self,"* if you cannot turn that, *"Self,"* off and do for others instead of only doing for, *"Self?"* What that, *"Self,"* becomes, is, *"Selfish."* And, here lies the problem...

If you come to a place thinking that place will give you something... If you come to a place only trying to rise yourself up... If you come to a place and do not care about others... If you come to a place and do not care what affect you are having... If you come to a place and do not reach out and put others before you... Then, where do you think you will end up? You will end up in a lonely, lost space, where others don't like you. Why? Because you only thought about yourself.

I have seen this so many times. And, it has been documented in so many documentaries, news specials, and even in the movies. People come here for, *"Self."* But, they leave destroyed because, *"Self,"* should never be the primary focus.

This is what I believe sets the true person, (the truly spiritual person), apart from the masses. They are not only focused on, *"Self."* Instead, they are focused on the greater good – caring about others instead of solely caring about themselves. And, they do for others instead of only doing for themselves. From this mindset, they put others first, they take others into consideration; they go out of the way to help others. Though they may pursuit their dreams, they are not lost in the belief that they are more than anyone else. From this, (while pursing their dreams), they make the whole world just a little bit better.

**Art for Art Sake**

16/Jul/2014 08:15 AM

Recently I've been invited to attended a few gallery shows and exhibits at museums. At *MOCA* I got to revisit a couple of the works of artists out of the New York School: Klein, Pollack, and Rothko; some of my all-time favorites. But spreading out for there one of the biggest realizations I had is that so many artists are simply doing what has already been done.

For example, at one showing I went to last week, there was a room full of twelve-by-twelve inch paintings on canvas that were solid colors. One was blue, purple, red, and so on. Now, when Malevich did the original, *"White on White,"* in 1918, that was revolutionary. It made a statement. But now, it seems so many artists simply rehash what has already been done. I mean, how many different artists have done a series of paintings of single colors on a canvas by this point in time? I'm sure when I was finding my artistic style I did it too. Plus, I am sure; you can get paintings like that at many department stores. There is just no revolution in that art. All this being said, somehow/someway these artists have developed enough clout to be shown in galleries and museums.

I also find it interesting how many cutting edge artists, of recent times, have been deducted from the walls of museums – though I am sure their works are still in their vaults. I really loved the German neo-expressionism that was prominent in the 1980. I found great inspiration in the works of artists like Baselitz and Fetting. Though many of the neo-expressionist are still around and working (including myself) ʊ they are no longer being shown like they once were. The same holds true for once popular artist like Schnabel, and one of my favorites, Morphesis. The cutting edge seems to have been cut.

Now, this is not meant to be a criticism, it is simple an observation. And, certainly the trends in life often times parallel that of art. We have been engulfed in a space-time where conservatism has continued to take hold and seemingly every attempted to break loose from this continuum has been dashed. The music has remained stagnant and culture has focused on the individual self. In this environment it is hard for art to take hold; particularly revolutionary art.

But, the revolutionaries are still out there: the old and the new. So, as is always the case, someone somehow, someway will eventually break through and kick the art world in the butt and from this, art may move to new levels of expression – not just the already been done.

## Why Psychotherapy Doesn't Work

14/Jul/2014 07:54 PM

There are two reasons why psychotherapy doesn't work. One is the patient. Two is the psychotherapist.

The science of psychotherapy is based around the concept of the patient telling the psychotherapist what they are feeling. Then, the psychotherapist asks various questions in order to peer deeply into the person, hopefully finding the causation factors that have lead the patient to presetting a state of mental imbalance and/or acting out in an inappropriate manner due to the emotions that they are feeling.

The first big problem in this equitation is the fact that the psychologist, no matter how well trained they are, only knows the facts about the patient as they are presented to them. The fact of the matter is, the asking and the uncovering of facts about a specific person may involve the person lying. From this, a completely altered reality may be presented to the psychotherapist. And, some people are very pathological about their lying. They lie to the degree that they may even believe their own lies.

Even is the patient does not intentionally lie, at best, they present all of their life stories from their own point of view. From this, the whole story is never truly understood by the psychotherapist. Thus, whatever diagnosis they make is based upon a limited set of defining elements.

The second problem with psychotherapy is the psychotherapist himself or herself. More than simply a mental health professional, a psychotherapist is also a businessperson. They make their living by guiding people's mental health. If they told all of their clients the truth about what they felt about them and what they thought the patient should or should not be doing, they would quickly have no clients. As such, they must guide their patients with kid gloves; hoping to help them but not lose them as a client.

Of course, both the patient and the psychotherapist will deny these facts or, at least, minimalize them with all kinds of rhetoric. But, these are the facts: the patient presents only the truth about himself or herself that they want to be heard by the psychotherapist. The psychotherapist must have clients to financially survive so they sugar coat the truth to their patients. Thus, psychotherapy is a very limited science; defined entirely by the people who practice it and the people who partake of it.

    I could go into a lot of stories and examples about both the patients and the psychotherapist I have interacted with over the years. But, I will leave that for another time. I will say that it is the participants themselves who make psychotherapy unreliable. This is why so many people need to go for so long and yet continue to exhibit the same emotional turmoil.

# The Reality of Dreams

13/Jul/2014 09:05 AM

Have you ever had the experience where you are dreaming and in that dream you become really angry at something someone you know does in that dream. In that dream, what they have done causes you to have all of the emotional and physically bodily relations of anger that you get when you are in waking consciousness. Due to the emotional reactions you are having you may even wake up. Though you are no longer dreaming, many of the side effects of the anger you felt in your dream may linger.

Very few of us, I believe, would transform that dream state anger into real life. We would not go and start yelling at the person who angered us in our dream in real life. We know it was a dream. Yet, strong emotional reactions linker in our body and our mind for sometime after we experience them. So, what occurred in the dream becomes a part of our living reality – though, in fact, it was not a part of our living reality.

Many fields of parapsychology and medicine have studied dreams; their affect on the body and the mind, and what they truly mean. Parapsychologists commonly have virtually no formal credentials so we will leave them out of this discussion; as they base what they claim more upon conjecture and speculation than anything else. Psychologist, however, are well-schooled and have been at the forefront of dream exploration since their science began. Though many a psychologists has studied dreams and their effect on the human body, and though some well-noted psychologists have published their studies, there is no absolute understanding to the causation factor for what dreams are or are not. This, in itself, is telling. For if the true professionals on the subject have no concrete answers about what dreams are then the science is left solely to personal interpretation.

All the being stated, as a foundation, we each enter the dream space every night. Once there, we encounter people that we know, and people that we don't know. As discussed, we may even become very angry with someone we know while in a dream.

Okay, here comes the defining factor of dreams that so many people and professionals overlook. Yes, you are in a dream. Yes, you encounter someone you know in a dream. They may even be sleeping in the bed right next to you. But, are they in the same dreams as you? No. Did they choose to do the thing that made you angry in your dream? No. Though they may too have been sleeping and dreaming at the exact same time as you, they were dreaming of a completely different storyline. Thus, dreams are not a universal pathway of communication or revelation. They are simply something that is locked in the mind of a specific individual.

Some say, a dream is a predication of the future. Some say a dream is the way a person experiences their deep inner feelings about someone or something while under the guise of sleep. Some say... That's just it, people talk, but there is no absolute knowledge about dreams. As such, all the conscious person can do is to let them be what they are; dreams. Let them exist in the place where they are encountered; sleep. And, do not let them defining our waking reality.

# It Is All What You Are Surrounded By

11/Jul/2014 10:43 AM

It is pretty easy to see, we are each defined by what we are surround by. Our family, our culture, our historical timeframe are each big factors. But, as we move through life, the subtle influences become more defining.

For example, you may be an American; sure. You may be from whatever city you are from; okay. You are living, wherever you are living; absolutely. But, then what? Then, it becomes much more subtle.

You become defined by the life around you. Who you work with, who are your neighbors, where you shop, what you do in your free time, all cause you to be emotionally influenced in one way or the other. From these emotional influences, it guides you into thinking about specific things. Meaning, if you work with nice people, if the neighbors that surround you are nice, then your time, in those environments, is nice. You are allowed to think nice thoughts and exist in a space of calm. This is, of course, the ideal environment.

For some of us, however, it isn't like that. Perhaps where certain people work there is a lot of competition and backstabbing going on. Perhaps where they live, they have bad neighbors. These factors all cause a person to loose their inner peace and, as such, they are set to a mindset of being forced into thinking about the more negative elements of life.

Certainly, it is easy to say, *"Get another job,"* or *"Move."* But, as any adult knows, doing those things is not always easy. There are financial constraints. There are bills to pay, so a job must be kept. Moving expenses can be excessive, so moving is not always an easy option, and so on.

It is also easy to see what may be causing a person to not be in a position of peace, but providing them with a pathway to a better existence is rarely easy. In fact, there is often someone stepping up, telling a person what they should be doing. But, what are they doing to move that situation along? Words are free. Words are easy. Telling a person what they should or shouldn't do is easy. But, what are the people that are speaking actually doing to help any person achieve a better place in life. The fact of the matter is, so many of these words promise false hopes, without verified outcomes, that the words spoken are hurting more than helping.

There have been many books written and lectures given about how to change your mind frame when you find yourself surround by a negative environment such as a bad job. Though some of these techniques may be momentarily helpful, all they are doing is providing a bandage to an open wound. All they actually do, at best, is to teach a person to exist in a state of denial. Denial is never a good place to dwell. The fact is, if you find yourself in a negative environment; surrounded by things that cause you to be driven into a space of anger, frustration, or emotional upheaval all you can do, (if you cannot immediately run away), is exist in that emotionally defining space.

Having dealt with some these factors in my own life, I can say from personal experience, it is troubling. For example, where I grew up, was very dangerous; it left me in a constant state of hyper-awareness as to what may be coming next. Which eventually caused me to be defined by anxiety. But, there was no way out. I was young. I was defined by where my parents placed me. As I have gone through life, there have also been times when I have found myself surround by places and in spaces that were very detrimental to me maintaining a sense of inner peace. And, sometimes, due to whatever foundational conditions, I could not leave these places; at least not immediately.

Many of us go through these types of life events. We must keep our jobs. We do not possess the funds to move, and so. From these life defining factors we must find a way to, if not rise above them, at least deal with them in the best manner possible.

The only workable suggestion I can give is that you have to let any negativity that surrounds you cause you to travel to a new space of personal realizations. Instead of simply existing in a space of anger, (which leads to all kinds of health issues and even physical confrontations), allow yourself to learn from what is around you. Study the people who are the source of the negativity and learn from their mistakes. By studying them, by peering into their being, this makes you more than them, instead of becoming less than them by descending to their level of consciousness.

Now, I am not saying this is going to solve anything. For this, you have to do things like get your financial resources together so that you can move on. But, what it may do is allow you to witness and study the flaws of human nature instead of being controlled by them. From this, you may gain some wisdom and perhaps become just a bit more peaceful in a peace-less environment.

**Some People Are Just Losers**

11/Jul/2014 08:58 AM

You know, every now and then I wake up to the fact that, *"That guy (or girl) is a complete loser."*

I believe that most of us go through life trying to be a good person. We are who we are and we do what we do but we do not mess with the lives of other people. If we do, we say, *"Sorry,"* and try to fix what we have messed up. Some people aren't like that, however. They are just a loser.

I always find when the, *"Loser Gene,"* comes out in a person it was something I knew all along and I feel really stupid for not acknowledging it immediately. But, I try to be a nice guy. I try to give people the benefit of the doubt. But, sooner or later it comes out – there is no doubt, they are a loser. They can't help it.

Sometimes I have even had tell people, *"You're a fucking loser."* I try not to do that, however. I don't mean to be demeaning. But, sometimes they just need to be told.

I've worked with a few losers. People who had the opportunity to do something really good and big in life and with their life, but they tossed it all down the toilet. Why? I don't know? I guess that's what makes them a loser.

Then there are the losers who always want to brag about themselves; tell you all of their great accomplishments – all that they have done. If someone has to tell you who and what he or she is, that means they are the only one believing it. So, what does that make them? A loser.

Sometimes, a person's loser quality comes at you like a flash of lightening. I know it has happened to me. For example, I was sitting in an on-line editing suite one day with this producer guy. We were syncing dialogue to film footage. He had his headphones on and he began talking really loudly. You know, like some kids do when they put headphones on for the first time; before they realize that you don't hear your voice as loudly when they are on, compared to when they are off. He was sitting there broadcasting every word. I am sure what he was saying could be heard all over the facility. It all became clear. I totally understood who and what he was. Loser!

Oh yeah, if someone wants to hear themselves talk, if they want to force their words on others – others who do not want to hear their words; what does that make them? A loser.

Some people lie and pretend to be something they're not. Loser!

Some people are liars. Loser!

Some people make up lies about others. Loser!

Some people steal. Loser!

Some people blame others for their own faults and shortcomings. Loser!

Some people justify their actions when they are downright wrong. Loser!

Some people, when they have done something wrong, lie about it or make excuses for it. Loser!

Some people don't try to fix what they have broken. Loser!

Some people, when they are presented with negative facts about themselves, instead of owning it and saying, *"Sorry,"* they try to turn it around on someone else. Loser!

Some people intentionally go out of their way to hurt others or mess with other people's lives. Big Loser!

This, *"Loser,"* list could go on… But, we all know what a loser is.

You know, many times you can go back to an individual's psychological make up and trace the causation factor for their loser-dom. But, that doesn't change anything. A loser is a loser. Losers choose to be losers. They could choose to be something else but they don't.

We should all get together and make a list of all the losers we have known. Let's set some ground rules first: we have to know them personally, because the only way we can confirm if a person is a loser is if we have had personal interaction with them. No hearsay. And, we have to be able to name at least one big, "Loser," thing that they have done. Pretty easy rules; right?

Okay, let's go! I image that this list will be pretty big. :-)

# Hypocrite

10/Jul/2014 02:34 PM

You know, when I was a young spiritual seeker we used to sit around and everybody would, *"Play pretend."* There were all of these groups and though each had their own particular focus, they each played the same game of pretend. Meaning, people were something while they were there, then they went off to become something different; i.e.; who they really were. Now, it was not that we were doing anything bad, but this type of behavior is deceptive – particularly to the Personal-Self, because it makes people believe in a false Sense of Self.

Here it gets a little complicated, because for those who have not walked on the spiritual path, you may not understand. But, as a lot of people go to church, here in the West, maybe this is a better way to explain it... People go to church, they listen to the sermon, the pray, they meet and greet, and they do whatever, but then they are gone. How many people that you know who go to church every Sunday live a truly Christian lifestyle? Very few I would imagine.

In spiritual circles, it is really no different; it is simply that the whole concept of spirituality is much more amplified. People become something new.
They are a *Sufi,* they are a *Yogi,* they are a *Sikh,* and so on. This becomes their definition, though it does not necessarily become who they are. A title; not an all-encompassing Thing or a product of True-Inner-Being.

When I left behind being a monk and a swami, it truly let me become who, *"I,"* was. Me, without the need for a formal title or definition.

Recently, as I have mentioned here in this blog, my childhood friend had heart surgery. As we sat around reminiscing, I was reminded how, *"Hard,"* we grew up. And, that, *"Hard,"* is part of who I am. ...That love for the streets and the street life. But, that has not stopped me from being spiritual. And, I use the term, *"Spiritual,"* for lack of a better word. When I came into my own I realized that I could embrace my roots but live spirituality as I see it. I make no claims to do anything else.

Most people are not like this, however. If they get involved in spirituality, they want to play pretend. They may, in fact, be something else, but they play pretend, *"Spiritual pretend."* And, they never reveal themselves while they are playing spiritual pretend. Thus, they are hypocrites.

Some time back I wrote a piece called, *"Let's play dress-up."* It's published somewhere. In it, I discuss how people get dressed up in their yogi garb but that does not change who or what they are at the core of their being. They are just pretending.

I do not hang out in what may be called, *"Spiritual circles,"* very often – for the reason that I don't like hypocrites. This being said, every now and then, (out of whatever weird *karma*), I am forced into being confronted by the spiritual game of, *"Let's play pretend."* For example, I have encountered people who may stand around, while stomping on the floor, screaming, *"Fuck me! Fuck me!"* over and over again. This, while the next day they are pretending to be a spiritual teacher. It is really a sad endless cycle. One could ask, *"Why doesn't a person simply own who they are?"* But, of course, the answer would be, *"Because they are a hypocrite."*

They are a liar. Maybe they are even lying to themselves. I don't know? But, what they are doing is creating a pathway of lies compiled upon other lies. And, that is not true spirituality. It may be the spiritual that is practiced today, but I believe we can all agree that it is not true spirituality.

If they are ever confronted with their lies, deceit, and inappropriate behavior, all they can say is, *"Who me?"*

They pretend they did nothing wrong and maybe even try to turn it around, back on the other person or someone else. Very sociopathic, don't you think? Yet, people like this are out there all over the place; especially in spiritual circles.

So, in closing, I think it is very important for each of us to look into ourselves and be real. Not only real to ourselves but to the whole world. For that is true spiritual. Don't lie about who and what you are. Don't try to deceive others by hiding your actions. Don't lie. Be! That is true spirituality.

Ultimately, if you want to be spiritual, (some do, some don't), but if you do, realize that you do not have to be something you are not. You do not have to memorize the words of others and state them as if they are your own. You do not have to, *"Play the game of pretend."* All you have to do is be honest and be yourself.

# Notoriety

10/Jul/2014 09:13 AM

It has long been documented how a stalker get some sort of distorted psychological gratification when the person they are stalking speaks about them. Stalking has taken on all kinds of new forms since the digital age came upon us. But, it is all based in the same distorted psychological mindset of, *"Lacking."*

The stalker lacks the understanding of true self. They lack the experience of accomplishment. They lack the understanding of being a true person, living a true life. Thus, they try to fill their lacking by grabbing onto the life of another person. They somehow feel that by getting close to that person their life will be fulfilled and they will no longer be lacking.

Then, there are the people who just do stupid shit to bring attention to themselves. Like the so-called journalist who threw water in the face of Tom Cruise or that one Ukrainian guy who jumped under the dress of America Ferrera, tried to kiss Will Smith, punched Brad Pitt, and so on. Though they may be more dynamic than a stalker who hides in the shadows, their lack of self-worth is very evident as they are tying to grab onto the presence of another person.

The other side of this issue is people who latch onto people who are successful. These people somehow gain some sort of misplaced (whatever) by claiming that they know and are, *"Friends,"* with so and so.

There is no art it trying to grab the spotlight from someone who has already earned it. It does not give it to you.

When I was young, a lot of people I knew did time in the various county and juvenile facilities. Some ended up with long sentences. There was a lot of pride that these guys possessed over their believed accomplishment of going to jail. Probably some of these people have spent their whole life in prison. I never understood why that was a badge of honor?

There is also the case of people who somehow think that they gain something by fighting and hopefully beating someone up. I saw a lot of this as I was growing up. In times gone past people have stalked and accosted me; they lost but the whole process was ridiculous. I'm glad I'm old now so that shit no longer goes on. But, that whole process is so animalistic and what does any of it mean?

You know, you look back to the people who have attacked known-individuals and no one remembers their name. They just are thought of that, *"Idiot,"* who did that. ...If they are remembered at all.

In the age of the internet many people have gotten loud. Loud and rude, spitting all kinds of bullshit, trying to make a name for themselves. But, just because someone has succeeded in internet publicity, to whatever degree, does not mean that they possess the credentials to be anything. For, as we all know, anybody can say anything on the internet. But, if a person has not been validated by earning the degrees, having their works published by respected publishing houses, or having their music, films, or whatever distributed by recognized distributors, than all that says is that the person has no true foundation for saying or doing anything that they are saying and doing. At best, they only gain a few brain-dead fans that have nothing better to do with their life. Again, this goes back to the whole case of stalking. People with no true sense of self, stalking someone. Even a fan can be considered a stalker.

Ultimately what all of this leads to is that people want notoriety; people want to be something. But, most people are so locked into their own head that they do not even comprehend that without a foundational basis and without a focused pathway from low to high, at best, all they will achieve is a momentary note and a place on the list of, *"Who?"*

As I have long stated, *"I am not a religious person."* That being said, the person who consciously leaves behind the desires and constraints of the modern world in order to enter into the world of solitude and service is a far greater person than anyone who seeks notoriety – especially those who seek notoriety by either trying to steal the spotlight from another or basing their desire for notoriety upon lack of foundation by only possessing a loud mouth. The religious person, however, gives up the desire of elevating self, giving way to a life defined by having helped and given to others, asking nothing in return.

Which do you think is better, notoriety or selfless service?

# The Way Things Should Be

09/Jul/2014 08:40 AM

We all want things in life to be the way we want them to be. We want to do what we want to do and we want to behave the way we want to behave. But, this isn't always possible. Most of us learn our lessons when we are young and we come to understand that we must curtail certain aspects of our behavior and the things that we do. In life, however, there are some people who do not remain conscious enough to step beyond their own negative behavior and, from this, they bring other people into their negative life space – when that other person has no desire to know anything about what someone else thinks, does, or how they behave.

Recently, I have been forced to interact, or perhaps better put, deal with, a few people who apparently do not possess the ability to step beyond the limitations of their own desire-full personality and think more about others than themselves. One example has been my rude neighbor whom I have discussed way more than I have ever wanted to, as I never wanted to be forced into dealing with his ongoing unconscious and unaware behavior at all. Life was fine before he arrived. I also recently had to deal with the ridiculous behavior of an editor that I went out of my way to help and, in fact, have helped more times, over the years, when he really needed it, than I can count. Another occurrence happened in the waiting room of the hospitable where my friend underwent heart surgery the other day. I thought I heard his adult daughter and his girlfriend arguing outside. Yup, in they come; the daughter trying to walk away and the girlfriend following, screaming at her. And, she wouldn't stop. My first thought was how could anyone behave like this with all of these people around – all of them in a state of concern and worry about their loved ones? But, there it was. The daughter kept trying to walk away; the girlfriend wouldn't let it go. Finally, I literally pushed the girl's fiancée into the middle and by raising his voice he finally got the lady to stop yelling.

...I mean, it wasn't my fight. There was nothing I could do.

Some people only think about themselves. Others are adult enough to keep their life projection(s) to a minimum, especially when other people are around. Then there are still others who apparently feed on this type of behavior, pushing until the other person pushes back, which is never a good thing.

In life, what annoys me the most about inconsiderate people is that there is no justifiably reason for behaving in the manner they behave. Yet, they are the ones who are quick to become angry when they are confronted about their behavior. If a person possessed a conscience, if they truly cared about people, they would be sorry. But, many are not.

It's a vicious circle that never has to happen. All a person has to do is be conscious and put other people before themselves. But, for some, I guess that is too much to ask.

This is why I am so vocal about my distaste for many of the so-called, spiritual teachers roaming around theses days. They are bottom dwellers and they are liars. Because if they are not one-hundred percent aware of their environment, conscious of their own actions, and in control of their own emotions then all they are doing is lying to the people they are supposedly teaching. They are not being true or honest to themselves nor are they being true or honest to the students they are trying to cultivate. We hear about this type of person all the time. I have personally witnessed this type of behavior in many a so-called spiritual teacher and have had to deal with its repercussions many times. This is why I always state, if someone is claiming they are spiritual you better think twice before you listen to a word that they say.

Care about people. Always take other people into consideration before you do anything. Think about them, before you think about you and this world will be a much better place.

## Anything Exciting Going On?

08/Jul/2014 01:14 PM

Whenever I meet up with someone, after the basic, *"How's it going,"* is stated, I generally follow up with, *"Anything exciting go on?"* Today, I bumped into this young guy I know and I ask, *"Anything exciting going on?"* He looks at me and says, *"Today."* Then, he studies me like, do you understand? This made me smile. Yeah, I understand…

On the other side of the coin, just yesterday, I was with my friend of over forty years as he went through his second heart surgery. The day before, in his hospitable room, we discussed the many people we knew that had already checked-out. It all goes by so fast…

The thing is, it is very easy to fall into the melancholy. To fall into the not taking note, the not truly living, the not noticing the time go by, the not living and appreciating this, *"Today."* Then, it is gone.

You know, you don't have to get all metaphysical about this. You just have to stop and take notice. You have to study the what you are feeling and the what you are living, *"Now."* And, then you simply have to live it to the best of your ability.

*"Anything exciting going on?"*
*"Today."*

**That's Not What I Want To Do**

07/Jul/2014 12:23 PM

One of the first things I realized when I entered the film business is that I could edit a movie very quickly. Most people, (at that time), would maybe get five minutes of raw footage put together per day. Me, it was very common that I would edit an entire feature length film over a weekend. I guess this has something to do with possessing an eidetic memory. Which is actually more of a curse, in life, than anything else, in that I remember everything. But, once I saw a scene I would remember it and I could put the best scenes together very quickly.

Many of the *Zen Films* Donald G. Jackson and I created were edited in this manner. We would go and rent a video-editing bay on Friday night and we would come out with a movie by Sunday. *Armageddon Blvd., Ride with the Devil, Lingerie Kickboxer* were all done in this manner.

From this ability, the people who financed Don, (in that time period), had high hopes that I would jump ship so they could finance my films instead of our films, as Don was very mentally chaotic. He never got things done. Or, it took him a long time to get things done. Me, I am bam-bam; see it, shoot it, edit it, soundtrack it, and done. They thought they could make a lot of money off of me.

But, I was born in the *Year of the Dog,* (in the Chinese astrological calendar), from this, I am told; I am supposed to be a very loyal person. Which, I guess I am. Also, one of my curses. :-) Anyway, I said, *"No."*

Back in those days, Don and I would meet at our offices in North Hollywood everyday, seven days a week, at about eleven; hang out, cast movies, talk with other filmmaker, shoot footage for films when the inspiration struck, go to screenings, see live bands, eat, and basically hang out and have a good time. This went on for a few years. And, we did make a few good films during that period. Most of the time, we had fun. Good memories, good times. But, times always change.

Though Don and I took, literally, more than a year to film movies like *Guns of El Chupacabra,* this was not the pattern I preferred. Ever since I made, *Samurai Vampire Bikers from*

*Hell,* (which we made over a weekend), my philosophy has always been to get out there and do it. Make that film. Get it done. Because it will be no better if you take two years or two days. Sure, if you need some pick-up shots after the fact, go out there and get them. But, the body of the film; get it done!

It's all about focus and organization.

From this ability, I have also had people coming at me wanting me to make films for them. But, I don't make films for money. I don't do exploitation. I do Art – at least Art as I see it.

As time has progressed and I have become more and more filled with distaste for the meaningless egos and the innumerable promises and lies prevalent throughout the film industry here in Hollywood, I have continued to minimalize and acutely focus my film productions. ...Bringing in fewer and fewer cast and crewmembers and focusing on specific characters to get the story told. This has been a very freeing experience. It has also lead me to create the next generation of *Zen Filmmaking,* the Non-Narrative Film.

So, though I still hold onto the belief that if you are filming a narrative film, that it should be done to get it done, I have also retreated to one of the practices that Don and I employed with *Roller Blade Seven* and *Chupacabra* – creating a film over time. For example, I have been filming the next *Max Hell Frog Warrior* installment for over two years. My feeling is, it will be done when it is done. So, for all of you out there who ask me what is going on with that project, there is your answer.

Don and I used to always say that the most important element of filmmaking is that, *"Fun is what it is all about."* Though working with Don, due to his numerous psychological quirks, was not always fun, I have personally held onto that belief. From this, it is has guided me down the road of removing as many obstacles as possible from the filmmaking process. And, the fact of the matter is, filmmaking is not easy. Dealing with the egos of people is not easy. Paying for a movie is not easy. Getting things done and making things happen on a set is not easy; nor is it always fun. But, as I hold onto the belief that filmmaking can actually lead to a state of *Satori* or *Cinematic Enlightenment* and that a film should not be based solely on the desire(s) of the filmmaker or the actors to feed their egos and/or their careers, or for financiers to fill their pockets, I continually have to tell people who want me to make a traditional film, *"That's not what I want to do."*

I'm about freedom. I'm about a happy experience. I'm about obstacle removal. I'm about art. So, ultimately, I'm about one thing, *Zen Cinema!*

**When You Believe**

07/Jul/2014 08:22 AM

I often speak about the downside of the film industry in an attempt to, if not protect people from the downfalls, than at least to warn them about what can happen. From my time at Hollywood High School onward, I have seen how the film industry has deceived many a person and has handed them belief but not the reality.

Personally, after receiving offers for many years to enter the film industry, I finally gave in at the ripe old age of thirty-two. I dove in headfirst. Looking back, I really should have become involved much earlier, as youth has a lot of benefits that are not possessed by the aged. But, when I was younger, I was doing other things…

Everybody wants to be a movie star, don't they? This is my belief. Most never possess the drive to go after this dream, however. But, some do. And, here is where the problems begin.

The thing about the film industry is that it is like this weird drug. There are all these promises – promise that never come to volition. But, once you step into the ring, they are always there, tempting you.

Producers and directors promise you roles in their films. Films that are never made. Auditions make you believe that you are getting somewhere. But, auditions are not being cast in a role. Being an extra (which anyone can do) on a big set makes you believe that you have what it takes as you are rubbing elbows with stars. You are in the same scenes with them, standing only a few feet away and all... But, the fact is, you are not one of them. You were not cast for your role they only put you on the set because you look the way needed to sell the live action and time period of the film. Ultimately, extra work only leads to more extra work. It is the biggest lie of all that it leads to anything more. This is why I don't use extras in my films.

Then, some people get roles in indie films. Most indie films do not pay but they are something. But, what is that something? Sometimes they are pure exploitation. Something you end up being quite embarrassed for even being a part of it. I have known beautiful young girls, (one in particular), that actually had sex on camera for a zero indie film. What did that equal? I also knew one girl in the *U.S.C. School of Law* who had her eyes on the prize of becoming a big lawyer but who was bitten by the acting bug and was persuaded to get naked on camera and simulate sex for a zero indie film. I am sure that has haunted her ever since.

The thing is, the film industry promises the ultimate illusion: fame, fortune, and stardom. All part and parcel of the ultimate American dream. But, for the very-very-very few that obtain it, most only look back with regrets.

In this day and age, making a film has become easier and easier. With this has also risen the number of films made by incompetent filmmakers. Incompetent filmmakers following the same dream to stardom and promising the same lies that have been handed down for a hundred years to the budding stars and starlets.

What does it all equal? Following a pathway of desire, dreams, and lies. None of them are healthy.

Hollywood is a no win game with the ultimate promise of achievement. Be carful where you step.

# Perfection of the Imperfection

06/Jul/2014 04:35 PM

Okay, here's the deal. When you step up to the doorway of death your life does not flash before your eyes as has been detailed by so many for so long. As someone who has walked up to that doorway, more than once, (not by choice, I must add), what occurs is that everything falls into an understanding of this equaled that and that equaled this.

Okay but then what? So many metaphysicians have tried to sell you a bill of goods that at this point, life all comes into focus and all things are understood to be perfect. Okay, but then what? If you died you are dead. What does any of it mean?

This is one of the biggest orchestrations of illusion on the path of consciousness. That your life will mean something. But, it does not. If you are dead/when you are dead then the, "You," vanishes and nothing means anything anymore.

People who have lived an unfulfilled life desire to hold onto the dream of the absolute. That there, in that place called heaven, (or whatever), it will all have meant something. That all the chances you missed, all the opportunities you didn't take, will all come to absolute fruition, and everything that you fucked up will be fixed – you will go to some never-never-land and your life will have added up to something. Lies...

What you lived, you lived. What you did, you did. And, that is that.

You can hope, you can pray that all of your sins will be forgiven, that all of your miss-steps will be re-orchestrated, but that is all the bullshit of the lying/thinking mind. What you did is what you did. What you lived is what you lived. When you are dead, that is the end of the story.

In life, we all want things to have been better. We all want things to have been lived in a better way. We all want to erase the mistakes. We all want it to have meant more.

But, all we have is all we have. No matter how much we want our life to equals something more, what we did and what we lived is all we have. That is the ALL of our life.

We can pretend. We can believe. We can hope for passageways to far off heavenly kingdoms where all our sins will be forgiven, all our missteps erased, and all our desires fulfilled, but that place does not exist.

All that there is, is all that there is. All that there is, is what we have done. All that there is, is based upon the choices we have made. Realize this, and it may cause you to make better choices in the future. ...That is, if you have a future.

Don't wait until you knock on death's door until you find this out.

# How Knowledge Expands

05/Jul/2014 07:52 AM

Knowledge expands by one person studying the previous research of another person and then expanding upon it. One studies and analysis what has been written in the past and then adds their own research and understanding onto the previously gained knowledge. From this, new understandings are born.

In the academic word, when one takes the knowledge of another and then publishes it, they are generally assigned the title of, *"Editor."* From this, they are understood to be the one who collected the research and then (perhaps) edited, reworded it, and presented it to the public. That is what takes place in the academic world. In the modern world, however, some people take the research documented by another individual and take credit for it themselves. They call themselves, *"Author."* Though this is what sometimes takes place, by the unscrupulous, that title is factually incorrect.

Somehow, in some way, there are the cases of people who have developed the credentials, either by hook or by crook, to gain a publishing deal. Then, once a publisher has accepted their proposed book, instead of doing the research and writing the text themselves, they turn to another person to provide them with the knowledge necessary to present information within the pages of the book. Then, they call themselves the author of that book. Wrong, yes, but it is not uncommon. It has happened to me.

I can tell you, from a personal perspective, that as a budding writer when I was asked to write a chapter (or more) for a book, by someone who I believed had the appropriate credentials and morals, I happily did it thinking that I was helping them and perhaps helping me. In this process I received little more than a mention in the acknowledgement page of the manuscript. This is just wrong!

Now, I am not writing this as some sort of a call-out to the truth about what is going on. What I am stating is that it does happen. And, it does happen quite frequently, especially in the works that conglomerate the information of a specific industry.

When it comes right down to it, the reason the so-called author contacted me is that they knew a simple fact – they understood that I could provide them with the necessary information and write it in a precise and readable manner. But, was I thanked for it either in monetary funds or by being given appropriate credited as one if the authors of the book? No.

Certainly, I am not the only one who has experienced this pattern of behavior. There are certain authors who base their entire career upon taking the research of others and claiming it as their own. Wrong, wrong, wrong! But, are they going to come forward and admit what they have done? That is very doubtful.

From all of this, one may question, *"Why do it at all?"* From my personal experience I can say that as a budding author, (when I was a budding author), I believed that it may accelerate my career. From a more personal perspective, I believed that I was helping someone. But then, that someone took all the credit from all my years of research and claimed it as their own, receiving all of the accolades and all of the financial rewards. Wrong!

As a researcher and as a historian, whenever I formally publish, I always reference my resources. And, the publishers of my works confirm those resources. In academic presses they generally employee the footnote system in referencing. In popular presses they usually simply put the references used at the end of the article or in the rear of the book. But, they are there.

It is really much more than this, however. It is about honor. We all gain from the knowledge based in the past. We all gain from the presentation of this knowledge. What we do not gain from is when one person takes the knowledge, obtained by another, and then profits from its presentation by calling it their own. That is simply wrong.

To this end, if you are a researcher or a budding author, though you will obviously have to jump through some hoops to get your own works published, be careful whom you deal with as many a so-called author may take advantage of your research and gain fame and fortune by calling it their own.

# Dodging the Reality of Your Reality

04/Jul/2014 02:14 PM

Have you ever had the experience when you are asked to do something for someone and then you really go out of your way to get it done – then when it is completed you realized that you were lied to or not presented with the whole truth and nothing but the truth so you bring this fact up to the attention of the person who asked you to do it in the first place and when you do they try to turn it around like you did something wrong?

Wow, that's a long sentence...

Recently, this happened to me. This one editor, whom I have known for a lot of years, came to me in desperate need of an article on a very specific subject. I stepped up and went straight to the source writing the article and really saving the day. I know I saved the day because the editor told me I did. But, in the process the promises made to me about the article, which I presented to the interviewee, were not held up, making me look like a liar. Though I, of course, have no control over a magazine's production, I do not like to be seen as untruthful. So, when the issue of the magazine was released I told the editor that he should send copies to the guy, (instead of me sending them), because the interviewee was probably going to be pissed.

Okay. That's the backstory...

So, then I go to this big martial art convention. The editor was obviously trying to dodge me, as he was nowhere to be seen – when he is always everywhere. Okay, I get it, he didn't want a fact-to-face. Then, a couple of days later I receive this very well crafted e-mail. Not a man-to-man phone call or anything like that but an e-mail. I could tell, it obviously took a long time to write. In it he alluded to the fact that he, the editor, (who gets paid a lot of money to do his job), had to work a lot on the article I gave him as it was not the article he had asked for. Liar! And, that the interviewee was not cooperative, which is why the issue of the magazine turned out the way it did. In other words, he blamed everyone but himself.

The e-mail was written as if it were for someone else's eyes. ...To cover his own ass. To make it looked like everyone else fucked up, but not him. Interesting...

I have heard about this type of behavior and e-mail strategy from my friends who work in the corporate world. From them, I have learned that you always keep a paper trail of e-mails as people often times try to lie and dodge responsibility for an issue and simply present an after-the-fact e-mail believing that is all that exists and, from their e-mail, they can make other people look bad and themselves look good.

Stupid ideology... But, the world is full of stupidity.

In times gone past I used to reply to these types of e-mails, stating my point of view and the facts as I see them. But, what does that prove? It goes round and round to nowhere. And, this editor has hit me with this type of e-mail in the past. So, I guess I should have seen it coming.

He dropped the ball and needed help. I stepped up and gave him the help he needed, and this was my thanks, being blamed for his mistakes.

So, what is the moral of the story? I really don't know. You can look at it a couple of different ways, I guess. One, always keep your e-mails. Two, don't go out of your way to do things for people you consider your friends when they are only in it for themselves and don't care about any impact they may have on your life. Three, just don't give a fuck and do what you do to do it. But, number three, that's not me... I care about people. I want to help everyone and make their life better. So ???

Life... Every now and then, it does throw you a curve ball. A curve ball when you were trying to do a good thing for all concerned. But, a curve ball none-the-less.

What do you do? I don't know? This is just life, live it to the best of your ability, I guess. But mostly, don't try to blame others, via e-mails or otherwise, when the causation factor was all on you.

# It's All About the Bottom Line

03/Jul/2014 09:27 AM

I think it is a sad reality of life that the majority of the people of this world, no matter what they claim, do not give a shit about anybody but themselves. This is especially the case when they are pushed up against the wall – particularly if it is the financial wall. They will say and do whatever it takes to get people to do whatever it is they need them to do to actualize their own personal reality and to keep their life financial life afloat no matter what it does to another person.

In life, there is always the captain of the ship. This person may be the actual captain, but most of us are not in the military, so it is more than likely a boss or someone in a position of authority that pulls our strings. As they pull the stings they have the potential to hire, fire, and mess with people's lives. Some people who rise to this position are very nice and do good things from their position. But, most people who rise to this level are not like that at all. They rule with force and they only care about the bottom line. As such, this bottom line philosophy flows from the top downward. People do whatever it takes, to whomever, to achieve the desired end result of financial fortitude. From this, each person in the chain of command keeps his or her position intact by doing what he or she does to keep the higher-ups happy. But, in doing so, the lives of many people, farther down the line, can become damaged.

A lot of bad and unconscious things have happened in the world due to people following this pattern. Mostly, these negative things happen to the people who actually hold onto the mindset of believing in people and believing in the betterment achieved by what they are doing. A clog in the wheel, yes, but all clogs are a necessary element to the overall functioning of the wheel. Yet, due to their belief in personal goodness, these people are commonly the first to be thrown to the wolves.

Now, it is not that the lower levels in the chain of command are all good and holy. No, many of them are trying to climb the ladder so they are willing to do whatever it takes to step up. Then, there are those who are only trying to survive, so they too, do and do – doing whatever it takes, even if that, *"Whatever it takes,"* means going against their own moral code in order to survive.

Life is a complicated mess. People need to survive. That survival is generally based upon financial income. From this, all kinds of unthinking, unkind, and/or selfish actions occur.

Has a person in a position of authority done you wrong? Perhaps it was a person you considered a friend? By whatever means you were asked to do something, (perform an action), and because you were asked, you did it. But, you later discovered that the ultimate outcome of that action affected your life in a negative way. It has happened to many of us, myself included.

The problem is, even if the person higher up the chain cares that you were damaged that did not stop them from doing what they did to maintain their own position in life. And, *"I'm sorry,"* means nothing, as it changes absolutely nothing. So, what can be done?

In life, we all need income. We hope that we can obtain the necessary financial sustenance through doing something we like and in doing it we trust it will not hurt our moral code, other people, or our extended reality. Unfortunately, this is not always the case. And, the thing is, rarely do we know that we are about to be sucker punched before the punch arrives. Promises are made. But, promises are not kept. By the time we find out that we are going to be fucked over, it is often too late – as we already have been hit.

Once you have been done wrong, you can quit and never be damaged by that person or that organization again. Some people can't do this however, as they need the income. You can yell and scream, but that changes nothing. You can apologize farther down the line to the person that your actions damaged, (caused by the higher-ups), but again, *"I'm sorry,"* changes nothing.

In many cases, all that you are left with is what you have done. Done... Guided by those who lied to you, farther up the chain of command.

Life is a mess. No one says it is easy. The farther you progress through it, the more obvious the lack of ease becomes evident. This is due to the fact that as you travel through life your responsibilities increase and the possibilities of alterable actions decrease. As such many people find themselves trapped in their job and their lifestyle.

Many a Self-Help book has been written on the subject of how to change your life; some are good, some are not. But, the ultimate truth is, most of the ideologies in their pages do not work because people remain trapped by the hands of their employer, needing to do whatever it takes to maintain their income.

In places like India and Thailand it is much more easy to say, *"Fuck it,"* and leave the world behind. Then, if you do this, everyone reveres you, as you are a holy man (or woman). The Buddha did it; right? He left behind his family and his child. Here in the States, however, if you do that the courts will be after you for child support. So, bailing to Holy-Land is not an easy option.

So, what can you do? Ultimately, all you can do is what you do. But, you need to guide yourself down the right road as early as possible in life, doing the right things. For the older you get, the harder it is to change. But, no matter where you find yourself in life, create a mental place in yourself where you are willing to walk away when and if you have been wronged – especially if that wrong involved you wronging someone else, guided by the powers-that-be.

Be more than your controllers. The world becomes a better place.

**What Have You Done Nice Lately?**

02/Jul/2014 09:00 AM

Most people spend much of the time doing what they are supposed to do. Whether it is in school, at the job, or taking care of the kids, they are taught and they understand the procedures and the protocols. They do what they must do. But, while they are doing, they are oftentimes thinking and wishing that they were not doing. As such, once they have been released from the confines of whatever environment they are confined within then, *"This is me time."* A time to do the things they want to do.

Okay... This is life. That is pretty much modus operandi for everybody. But, there is a big gaping hole in this mindset. What about others? What have you done for the betterment of anything? What have you done nice lately?

The fact is, many people don't care. They never thing about others, they only think about themselves. So, why should they care about and/or do anything for anyone but themselves?

When you hear it put in these words, many will immediately think, *"That is pretty selfish."* But, ask yourself, *"How much time do I spend actually doing anything for anybody?"* Now, I am not speaking of friends, family, or coworkers. These are people that you are expected to do things for. But, the question then remains, what are you doing simply to do? What are you doing to help and to make things better?

Some people orchestrate their lives so they are constantly giving and doing for others. Certainly teachers give a lot. They give a lot for a very little amount of money. Teachers in the grammar, middle, and high school levels all must contend with a lot of adversity, yet they continue to give. What they give to their students is fundamental for an individual's passageway through life.

Teaching in other areas is not, necessarily, so giving by its definition or in its nature. For example martial art teachers are often full of ego. Dance teachers, much the same. Even yoga instructors base much of their motivation not solely upon helping but in the claiming that they are helping. None-the-less a martial art teacher teaches something that can be used throughout a lifetime. This is also true of the yoga teacher and so on.

But, what can the average person do to give? As I have long stated, you don't have to join the Peace Corp, you don't have to perform great acts; all you have to do is be nice and do small things. Smile at people when you walk past them.

Smile, even if they have scowl on their face. Open doors for people. If someone drops something pick it up for them. If something has fallen off of a rack or a shelf in a store that you are in, pick it up and put it back in its place. And, be nice. Being nice to people goes a long way.    From these small things, all of life gets better. It gets better in small ways that expands to bigger ways. Do good instead of doing bad. Be nice instead of being egocentric, self-involved, or mean. From this, everything in this Life-Place slowly gets better.

# Made in China

01/Jul/2014 08:14 AM

En route between L.A. and Vegas there is this large Outlet Mall. For those of you who may not know, an Outlet Mall is a place where name-band companies set up shop and sell things from their store at a discount price. Sometimes when we make this drive, my lady and myself, stop there to shop.

Personally, I am not too much into them. The prices never seem that great and a lot of times they are very crowded. I don't like people or crowds. But, as my lady is into this one particular handbag label, we periodically stop to check out this one store. This we did yesterday.

As has been well-documented one of the biggest groups to come to visit the U.S. these days are travelers from the P.R.C. – the Mainland of China. Once almost impossible, now with the rising economy many have the means to make the journey. As such, the tour buses pull up to these Outlet Malls.

So, there we are, inside *Coach*, looking at purses. The shop is full of women and their men from the P.R.C. In fact, so many shoppers come from China to visit this store a large percentage of the staff are native Mandarin speakers.

There I stood holding a handbag that my lady was thinking of purchasing. Grab, this woman pulls the purse from my hand. What??? She wanted it, so she literally grabbed it from out of my grasp.

Now, I have heard about stuff like this happening at *Black Friday* sales and at places like that. But, it had never happened to me. I stood there laughingly dumfounded.

There is no doubt that Chinese people are rude. Yes, yes, that is a stereotype. But, cultural stereotypes are generally based in fact. Having lived in China and having spent a lot of time there, the stories I could tell. But, this was a first, having something grabbed from my hand.

I suppose had my lady really wanted the purse I may have put up more of a fight. But, I just stood there, looking the Chinese grabber in the eye, shaking my head. If you want it that bad…

The funny thing, and the point to all this is, *Coach* handbags are no longer made in the U.S.A. or Italy or any other cool place for that matter. They are made in China. But, they are only distributed there in very high-end boutiques. So, Chinese tourists must come to the U.S. to buy a bag Made in China for a reasonable price. That is if you consider one-hundred plus dollars a reasonable price...

I don't know, the purse was Made in China, the people were Made in China. There is simply something very bizarrely wrong in that equation. I don't get it?

Desire, it does drive life...

# The Teacher Takes on the Karma

27/Jun/2014 07:49 AM

No matter how you come at the subject there is one very clear fact of life, the moment you teach somebody something/anything, the moment you give someone advice you take on the *karma* for their next set of actions. Why? Because it was you who guided them.

Since the dawning of the New Age, and for centuries before, people have stepped to the forefront with various ideologies and teachings that they believe will help a person become more and better. In times gone past, this information would be passed along, directly, from person to person. Since the modern technological age came upon us the dissemination of this information has vastly expanded. As such, the method for the transmission of providing an individual with advice and teachings, (spiritual or otherwise), has increased multifold. From this, a lot of people have discovered their voice. But, was their voice their own?

If you listen to any of the self-help, get-better, be-better teachings that go around, there is one thing that will quickly be revealed, that revelation is that pretty much everyone who is speaking is saying exactly the same thing. Yet, they pretend the words are their own. They are not.

Listen to the self-help teachers and what do you hear? The same words and promises made over and over again. The same words and promises that were spoken by some other person a day, a week, or a year ago.

Listen to the rhetoric and you will hear that one person is saying the words they heard from another person. If you spend anytime listening, you can actually trace the words spoken by one person to that of another speaker.

Though word are all well and good. And, some words are meant to make you feel better and be better. But, this is not the point. The point is, no one is saying anything new. They are simply regurgitating something that they heard somewhere else and then are pretending, to themselves and to others, that they have something worth saying.

What has occurred from this process is that a lot of people have been propagating the same message by stealing the words of others. But, these words, as they are not organic in their content or message, have come to mean nothing.

Most people, particularly so-called, *"Spiritual teachers,"* are like parrots, they do not speak from a place of inner-knowledge; instead they speak from a place of memorization. Others are more like a ventriloquist dummy in that they simply say what they are told to say.

The point is, none of this is real. It is not enlightened knowledge. It is simply the repeating of words spoken by another. This is why there are so many false teachers out there. They hear something they like and then they repeat it.

All of this takes us to the point of fact that is, these false teachers possess no true inner knowledge and what they speak is not instigated from a place of pure knowledge. Thus, what they say is simply based in ego. *"I am telling you what I think you need to hear." "I am telling you what I think you should do."*

What is born from this type of instruction is *karma*. The *karma* that will be transmitted back to the teacher due to the words he or she speaks, the advice he or she gives, are not based in the suchness of true knowledge but are instead based in memorization.

If you tell somebody what to do and he or she does it; that becomes your *karma*. Just because you are telling them to do something nice does not mean that you will not suffer negative repercussions. Why? Because all action equals reaction, just as one action equals the next action. As such, what is born in one action leads to the next and the next and the next. This goes on throughout eternity. And, here comes the kicker; what is positive to one person may be negative to another. The action thought positive by one person, may be understood to instigate negativity by another.

There is no one good. There is no one universal truth or ultimate understanding. There is only personal interpretation. From this, words equal actions and actions equal *karma.*

This is why the true sage listens when people speak but does not respond. The true sage never suggests what someone should do. The true sage never believes that they have something worth saying. As they are silent, the true sage creates no *karma* and the world is left just a little bit better.

Teachers, turn off your ego and stop creating *karma.*

# Different Perceptions of Reality

26/Jun/2014 08:16 AM

Each of us possesses a different perception of reality. We have the, *"What is okay,"* and the *"What is not okay."* Though many of these definitions span the globe and are universal, many are very individual.

The country, culture, city, neighbor, and socioeconomic factors that a person grew up within each defines what an individual deems is acceptable or not. Here lies the foundation for our perception of reality.

From a very limited perspective, personal space is one of the first things that many people bring up when they travel to different countries or to new locations. For example, in the western part of the U.S. people have a very large bubble that they consider their personal space. They do not like it to be invaded. They do not want to be too close to other people – especially someone they do not know. People from the eastern region of the U.S., particularly those hailing from large citied like New York, Philadelphia, Pittsburg, or Boston, are much more forgiving of the closeness that must be encountered. This is due to the fact these city dwellers grew up surround by people, where personal space was much less spacious. When one travels to other countries, particularly in the Middle East or South Asia, again, many people quickly realize that personal is not expansive. The personal bubble is very small. Many dislike this fact.

But, more than simply the physical aspects of life, each person perceive reality in a differing manner from other people. This is based upon religious ideology, cultural training, or simply by choice.

The fact is, the way an individual perceives life may or may not be grounded in reality. And, this is the thing about reality, it is speculative. There is what is considered, *"Common Reality,"* a place that most of us deem is acceptable and then there is "Personal Reality." This is place where each of us lives in our own heads.

Most of us accept *Common Reality* and do not step too far away from its boundaries. Some people, however, either do not possess the mental skill set or do not have enough of a conscience to choose to be defined by it. Here is where many of the evil acts, witnessed by this world, have been instigated.

People who exist solely in the mental space of *Personal Reality* are dangerous. They are motivated by any number of things but the outcome of their motivation is always damage because they focus on themselves and what they believe first, before ever taking anyone else or even accepted *Common Reality* into consideration.

The world, and human consciousness, as we understand it, is defined by a prescribed set of parameters. In this place, it is understood that good is good and bad is bad. Doing good should be rewarded, just as doing bad should be punished. But, once a person steps outside of this defined realm of reality anything goes.

There are many, even many who walk upon various (so called) spiritual paths that instigate behavior based upon *Personal Reality.* Some even believe and claim that once a particular action is taken then all of humanity will emerge in a better space. But, let's not forget that this was (and is) also they motivation for war, human sacrifice, and torture. Reality based in this mindset is never good.

This is the point where everyone needs to take a long hard look at what they are doing and study the foundations for what they believe. For if what you believe in was or is based in the destruction of anything (especially people) than from the understanding of *Common Reality* it is wrong. Hurting, killing, destroying, damaging, lying, cheating, deceiving; it is all-wrong. And, no matter how much a person, a society, or a religion justifies the reasons for having done what it has done, by our own defined *Common Reality*, it is wrong.

This is the place where life gets complicated as most people are defined by their religion and their society. They, in many cases, are very proud of their religion and their society. And, even if they know the history of their religion and society; they justify its action. That was necessary for us to get to here.

But, many people never take the time to question the foundations of their beliefs. They simply believe. This is the place where, *"Mind,"* tosses out, *"Reality,"* and people simply becomes a pawn in the propaganda of culture, religion, and life. This is why the acts of war still go on. This is why the damaging and hurting of others still goes on. This is why that though the technology surrounding physical life may have evolved, human life is still trapped at its most animalistic level.

This is the point where you must ask yourself the question, *"What are you going to do about it? Are you going to continue to buy into the lie or will you step beyond it?"*

This is a complicated question, but it has to be answered by you. Are you going to continue to make excuses for the negative factors that formed your culture, your society, and your religion or are you going to choose to rise above them?

# Mad At Me Because I'm Mad At You

25/Jun/2014 07:55 AM

I always find the concept of anger and how it is implemented very interesting. Individually, we each get mad at a person or a situation for our own set of reasons. Some are very logically – reasons that anyone would understand. Others are a bit more speculative. But, none-the-less, we become angry.

Anger goes hand-in-hand with the human experience. Yes, some people train their mind to immediately let go of anger once they begin to experience it. And, this is a very good mental training. But, there is a fine line between being able to consciously let go of anger or redirect it and that of simply repressing it.

From a psychological perspective, repression is never a good thing. But, far worse is that of allowing anger to control you and you acting out upon this fleeting emotion. And, that's what anger is, a fleeting emotion. It will be here but then it will be gone.

Many people become locked into the mindset of expressing their anger. When they are angry, they blow up. They lose all control. Or, maybe better put, they choose to loose control.

Perhaps as a young child they came to understand, whether consciously or unconsciously, if they threw a big enough fit they would get their own way. In other cases, people learn that if they throw an anger-based-fit they will get their own way do to intimidation – as in some cases, an angry person can be a pretty scary sight.

The fact is there are some branches of psychology that tell people to express their emotions no matter what they are. But, here comes an important distinction between a person who is in control of themselves and one who is simply a screaming spoiled child. Yes, we all feel emotions. Yes, we all become angry if we have an opinion. Yes, we all become angry if we have a desire. For if something is not going our way, (the way we want), then that angry emotion is triggered. But, anger is a powerful generator of negative action. Think about this, when you have felt anger and you acted upon it, were your actions positive movements that makes you and the all of humanity more and better or were they destructive performance that damaged things, other people, and possibly even yourself?

One of the curious things I find in life is that many people when someone is angry at them, for whatever reason, then they become angry at that person. They do not care to take the mental time to try to understand why someone is angry at them or what they have done to make that person angry. Instead, all they do is repay the favor; you are angry at me so I am angry at you.

When you think about this it is pretty ridiculous. But, do you behave in this manner? Many people do. Do you become angry with someone after you have set a course of events in motion that has caused a person to become angry with you? Even if you understand their causation for anger, do you choose to change yourself and stop being the instigator of that anger? And, if you have taken this action does that action burn inside of you causing you to generate more anger? Or, do you simply blame everyone but yourself and become angry at them for being angry at you?

Life is a complicated sphere of interactive reality. We, as people, all have our own set of definition about how this sphere of interactive reality is supposed to operate. We have developed this mindset by the experiences we have encountered throughout our life. But, the one fact that is universally true is that all emotion is born within you. What you do with it is ultimately your choice.

You can become angry. You can be mad a people, life situations, or even god. But, it is you who is deciding to feel that way. Then, it is you who decides how you will encounter life with the motivation of that emotion.

If you do bad things based on desire, ignorance, or emotion then your life becomes defined by those actions. As such, this will also affect the reaction of others who encounter you.

The truth of life is, if you define yourself by emotions, creating other emotions, and emotions in others, all you will experiences is a life of chaos: of loves and hates or people that may love you but most will hate you because you are not in control of yourself.

We each feel emotions. We each react to the emotions others have for and towards us. But, the universal truth is, we can let our emotions control us and guide us down an emotion based road of anger and destruction or we can be more. We can know what we feel but not be controlled by it. We can understand the truth of life that emotions, practically negative emotions like anger, come and go. By knowing this, we can learn to control and not be controlled by these emotions. If we feel them, we witness them, we do what we must do from a conscious perspective to keep them from reoccurring, and then we move on. We move on to live life in the most conscious, refined, and self-controlled manner possible. From this, our anger and the anger of others is never our motivating factor. This moves us closer to Zen.

## What Do You Believe In Scott Shaw?

24/Jun/2014 08:30 AM

As I have written a lot of stuff in my life; particularly on the subject of Mind-Stuff. And, as publishers and people have said a lot of things about me, (some true, some not), I am often questioned, *"What do you believe in Scott Shaw? What is your philosophy?"*

I always think that it is interesting that when you write a book the publisher immediately assumes that book and its contents describes exactly who you are. You know enough to write a book about a subject that must be what you practice. ... Practice what you preach and all that. Not necessarily... From this ideology, several publishers have claimed that I am something when, in fact, I am not.

I also find it interesting how when you write books and articles like I have, the publishers forever place you in a defined category of the writer of, THAT. This has certainly happened to me. A lot of times I will be contacted by publishers and asked to write an article or a book on a particular subject. Many times, however, I turn the offer down, as I believe I have said all that I have to say about a particular subject. The adverse has also happened when I have presented a proposal to a publisher and they have turned it down believing that I am only an author on the subject of, SOMETHING ELSE.

Now that I have attempted to tell you what I am not – even though other people have said that is what I am, I will try to get more to the point and attempt to give you a definition of Scott Shaw – at least from a metaphysical perspective.

When I was very young I walked into a bookstore on Western Ave. in L.A. and I was drawn to a copy of the *Tao Te Ching*. I read through it in the store, then ran home and asked my mother for the money to buy it. She gave it to me. I returned to the store and purchased it. I took it home and read it over and over again.

If there is one book that I believe possesses the simplest truth and most prefect pathway to enlightenment, it is the *Tao Te Ching*. There are many translations and some aren't as good as others but it is a great book. I even translated it once-upon-a-time. I will have to look for that someday and maybe seek out a publisher. In any case, I believe the truth is all there.

This being said, and though it would have been the easiest and best decision of my life to just stay true to those few and simply words presented in that book, easy has never been my best quality. Nor has not seeking; looking under every nook and cranny. As such, as has been well documented, I have danced around deeply into a lot of Eastern and Middle Eastern religious ideologies. I gained from each of them. But, I left them all behind, because at their core they are all way too complicated.

If there is one thing that defines me, it is the quest for refined simplicity – leaving behind all of the structure and all of the dogma and emerging into a space of wholeness that is ALL and EVERYTHING in and onto itself. I don't believe religion can take you there. Religion is far to bound by the structure of what you must do and how you must behave. Even formalized Zen Buddhism is so bound by structure that it defeats its defined essence.

People, who have the inclination, seek the truth: the truth about god, the universe, themselves, and the answer to the question, *"Why?"* From this, they turn to religion and to soothsayers. But, none of these hold the truth because I believe that the truth can only be found within yourself. And, it is only there if you are free enough to step beyond the structure, step beyond who and what you think you know, and even step beyond how you want to project yourself to the world. There, I believe, in that space/place of freedom and emptiness where absolute knowledge can be experienced.

To this end, and to answer the question, I believe in nothing. I believe in the perfection of nothing. For in nothing, all things are.

**It Never Rains in Space**

23/Jun/2014 08:54 AM

Since the dawn of humankind and the ever-evolving realms of human consciousness man (and woman) has stared at the stars with wonderment. From this, there have been all kinds of fantasies and works of literature created. The human mind traveled there since the reality of sense separation and the defining of human boundaries came into play. People wrote stories of the possibilities of what is out there since long before man ever made his first steps into the realms beyond this earth. Someday, perhaps, man will have developed the ability to actually travel into and streak across the galaxies as has been depicted in so many novels, movies, and television shows. Then is not now, however. Now is now.

In life, we are defined by life. We are defined by our available options. Our mind can wander, we can believe in anything we wish to believe in; we can hope and we can fanaticize about anything that we want – we can even take steps in making the next evolution of humankind possible. What we cannot do, however, is to change the reality we are defined to live within. Here, in the space and the time we find ourselves inhabiting is all we have. Meaning, we are defined by where we are.

Many people speak of what is, when it is not. They claim all type of aberrant realities. They make people believe in heavens, hells, parallel universes, and altered dimensions. This is why the proponents of the counterculture, which took hold during the 1960s and 1970s, were so able to establish themselves and their place in counterculture history by preaching the benefits of the use of hallucinogenic drugs – for in that altered reality, anything was possible.

The problem with the use of hallucinogenic drugs and their ingestion as a causeway to expanding consciousness is that there is never one-reality. Though two people may take the exact same drug at the exact same moment, their experience and what they each, individually, experienced will be completely different. Thus, hallucinogenic drugs are not a pathway to a new kingdom. If they were, everyone would arrive at the same place. They do not.

This same basis of individual consciousness, equaling religious ideology, is also easy charted. Though people may follow the same religion and even exist within the same sect or have the same teacher within that religion; each will have their own mental picture of what is what. If you speak to them, if you ask them to describe their religion, if you ask them to step beyond what is stated in their scriptures, than each will come to their own conclusion about the definition of life, reality, god, and the cosmos. Though, compared to the altered mental reality of an individual who ingests a hallucinogenic drugs, there will be more of a common thought process and definition, none-the-less, there will still be large gaps, revealing large differences, in conceptualized reality.

When you enter the more abstract and metaphysical levels of human consciousness and those who talk about and teach these realms, the sky is the limit. They can say anything because there is no common ground and basis in or of fact. In fact, the more grandiose the claims made by these practitioners, the more they elevate themselves to a place where they may be believed to be more than the common individual. In other words, they are claiming, *"I am able to experience something you cannot, as such, that makes me more than you."* Some feeble minded people buy into this. From this, all kinds of nonsense and devious deeds have been unleashed throughout the evolution of humanity.

Human life was formed and, at least for now, it exists predominately upon this earth. Here: there is life, there is death, there is human conflict, there is success and there is failure. Here, there is weather. It rains here on earth. It does not rain in space. That rain gives us needed sustenance. In space it is absence. Thus, it is not where we are supposed to be.

No matter what our mind chooses to believe. No matter what we do or whom we choose to follow, there is one simply reality. That reality is, all we are is all we are.

We can fantasy, we can pretend, we can follow those we believe to be holy or who claim holiness. We can alter our reality with hallucinogenic drugs, but, at the end of the day, we will come down from that drug and who and what will we be? Who we will be is simply who and what we are. No more, no less.

No matter what we believe, no matter what holiness a person does or does not claim, they too will die. Though some claim they can transcend this realm and communicate with those who have left this life, this too is a falsity based upon the creative mind of some novelist from times gone past. To prove this point, try this, put two of the people who claim they can communicate with the dead together, will they speak they same words supposedly voiced by that person who now dwells in the great beyond? No, they will not. Thus, like hallucinogenic drugs all reality is based on the individual. There is no absolute definition, no defined absolute knowledge about this life space or what is beyond our life. There is only what we have here and now. Accept that and you are free.

# Philosophy Equals Bullshit

22/Jun/2014 08:43 AM

There is a simply reality of life, there are those who do. They go through life with little thought of the absolute meaning of human existence, nor do they seek the absolute truth. They simply live their life, doing what needs to be done to sustain their existence.

Then, there are those who think, the try to explain the reason(s) why and for, they try to add definition and justification for all that is taking place in this human landscape. They find reasons and deceptions to justify what they are thinking, what they are feeling, why they are acting the way they are acting and what they are not doing. Plus, they attempt to define why the other people of the world behave in the way they behave. Though all that they say may equal a nice complication of words, in the end, it all equals nothing. Why? Because with out the non-thinkers, the thinkers would have nothing to eat, nowhere to live, thus, they would not be able to survive.

From time immemorial, people have placed the thinkers; i.e. the philosopher at the top of the food chain. Why? Because they present philosophic hypothesis that may be but probably are not true. Mind stuff is not reality. It is just mind stuff. At best it is food for thought and something to occupy the mind as the body passes through life.

Here lies the problem, there are those who are the doers and there are those that are thinkers, but in between are the people who buy into the bullshit presented by the thinkers. They are the people who have time for thought but are not capable of developing their own philosophy, thus they follow those who have previously written and spoken and/or are currently developing their individual philosophic school of thought. These people are the enablers of the thinkers.

The doers do. The thinkers think. Those in between follow. Who are you?

If you did not have time to think, if you were not financially comfortable enough to have time to think, what would you be doing? What you would be doing is that you would be forced into doing. You would be forced into finding food and shelter. You would be forced into the most animalistic level of existence. Though it has long been prorogated that society has risen above this, it has not. Look at war zones where treachery and animalistic behavior abound. People are forced to employee their most basic survival skills. Thus, if this is the basis of human sociological behavior and as we have not truly risen about it, this explains the obvious; the doers are the truly blessed. The thinkers are simply dishing out the bullshit. And, those in between are lost, seeking a reason for their existence.

# Love Your Dog Because Your Dog Loves You

21/Jun/2014 08:37 AM

I was driving down the street and I encountered an interesting spectacle. There was this white Mercedes driving near me. All well and good. Quite normal... The interesting thing was that next to the car was prancing this rather large, mixed breed, brown dog. The car wasn't going too fast, so the dog wasn't really running.

As the car moved along, the dog continued to pace itself right next to where the driver was sitting. As the two progressed down the street, you could see that the dog was looking up at the driver.

The car pulls up to a stop sign and stops. The dog right next to it stops and is staring at the driver. I was initially a little behind the car but I tried to alert the driver as to the dog's presence. But, they did not take notice of the dog standing there staring at them or of me trying to let them know that the dog was there.

The car moves on. So does the dog.

The car stops at the next stop sign. Finally, the driver can see me. I point at the dog standing right next to her door. She looks down, opens her door, "Get in the car right now," she exclaims. With this, the dog jumps over her and into the passenger seat. She closes the door, drives off, makes a U-turn, and I assume heads home.

You could see the love in the dog's eyes. He probably loves this lady so much that he somehow got free from where he was and only wanting to be with her, followed her down the street. It was really a great sight to witness this much love. It was also worth noting the owner's frustration at the dog's love. The two differing sides of the same coin.

I understand that it probably not a good thing for your dog to follow you down the street, jogging next to your car, but I hope she didn't discipline him due to his love.

I am sure there is some metaphysical parallel to life and spirituality in all of this. But, all I can come up with is, *"Love your dog because your dog loves you."*

# The Silence In-Between the Sound

20/Jun/2014 08:38 AM

I was woken up by some noise outside on the street this morning. It made me think back to another time...

I had this condo in Redondo Beach for about six or seven years. The building was right up against the water. So, it had specular views and the sound of the waves caressing my ears. When I first saw it, I feel in love. I felt it was exactly where I should be.

When the real estate guy showed it to me, it was in the evening. I noticed on the other side of the building that there was a bunch of scaffolding. I asked about it. He told me that the building cooperative was cleaning all the windows. Okay... That sounded all right. I put my money down and I moved in.

I had previously been living about a block away so as soon as the deal was done I grabbed my Mac, a couple of pillows and blankets for my lady and me; walked them over, and I was there. I was in heaven.

AM rolls around. I start to hear all of this loud pounding and cutting off in the distance. It kind of made the building vibrate. As it turns out, the real estate agent had lied to me. They were not cleaning the windows. They were retiling all of the patios. Now, this was a big tall building, there were several hundred units, and they had just started the job. I got screwed.

I thought to sue the real estate guy, as it would have been an open-and-shut case of deception but I pulled back. My lawyer was mad at me. He gets mad at me frequently as I always stop him from suing people even though he knows he will win. I'm his worst client. I know this because he tells me I am.

The big problem in the equitation was, they had started on the other side of the building. As they moved around to my side of the building the pounding and the tile cutting got louder and louder until it reached a fever pitch when they were working near my unit. It was really deafening.

During this period I was teaching a lot of classes at the university. For those of you who may not know, it takes a lot of time to prep a class; especially a class on filmmaking. You don't just go in there and spit out wisdom; you have to have it all well organized with lots of cinematic examples. The noise killed me.

I was also writing a lot. I was working with this publisher that really liked what I wrote. Pretty much once I finished one book, they would ask me for another. This, plus, I was writing articles and making movies. So, the noise was not good.

If you were one of those nine-to-five people, like my lady, it was no problem. She never understood all my complaints. She would leave before it started and come home after it ended. People like her never had to experiences the blunt force of the trauma. It killed me.

But, I had to exist. I had to create. All I could do was to formulate a plan.

The tiling would start every morning around 8:00 AM. So, I would get up prior to that, try to get some work done, and then go out and have breakfast, shop, visit friends, and do stuff like that, once all the chaos began. The crews would go to lunch from 12:00 to 1:00 so I would come back and try to get some more work done for an hour. They would re-start. I would re-leave. I would work out or teach some MA. They would quit around 4:00 PM. I would come home and get busy. When I was filming movies, during this period, it wasn't so bad because I would be out doing it. But, when I had to do stuff at home, it was very problematic. This process of retiling the patios took about six-months. It was bad!

Now, when they were done, when all the tiling had been completed, life became better. But, then arose a new problem. This was at the time when every one was getting into hardwood floors. I've never liked hardwood floors very much. I like carpeted floors. But, to each there own.

In any case, many people in the building began redoing their floors. The way this building was constructed, out of concrete, I believe, sound vibrated through the structure – especially the sounds of construction. So, every time I thought it was all over and I was back to simply listening to the waves and creating: bam, bam, bam, cut, cut, cut. Heaven again became hell.

When construction wasn't going on it was a great place to live. When it was, it was not. Eventually, all the noise caused me to move. But, I was there for a lot of years. The noise and my figuring out ways to work in-between it makes me think to the old Zen proverb, *"If a tree falls in the forest and there is no one there to hear it, does it make a sound?"*

I think if we look at this a different way, the sound would be the distraction in the solitude of the forest. It would be disruptive to the peace and the serenity. So, when the tree falls, the noise it makes interrupts this peace and serenity. But, once it meets the ground, again there is silence and all things can return to being as they naturally are.

This is the place of meditation; of *Zazen.* This is the place we all seek. We may have to wait until the world around us becomes silent. But, if we wait, we can find it. Even if it only lasts for a moment; in that moment, *Satori* can be found. It can be found if we do let the disruption of the noise linger in us and control our inner-being.

# Venture Capital

19/Jun/2014 09:35 AM

Venture Capital is the process of taking money for an idea that you have. Venture Capitalists are people that seek out others with what they consider to be a good idea. They then fund that idea. This funding is usually for a company. But, in some cases it for some other sort of idea or product. Certainly, in the film industry, people pitch their movie ideas all the time and ask people to give them the money to make their film idea a reality.

Most people, as they start out in life, do not have the funding to actually begin their business. Because of this, turning to a person with money is an obvious idea. For small ventures, turning to a family member is commonly the first choice. I know when I opened my first martial art studio it cost me all of $500.00 to get it going. (Wish it were that cheap now!) My mother was happy to lend it to me. I understand when my father opened a restaurant in the early 1950s he took the money he had saved up and combined it with money from his father and my uncle to open the restaurant which became very successful. Easy... All well and good.

Recently, I was watching an episode of, *"Bar Rescue,"* where a son had driven a bar his parents had financed a million and a half in debt. All on his parent's dime. That is the other side of family money and family psychological politics. I am sure that kind of goings-on happen all the time.

In the film industry, I have known a number of people that have driven themselves and their parents into bankruptcy all on the belief of making a movie that would change everything. Due to all the hype that is out there, that is a very easy trap to fall into. Personally, I used to be contacted a lot from people asking me for money to finance their film. I will have to find an article I wrote on that subject a few years back. They all believed in their idea. Some even had a good pitch. But, funding someone else's film is not my thing. I have seen and experienced too much of the dark side of the film industry to ever go down that road.

In the last few years, crowd-funding websites have sprouted up. There, people ask for money for whatever idea they have. Simple enough. But, there are no promises. I have known, and known of, a number of people who have put up nice pages, some even got all the money they asked for. But... What happened to the product promised? Nothing... Even a couple of established filmmakers I know of have taken and kept the money. No film. Uncool.

With no oversight, there is no necessity to do anything with the money but blow it. I saw this so many times with Donald G. Jackson. He took money for a film and never made it. Promised people the world but never came through. Told people they could write the script, produce, star in; but then nothing. Due to his behavior, a lot of people hated him. He had to be very carful where he waked. That was why (I discovered) he always had someone like me around him. Someone who could and was willing to fight. A bodyguard in other words. That is not a good way to live one's life.

I learned a lot through example. This is why I never ask anyone for money to make my films. Which sometimes (oftentimes) means I don't get to make films. But, I am willing to pay that price to keep my *karma* clean.

Money is a tricky thing. It is the substance, the energy that we all need to survive. It is what takes us from here to there. It is both allusive and easy to get. Easy to get for the person who claims to have something that can be the basis for promising someone the ability to live the dream that they have long desired to live. I have seen so many people give their money to film producers who promises them big figure returns, only for them to end up broke and with nothing. It is very sad. But, the producer had an idea. They had a promised product. They made that promised product. That is the American way, right? But, when it came to the payout, where did that money go?

Venture finance is a tricky busy. There are a lot of risks. That is why venture capitalist always take a percentage of any company or idea they finance. This is why, when you see in the news, that the creator of a company is getting the axe. How did that happen – he created the company? How that happened is that he gave his power away for the money to get started and once he crossed a line that the powers-that-be, that the money, did not like, that was the end of him or her.

In some ways this is a good practice. There is cause and effect. Most of life is not like that, however. There are those that make a practice of taking. Some even have developed it into a science. Others, like venture capitalists, give so that they can eventually make and take on the idea of someone else. It is all a complicated *negative-karma* game. Yet, many people rise to the heights of financial wealth based upon this system.

This is always the question that the person of consciousness needs to ponder. Yes, we all need money to survive. It is the energy that keeps us functioning. But, what are we willing to do to get it? I can define my boundaries. You need to be able to define yours. Because, at the end of the day, all we have is what we have done. That is our legacy. If what we have done has taken from, hurt, or damaged others, than no matter how good the idea, all that is left is ruination. Is that how you want your life to be defined?

# Angels, Demons, Charlatans and You Talk Too Loud You Inconsiderate Asshole
18/Jun/2014 02:36 PM

I have been forced into thinking a lot about angles and demons over the past year or so due to the fact that a very loud and rude neighbor has moved in next door to me. I have spoken about him, a couple of times, in recent blogs but the inconsiderateness of his nature, continues. The fact is, I virtually never thought about the subject of angels and demons prior to his moving in next door to me and broadcasting his beliefs out to the ethos. I mean, sure, I have seen movies that send the mind in that direction, but I do not like that subject matter – far too negative for my tastes. Me, I am much more into the Zen of life: making the everyday and the mundane the pathway to enlightenment, living life to the best of your ability, helping people as opposed to hurting them, seeing the good in everyone, and forgiving the sinners. But, I have been forced to listen to him day in and day out and it never seems to end.

This guy claims to be some sort of a something... I spoke to him once when he first moved in. He seemed all right... I assumed that he would soon understand that he talked way too loud and no one around him; none of the neighbors, (most certainly myself), wanted to hear what he was saying. But, he never really took the hint. Which has forced me (and others) to listen to his ongoing nonsense.

In any case, he claims he summons up some sort of entity that takes over his being and communicates though him. My first thought was and is, *"Bullshit."* But, it is apparently what he believes and who am I to judge a person's beliefs?

To conjure up this being, prior to the discourses he gives over the phone, over the internet, or wherever – he does this loud invocation. It sounds something like a child making up the sounds that they believe someone like a Native American Shaman would make. It is no language and it sound pretty ridiculous. I won't try to spell it out for you, because I wouldn't know how, but you get the idea. He chants this chant very loudly.

As someone who has studied Sanskrit... Hell, I wrote a book on the subject. Wait, I shouldn't say, *"Hell."* I'll explain that in a moment. But anyway, due to my background and my involvement in Eastern spirituality, I have studied Sanskrit and, of course, other Asian and Middle Eastern languages to varying degrees. Plus, I have spent a lot of time in Asian and the Middle East, so I know a, *"No Language,"* when I hear one. That is what this guy chants.

Anyway, after being forced into listening to this guy's un-neighborly behavior for so long, (that has really damaged my life), I finally decided to go and talk to this elderly Catholic priest that I have known for a lot of years about the subject. Immediately, he was both amused and concerned when I told him what was going on. He questioned, *"Do you ever wonder why people who claim these abilities never come forward and speak to a person like myself?"* Actually, no, I know exactly why people like that do not go and speak to priests and tell them what they were doing.

I questioned him about how throughout Catholic history there have been those who have been understood to communicate with ethereal beings like angels. His immediately response was, *"Look to how those saints lived. They were of god. They were not of man."* Good point.

I even asked him why I would have to encounter someone like this forcing his words and ideologies into my life. His answer was, *"Only God knows."*

We spoke for a long time on the subject and then he blessed me with a prayer of protection, warning me to not let this man's, *"Blasphemy,"* (the word he used), enter my being. He concluded that, *"These people know not with whom they speak, as no angel would speak through a soul that was not in the grace of God. Thus, if this man is not simply a charlatan, he is probably in communication with a demon from Hell."*

Heavy stuff. You see why I don't like to think about it.

He told me to pray to God asking for protection and that the man would move away. *"Nice thought,"* I laughingly thought but I fight my own battles. And, I am sure God has better things to do than to listen to me.

You know, we personally let some people into our lives and they damage our existence and us. That is our fault. But, I think many of us have encountered situations like mine where we are forced into dealing with someone or something that we have no desire of encountering. Whether it is a person, the unconscious actions of a group, climate, illness, whatever... We are forced into dealing with something and that something or that someone damages our life. This has certainly been the case with what my neighbor has done to me.

I could go into the subject of *karma* here, but it is much more than that and also much less than that. For if we look to our lives we will quickly see that it is only ourselves and a few close people around us that truly care what is happening to us. Think about this, we see tragedy on the news all the time but what do we do about it? We hear of people being hurt by others all the time, as well. What do we do? What can we do? Once the damage has been done all we can hope for is that the instigator of the damage receives their *karma* and/or the punishment they deserve. But, all of this changes nothing. The unconscious, uncaring, or intentionally hurtful actions of another person, or even something beyond human control, has entered our realm and damaged our life. What do we do then? And, who truly cares about the pain we are suffering? This is one of the sad realities of life.

I have spoken to the neighbors about the loudness of the guy; well actually they have brought up the subject to me. They have each questioned what they could do about it. But, the subject is the guy. He is the problem. He is so locked up into whatever it is he is locked up into that what can anyone do until he fades from our *karma*?

People commonly falsely hold on to the ideology of, *"This is my space, I can do whatever I want in it!"* Maybe that is his ideology. I do not know. But, this is never the case with life. Whether you live far off in the country or in the city like I do, your choice in action has to be defined by your environment or you have the potential of damaging the life of another person, just like this guy has done to my neighbors and particularly me. If you perform actions like this, no matter what ethereal being is supposedly speaking through you, what can be the results? The result is the distaste of those surrounding you and blogs like this being written.

You know, there have been so many times that I have just wanted to scream, *"Shut the fuck up, you inconsiderate asshole!"* But, what would that prove? Until a person comes to the realization that they must care more about others before they even think about themselves, then no true spirituality, no inner truth, no absolute knowledge, no religion can be actualized.

So, for you people that pray out there, I guess I will leave it to you to pray for me, as I'm not very good at it. And, you see, everybody has stupid shit happen to their lives. Everybody... In my case, it has just been brought on by some guy who claims to be something. Maybe he should go and talk to a priest or a shrink? But, whomever he chooses to talk to; I just wish he would stop making me listen to him talk. :-)

# Thought Verses Action

17/Jun/2014 09:38 AM

Many people think about what they would like to do. They think about what they could do. They also think about what it would feel like to be doing what they are thinking about doing. The problem is, this is all in the head. It is not out in the real world.

There are some that claim that simply having a fantasy, in some way, makes that fantasy real. Maybe... But, a fantasy, just like a thought, is only that. It is simply a mind-thing located inside your brain. So, if having a fantasy is real, on some plane of consciousness, than it is only real to you.

Most spiritual traditions lead one away from focusing on fantasy. Most tell the aspirants that it is far better to let go of lust and desire than it is to focus and think about them, for this can cause one to fall from the path. Just as when you see something that you desire and your mind becomes fixated upon it; fantasy leads to fixation. And, fixation is never a space of refined consciousness.

In the spiritual teachings of Hinduism, and to a lessor degree Buddhism, it is understood that the more you think about something the deeper that thought becomes burned into you brain. If it is a spiritual thought or invocation such as a mantra, than good can come from this focusing. If it is geared towards something of the material world or something solely based upon human desire, however, than it can lead you down the wrong road.

Basing your thought patterns upon spirituality, however, is not an essential factor in understanding that fantasy is not action. Action is action. And, though we all spend our childhoods, to varying degrees, lost into the realms of what could be and what may be, as we move foreword in life, if we do not come to understand that focused action is the only way of achieving our dreams than our dreams will never be fulfilled. Meaning, if we stay locked in our heads, nothing we desire will move out into the realms of accepted reality.

This being said, what we desire is what we desire. But, simply because we desire it does not mean that it is achievable. This is particularly the case when it involves other people. You have your desires, they have theirs, and sometimes the two do not coincide.

This is also the case for people who desire big things like being loved and accepted by the masses. Be that in the form of politics, stardom, or whatever. In cases like this, many-many people must approve of your move upwards and forwards. As such, very few will ever experience this level of human acceptance, though many strive for it.

The simple answer is to keep your desires small, then they will be much easier to achieve. The reality is, however, if certain members of humanity never desired to take larger steps then vast changes in our human landscape would not be where they are today. But, this goes for both the good and the bad elements of our human landscape.

Life is defined by you and what you decide to attempt do. If your desire is to overrun, not care about; hurt or damage others, than you can pretty much be sure you will not succeed. Though, in truth, some have. Why? I do not know. That will forever remain one of the eternal questions of life.

This being stated, if you have concluded that you want to go after your desire, if you are focused upon achieving a particular prize, then you must remove the fantasy and make it a reality. You must move towards its actual achievement or nothing will ever be actualized.

But, you must also understand that there is no guarantee that you will achieve it. It is essential to note, simply because someone else has done it, does not mean that it is your destiny to do the same. To this end, you need to be honest with yourself and fair to all those around you. You need to learn to adapt your desires and your fantasies. Take positive action to achieve them. But, do not hurt others in your quest. Do, but do not undo. Then, at the end of the day, you must be honest with yourself if what you desire is not taking form. At that point, it is time to not let that desire control you. Instead, you must control it. Let go and reshape your mindscape to be willing to let go and move onto what may actually be your calling and your destiny.

Just because you want something does not mean that it will come to pass. But, if you do not take action, nothing can or will ever happen.

But, remember, the true sage desires nothing. They are the ones that are truly fulfilled, truly free.

## Do You Think That You Don't Have to Pay for Your Karma?
16/Jun/2014 08:17 AM

The question that must be asked is, *"Do you think that you don't have to pay for your karma?"*

Most people dance thru life, doing what they do, with little thought about the effect they are having on others. But, as they are doing what they are doing, with little thought, they are creating tons of *karma.* Then what?

If you are impacting the life of another person or persons, what are the ramifications? Do you think that you do not have to pay the piper?

Many people do not. They are all about getting over – doing what they do, when they want to do it. And, if doing what they want to do makes them feel okay, even for a moment, then all is well with the world. But, what if what you are doing is damaging the life of another person? Then what? What are the consequences to you and what are the ramifications to your life?

There are so many people out there who do not care. They take and they take, they do and they do. They may even think, *"Why care about anyone else?"*

Some people wake up; they see what they have done. They realize that they have hurt the life of someone else. But, then what? If you have come to understand that you have messed with the life of another person, are you going to fix what you have broken or are you simply going to sit in the realization that you have done someone wrong?

The fact of the matter is, you can stop doing what you are doing that is damaging other people or this life-space but if you do not fix what you have broken what does your realization prove? You must ask yourself, *"What have I done to fix or undo my previous actions?"*

You see, this is the ultimate flux point in life. Most people don't care, until they are forced to have a reason to care. They only care, when what they have done has caught up with them and has begun to affect their own life in some negative way. Then, they wake up. But, waking up is not correcting what you have done. Correcting what you have done is correcting what you have done. So, what is it you are going to do to recreate life and fix the *karma* you have unleashed?

There is, no doubt, that this is a complicated question. But, if you actually care about the other people on this earth and if you actual care about the damage you have created, it is a question you must ask yourself. And, it is question that you must find an answer to. For if you do not fix the negative *karma* you have created all it does is to perpetuate itself and keep spreading out across this life-space. And, as you are the sourcepoint, who do you think it will ultimately affect the most?

Negative only equals negative, just as positive only equals positive. What are you going to do to fix the bad *karma* that you have created?

Even if you come to the conclusion that you only care about yourself, it is essentially important that you think about the effect your actions have on others and stop them before you unleash them and/or fix them if they have already been unleashed. Because if you don't, what do you think will happen to you, your dreams, your life, and your life's legacy?

You want a good life? It being with what your do.

# Don't Say Yes

14/Jun/2014 08:19 AM

On a funny note...

As you can imagine, I am asked to be interviewed quite a lot. ...All the crazy movies I've made, the *Zen Filmmaking*, the martial arts, and all that...

Do I say, *"Yes?"* Sometimes... But, I'll get back to that in a minute.

The first time I ever saw an interview take place, (and what can go right or very wrong with it), I was like seventeen. A few of the close disciples and I had gone to a local TV station, here in L.A, with my teacher, Swami Satchidananda. He was to be interviewed by this longtime L.A. newscaster and talk show guy, George Putnam, for one of those morning shows. Putnam was a real conservative but I had seen him on TV my entire life. So, I expected only the best.

Now, *Gurudev* was a fairly important guy. He was the one they had asked to open *Woodstock,* he was giving lectures all over the world, writing books, you name it. So, when he went in there I am sure he was simply expecting the usual questions. But instead, Putnam went after him. Said things and when *Gurudev* attempted to respond, *"Oh the Swami is upset..."* *"I'm not, feel my pulse,"* was his response. But, it was real hatchet journalism.

After seeing that I was always a little leery about what can happen during an interview – particularly a live interview. Certainly, I think we all have seen when the interviewer goes after the interviewee on TV or heard it happen on the radio. And, so many hatchet job articles have been written about people who simply thought they were going in to talk over whatever they were about.

For me, I have always been pretty lucky. Everyone who has interviewed me has been fair and has done a good job. In fact, I think back to an interview I was asked to do in the 90s for a martial art magazine. I said, *"Yes."* Then, the editor contacted me and said, *"Why don't you just write it yourself and put my name on it."* Of course, this made me smile. I wish all of my interviews could have been like that – getting out there what I wanted to get out there.

The things that go on in journalism that most people never know about...

Anyway, since the dawning of the age of the internet a lot of people have gotten busy and that is great, I always appreciate people who go after making themselves more. There has been a lot of internet journals go up, then came podcasts, and internet radio shows. And, of course, there been cable access shows around forever. There are a lot of all of those. So again, I get asked to be interviewed quite a lot. And, I always appreciate the offers.

It terms of the journals, those are easy. They email me a set of questions and I answer them. But, podcasts and internet radio shows kind of worry me. You know, it is very easy to say something that can be taken the wrong way or something that people well read their own meaning into. So, I walk that road very-very carefully. And, if I don't know the person who is asking to interview me, (as there are so many people doing podcasts and internet radio out there nowadays), I don't want to lead myself into a bad situation like my guru did.

So, to the funny part... When I am asked to be interviewed, I am way too congenial and accepting. I am, until I am not. So, people ask and I generally say, *"Yes."* But then... Then, I rarely show up for the show.

My manager had a long talk with me the other day... *"Scott, don't say yes,"* came the words... So, I have been trying to turn the eternally nice guy off and say, *"No."*

In fact, this one guy, who is a successful independent filmmaker onto his own right, recently asked me to do his internet radio show. He had actually taken one of my seminars on filmmaking way back in the way back when. Good guy! And, I certainly did not want to mess with him. So, there was the test. In times gone past I may have said, *"Yes,"* but not shown up. So, instead, I said, *"Thanks but no thanks."* ☺

So, to all you internet entrepreneurs out there, I'm not saying, *"Don't ask."* Because I may do it. Just please understand if I decline.

I'm making progress...

**Don't Be Cruel to Animals**

13/Jun/2014 08:55 AM

I was watching the news last night and a young next-door neighbor had taken a cellphone video of this twenty-one year old guy beating his dog with a stick. It was hard to watch. Thankfully, the young boy got in touch with the authorities and the Human Society came and took the dog away from the guy. The guy, of course, tried to lie about his behavior, *like I so often state, "Everybody lies,"* but they had video proof. They should have put the guy in jail but they let him skate. At least now the dog is in the hands of a loving new family.

Animals are great. They are great in the wild and they are great as pets. But, people do bad things to pets. And, that is just wrong!

I've known people who have kicked their dogs, beat them with a belt, made them live outside in the cold and the heat, forced them to breed just as a means to make money. Wrong, wrong, wrong!

I've known people that smack their cats around and have breed their cats to make money. Very-very wrong! I've known people who have had their cats declawed. *"I need to protect my furniture,"* they have claimed. Fuck that! Those people and the vets who perform that operation should be declawed because basically what they do to a cat when they declaw it is amputate the front part of their paws. That is wrong and the cat is never the same!

A lot of people let their cats go outside a night. That is wrong. They get in fights, get diseases, get abused by kids, and may even get run over by a car. Wrong!

Though you shouldn't let your cats out at night, cats and dogs are not solitary animals like some foolish people claim. They are social animals. They do not want to be alone. Don't have one cat. Don't have one dog unless you are taking him or her out all the time and letting them interact with other dogs at the doggy park or other places. Don't force them to live a life in solitary confinement!

I could go into all kinds of personal stories about what I have learned from my pets and what I have seen other people do to theirs. I won't. But, animals will love you. All they want is love and affection in return. If you are going to take on the responsibility of having a pet, treat them right. Make them have a glorious life. It is not hard. Just love them.

**It's Not About You**

13/Jun/2014 08:28 AM

Fade In:

You know, the entire reason that I stopped blogging the first time around was due to the people out there in the great beyond of the internet. As I describe in detail in the introduction to my book, *Scribble on the Restroom Wall,* (which is a book based around *The Scott Shaw Blog 1.0),* people would just haunt me. There were people reading all kinds of things into what I was saying – things that weren't there and then they would contact me about them. But, more than that, there were people that were saying things to and about me online to get me to write about them. Annoying. Get a life! People would also stalk me, showing up at places that I mentioned. But also, a large part of the weirdness came from people thinking that a blog I wrote was about them, when it was not. I learned a lot of lessons about the weirdness of internet man (and woman) kind...

I took some time off then I went for *Round Number Two.* Though I foresaw some of the oncoming danger and, as such, changed some of the things I wrote about; it happened again. So again, I stopped. Equal, *The Chronicles: Zen Ramblings from the Internet.* Again, I had learned some lessons.

But, as I write a lot anyway, I eventually figured, *"Why not? Let's do it again."* Thus launched, *The Scott Shaw Blog 3.5,* which started a bit after I begin 3.0, but briefly put it on hold due to travel and a couple of films.

In any case, from a recent blog I wrote, I received four messages and one phone call, all from people who thought I was writing about them. I was not! As curious/interesting/amusing as that is, it has caused me to feel like I should state a few things...

As most bloggers do, I write about what I am experiencing, what I have lived, my views, opinions, and what I am thinking about. I am not about putting people on Blast. If I were, I would do it in a much more devastating way than to speak about them, in relation to me and my life, in a person blog. Though this blog is up around six thousand hits a day, it is still a personal blog.

I write about me. I don't write about you. I write about what I am experiencing. I don't care what you are experiencing. This is my psychotherapy, not yours. :-)

So, if you want internet fame and fortune, seek it somewhere else. If you are paranoid and think I am writing about you, stop reading this blog. If you don't like the things I say or my point of view, again, stop reading this blog.

*The Scott Shaw Blog* is not about you. It is about me.

Fade Out.

**Do Angels Do Bad Things?**

12/Jun/2014 09:19 AM

Throughout history there has been all kinds of stories propagated about angels and demons, witches and warlocks, and forces from the great beyond. In various parts of history people have believed in these forces so much that they have performed sacrifices to appease these deities. On the other side of the spectrum people have, in fact, been put to death over the belief that they were in cahoots with powers beyond the realms of sight and sound.

Certainly, in modern times, though most of these exaggerated practices have subsided, there are still those few people who do diabolical deeds based upon their personal believes that they are acting in the name of some unseen force. Most of these people are simply understood to be mentally ill. But, some simply believe. And, belief can be a bad thing – especially in the mind of the wrong person.

All this being stated, many people, even in this modern day, hold firmly onto the superstition of religion. Look how many fundamentalists there are, by whatever religious name, living across the globe. They turn to the various religions and their offshoots to find guidance and meaning in their lives. Then, once they believe, they believe, and nothing will stop that belief.

A lot of bad things have happened via the hands of these people. Yet, many still hold fast to their fundamentalist beliefs.

I have long written about how many people who walk the spiritual path, by whatever name, are lured into, *"Magical thinking."* ...Believing that this equals that and by doing this one will get that. It's dangerous. Because there are no set rules and standards about magical thinking.

In the West, many of these, *"Magical Thinkers,"* are practitioners of the various forms of Christianity. Christianity and its, *"Holy Bible,"* are full of stories and tales that set the stage for magical thinking and the belief in and/or the worship or worry of the powers of the forces beyond the seeing eye. Certainly, the belief in supernatural, other worldly being, such as angles and demons, is spoken of throughout the bible. There are also an untold number of stories that have been told, books that have been written, and movies that have been made based upon the, *"What could happen,"* based upon exaggerated ideas found in the Bible.

In Christianity angels are a common focal point. There are three archangels that have emerged in the Catholic tradition and seven spreads throughout wider Christianity.

Christianity, just as the Bible, has evolved throughout the centuries. So, this number is not exact in origin. But, from the understanding of supernatural beings such as the Nephilim, originally detailed in the *Torah* and the *Book of Genesis* onwards, there have been discussion of angels and other worldly beings and their interaction with man (and woman) throughout the various scriptures.

In terms of demons, from their mention in the *Book if Enoch* forward, demons are believed to be in existence and are depicted as the disruptor of the body, the mind, and the lives of the faithful. But, for those who have actually read the Bible, and studied its evolutionary history, it is clear to see that most of the deities, attributed as demons, originate in other religions and were labeled as such due to the founding fathers of Christianity desiring to pull people away from their native religion and to gain a reason for those who practiced Christianity to remain true to the faith. As that is what Christianity and other religious are based upon; faith. From this motivation, some of these demons have been provided with extravagant powers. Simply the thought of them can cause the mind to become fearful. Those who have proselytized Christianity have used this to their advantage.

Hand-in-hand with faith comes superstition. Religion is full of the promises and the rewards that will be bestowed upon the obedient and the faithful. It is also full of what happens to the disobedient and the faithless. This is where the belief in angels and demons and how they can affect mankind is based. And, this is where all those who proselytize these other worldly beings find their basis for dialogue.

Just as in Christianity, in Eastern mysticism the sub-gods known as, *"Devas,"* or *"Devis,"* (male or female deities), are often the focus of the person seeking help and guidance. As some branches of Christianity pray for protection and guidance from the Christian angels and saints, so too do Hindus prey to the *devas* and the *devis.*

As Eastern mysticism is far more focused upon human asceticism than is Western religions, teachers forever warn about employing the help of these ethereal spirits for once they have been allowed into the mind, they do not let go. Thus, those who walk the ascetic path of Hinduism rarely delve into this branch of their religion. This too is also true of ascetic Christians.

The teachers of Christianity, particularly earlier Christianity, also warned against employing ethereal powers. In these cases, the Christians were much more focused upon the worry of calling up demons and allowing them to invade the mind. Throughout history, however, there have been those who claim that they can communicate with angels, demons, and the dead. Though this promise offers hope to those who are unhappy with their current life situation or are missing a person who is deceased, this practice is, in fact, against what the Bible states is acceptable Christian behavior.

In we look to the *Book of Deuteronomy 18*, (King James Version), we see that it states, *"When thou art come into the land which the LORD thy God giveth thee, thou shalt not learn to do after the abominations of those nations. There shall not be found among you any one that maketh his son or his daughter to pass through the fire, or that useth divination, or an observer of times, or an enchanter, or a witch, Or a charmer, or a consulter with familiar spirits, or a wizard, or a necromancer. For all that do these things are an abomination unto the LORD: and because of these abominations the LORD thy God doth drive them out from before thee. Thou shalt be perfect with the LORD thy God. For these nations, which thou shalt possess, hearkened unto observers of times, and unto diviners: but as for thee, the LORD thy God hath not suffered thee so to do."*

In the English Standard Version of the same book, the words that are used state, *"When you come into the land that the Lord your God is giving you, you shall not learn to follow the abominable practices of those nations. There shall not be found among you anyone who burns his son or his daughter as an offering, anyone who practices divination or tells fortunes or interprets omens, or a sorcerer or a charmer or a medium or a necromancer or one who inquires of the dead, for whoever does these things is an abomination to the Lord. And because of these abominations the Lord your God is driving them out before you. You shall be blameless before the Lord your God, for these nations, which you are about to dispossess, listen to fortune-tellers and to diviners. But as for you, the Lord your God has not allowed you to do this."*

Now, this is just one example. The Bible is full of them. Yet, Christians, and others, commonly turn their minds towards the ethereal and seek out those who can channel forces beyond this world in order to gain a personally desired end.

Here is the place where the question must be asked, *"Does a person actually follow the law of their religion or do they simply follow the path of getting what they want, even if that means sidestepping the dogma of their religion?"* Getting what they want, whatever that, *"Want,"* may be?

The fact is, in whatever religion a person finds himself or herself, most do not study their scriptures. They may listen to a priest on Sunday but they do not take the time to investigate the foundations and the basis of their religion on their own. *"I'm a Christian." "I'm a Hindu." "I'm a Buddhist." "I'm a whatever,"* and that is that.

But, the other side of this is that there is interpretation to be found in the many words that make up the many religious scriptures that are out there. People read a passage and interpret the words in a manner that will suit their own needs. Perhaps this is the biggest fault one can find in religion; anyone can say anything and find a passage somewhere to substantiate their point of view.

Now that we've laid the foundation, we come to the primary point of this discourse, *"Do angels do bad things?"* The answer is simple, *"No."*

Angels, (or even demons), do not do bad things. People do bad things.

People who believe in whatever religion or mystic force they believe in and claim they are doing something based on that belief have performed a lot of bad deeds throughout the centuries. People have invoked negative energy and have embraced its power and then have claimed it to be supernatural. And, people who claim that they can guide a person from the powers of the great beyond, have guided many a lost soul down the road to damnation.

Think about the stories you have heard about the wealth and bodily gratifications gained by channelers, clairvoyants, and spiritual teachers who were later decided to be frauds. They took money from people, guided them to do physical things, that they were not naturally inclined to do, and the list goes on. Yet, people who are unhappy with their life seek the guidance of these people hoping to find relief, absolution, and happiness. And, people seek out and pray to gods and goddesses, angels and demons hoping that they will get what they want.

At the core of life, no one has all of the things that they want. This is why Siddhartha Guatama, the Sakyamuni Buddha stated, *"The cause of suffering is desire."* If you are living in a space of desire, you will never be fully happy. Thus, you seek things outside of yourself that promise to fulfill what you believe you are missing. The answer to instantly cease this pattern of, *"Lack,"* and lack of fulfillment in your life is to STOP. STOP the desire. Let go. Release. If you live in this space of freedom then there is no need to pray and conjure up forces that none of us truly understand, no matter what some people claim.

Angels, demons, *deva, devis* are only empowered when you live in a world of desire. If you let go of desire, than what do they have to offer you? They can be free to be who and what they are (if they are) and you are free to exist in a place of perfection.

This is Zen.

# Jerk

11/Jun/2014 10:31 AM

Don't you hate it when you are nice to someone and then they turn out to be a jerk? I believe we have all had this happen to us. We meet someone, we are nice to them, we lend them a helping-hand, we say kind words, we have an informed discussion, and then they either backstab us or they turn out to be a really inconsiderate, selfish, or a flat-out bad person. Uncool...

By my nature, I am a very friendly person. And, that is perhaps one of my biggest faults in life as I see everyone as a friend. I like and trust everyone until they give me a reason not to. Most people are the opposite and that is probably better. They don't like people, they don't trust people, they don't see them as a friend until they have a reason to do so. That's better I think...

I speak about this a lot, but in this life-place, we are all what we are. We are born into a psychological mindset, we are raised and educated through our family, peers, and our interests, then we are schooled in the methods of human interaction by our societal surroundings. All this being said, these factors all become excuses. For people always bring them up when they go wrong and/or do wrong. But, if we are not personally in conscious control of our every life action than who is?

Now, here lies one of the primary problems in life, most people can only see themselves in the mirror. They tell themselves that they are doing right. Or, they tell themselves they have the right to do whatever it is they want. In either case, from this they live their life with little or no regard for others. What I am saying is that many people exist in a realm of sociopathic behavior. And, because they are locked into this mindset, they do not possess the ability to step beyond their own realms of selfishness.

People who are not married, or in a cohabitational relationship, people who do not have children, people who are not interactive on an everyday basis with another or other people, live in a realm of thinking only about themselves. As they are alone much of the time, they have not developed the ability to be aware or conscious of the needs of others. Thus, they just live in a realm of self. For if you are in a close interactive relationship all of the time, then you learn the skills that it takes to be with others; i.e. you have to give in and you have to be considerate.

When people reach young adulthood, they oftentimes leave their family home and go off on their own to live alone. This is a natural process and a time to learn about and define personal self. But, there comes a time when most people move towards interactive relationships. That too is natural. But then, there are those who do not find them. There is a reason for that. That reason is that individual. They have not developed the skills to put others first over self. Thus, they live in a space of only thinking about self and some even claim it as their choice or their right. But, it is not.

Now, it is not only people who live alone that are defined by erratic, inconsiderate behavior. I think back to this couple that were parked in their car one day right in the drive-thru portion of a parking lot. They sat there, with their two young children in the backseat, forcing all the cars that entered to find a way around them.

After I parked, I walked past them, and as their windows were open, I nicely mentioned the fact of where they were parked to them. Instead of saying, *"Oh really."* Or, *"Excuse us."* They went into a major, *"Fuck you,"* rant. All this with their small children in the backseat witnessing their behavior. Now, there is a part in most of us, I know there is in me, (You can take the boy out of the jungle but you can't take the jungle out of the boy), that was about to come right back at them with, "Fuck you, you inconsiderate asshole!" I mean, kicking the ass of that guy would have been easy. But, what would this have proven? So, I took the high road. I said, *"Do you realize how you are talking in front of your kids? Do you realize the example you are setting?"* Of, course, they responded with, *"Fuck you!"*

You know, if you watch shows like, *"COPS,"* you can see this type of behavior all the time. It is not good. It sends a child down the wrong road. But, it happens all over the place.

Whether a person was raised in one of these unhealthy environments or not really becomes inconsequential to the overall choice of who a person becomes and what actions they will perform. For, if you do not define your actions by all those around you, if you cannot put others first, if you cannot choose to be less to make other people's lives better, than what does that say about you?

Here lies the definition of the space that people who turn out to be a, *"Jerk,"* inhabit. They only think about themselves. And, from this, they are left alone, lying to themselves that they are, *"Good,"* that they are, *"Something."* But, they are not.

If you think about yourself before you think about others, if you hurt people, if you damage the lives of people, if you cause anger to rise in people, if you are a jerk – no matter how much you lie to yourself as you look in the mirror, the truth remains self-evident.

Being nice, caring about other first, doing as opposed to undoing, is the true key to life.

# Change

10/Jun/2014 09:20 AM

I think it is forever interesting how people never want you to change. They knew you when and think you are still that. But, change happens to all of us.

I remember I bumped into Buk (Charles Bukowski) in Pedro in the latter stages of his life. I knew him when I was a young teenager in Hollywood. He told me that everyone expected him to be the same person he was when he was forty. He was not. Times had changed. Yes, he still wrote of that life and that time. But, that time was no more.

Me too.

It is not that I don't remember all the times gone past and all the craziness I lived. ...Because I did live a lot of craziness out there in the long-lost nights. I wrote a lot about those adventures – travels into the forbidden realms of enlightenment. But, now I live a different life. And, it is not just that I have changed but the world has changed, as well.

Some people forever run after what was. They try to recapture their youth over and over and over again. I think that is sad. Be who you are when you are. That is more of the true key to happiness.

You know, it is just like Japan... I used to spend a lot of my time there. Then came Fukushima. I was in Japan when that happened.

...The thing is, I always expected something like that to happen in China. I mean they have so many nuke factories up and running. Someday, it will be a mess. But, I never expected it in Japan.

I was there and I couldn't leave. It took me three days to get a flight out. I'm probably still radiating from all that juice. It changed my whole perspective about Japan.

Then, there is Cambodia. I was just speaking to a lady this past weekend that was thinking about going there with her eighty-something year old mother. I told her, yes it is interesting, but she really needed to be careful. I mean, for those of you who know about the five little guys that decided to accost me and me thinking these are just five little guys. Then, slash, a knife across my face. In other words, it got serious. But, that was their mistake. After what occurred, to them, I don't think I can go back there anymore...

Hong Kong's cool, but China, the mainland, they won't give me a visa. ...Wrote a book, did a documentary... Unwelcomed...

Thailand, it's sketchy... After my book, *Junk: The Backstreets of Bangkok,* got translated into Thai a year or so ago, I don't know... When you can't trust the local law enforcement, whom can you trust?

And, this list goes on. I did burn my bridges. But, I lived! I lived, but I also changed.

By nature, I am a very ON sort of person, so I previously enjoyed the devastating hangovers that I would get after partying with by buds like Venchenzo or my father-in-law – as I would finally take the time to lay back and do zero for a day. But, Venchenzo had a kid. My father-in-law died. Gone are my drinking buddies. But, that's probably better... At least for my body.

And, that's just it. We all are who we are until we are not that any longer. By hook or by crook we all change.

Now, the Zen has caught up to me. I have run from it for years, choosing the enlightenment of the streets to the sublet shades of the same. But, it has now enveloped me. Subtle abstraction in a life that pounds on around me. Now, I enjoy the sublet solitude of doing the necessary and the obvious, of kicking back into meditative mediocrity.

Fuck! That sounds like a poem. I better shut up.  :-)

# imdb.com: Fact or Fiction

10/Jun/2014 07:33 AM

*The Internet Movie Database* or imdb.com is the worldwide source for information about film and television production. But, just like *Wikipedia,* much of the information provided to imdb.com is done so by people who possess minimal or highly biased knowledge about a subject. In the case of imdb.com, the majority of people who submit or alter information were not actually a part of the production that they are submitting to. As such, they possess, at best, a limited knowledge and understanding about that production. From this, just like on *Wikipedia,* a lot of information on imdb.com is highly biased and, in some cases, just plain wrong!

Let me step back in time for a moment…

A programmer named Col Needham launched imdb.com in 1990. By the early 1990s it quickly becoming the industry standard for film and television information on the internet. Back then; as everything was in DOS, if you wanted to submit any new information or changes to imdb.com, it had to be done in a very precise manner that Needham's program would understand. This generally meant submitting the information several times before it was deemed ready to be uploaded. It was a real hassle!

Back then, anybody could submit anything. So, there was a lot of self-publicity going on and there were a lot of films posted that were never actually made. But, that's Hollywood.

As imdb.com's protocol loosened, this is where the real problems began.

I'm not going to bore you with the numerous stories I have about haters or people who didn't know anything about what I was doing but would do things like have my movies removed or they would combine two of my films under one title, they would also remove and/or alter credits, and all kinds of stupid stuff like that. And, this is not just about me, everybody I know who is in the game experienced the same set of occurrences. The problems was, as submitting was so difficult, getting stuff fixed or put back up, once it had been altered or removed, was a big-big hassle. In fact, in the later

90s there were actually companies set up that promised to fix your imdb.com info. ...For a price, of course.

As there is so many shenanigans that go on upon imdb.com, I sometimes get contacted by people asking me if something on the site is true or false – either about my films, my cast, my crew, or about me. The fact is, there have been so many mistakes up there over the years that I rarely even bother to check any more. But, whenever I do, there are a lot of inaccuracies.

The reason for this, I believe, is that, in some cases, people are trying to get their assumed knowledge about films out there. That's great! But, this being said, many times they are wrong. I know I have seen numerous inaccuracies put up in association with films I have created.

Then, as mentioned, there are always the haters out there. They submit things just to fuck with people. Uncool!

And, of course, this being Hollywood, there are always people who try to get their film or themselves mentioned in association with some big film or big star in order to get some free publicity. This forever makes me smile. ...My advice, in regard to this practice; go do your own stuff and make yourself worthwhile instead of piggybacking on top of someone else!

There's also reviews and discussions about film projects and people on imdb.com. I always find reviews, especially negative reviews, funny – as reviews are just a way for the adolescent and adolescent minded people, with nothing better to do, to vent and get their frustrations out. But, here again, lies the problem with imdb.com; many of the things stated in these reviews are just plain wrong. For example, in regard to my films, they have been wrong about my methodology, my equipment used, my locations, you name it... But, such is the truth of the internet.

Though my personal opinion is that imdb.com should only allow the Producer of a film to submit or alter information about a project, I am sure this is not going to happen anytime soon. And reviews... Well, reviews are just reviews...

All this being said, as someone who has made a lot of films, I can tell you to be skeptical about the information you find on imdb.com. A lot of times, it is incorrect. And, to this day, getting things fixed on imdb.com can be insanely difficult and time consuming. So, like all things on the internet, (and in life), see something for what it is and do not put your faith in a false god.

And, please people, unless you a fixing an obvious, *"Fuck you,"* stop altering other people's film listings. If they are up there the way they are, that is probably for a reason. Stop believing that you know more about a film than its producer or its publicist.

# Respect the Coffee

07/Jun/2014 08:46 AM

There's this really good vegetarian restaurant that I eat at all the time in the Village in Redondo. It has a great atmosphere. I really love a restaurant that focuses not only on its food but on its atmosphere as well.

Anyway, I am told by the owner of the restaurant that the Redondo Beach Heath Department has this law that they can't serve coffee in those glass coffee pot things that most restaurants use. They must provide their coffee refills with this large metal container. It always seems kind of cumbersome when they have to carrier it out to the tables.

A week or so ago I made a joke about this fact to one of the servers and he immediately came back with the fact that if you leave your coffee in those glass coffee containers, that we all use at home as well, that it will actually burn the coffee as it sits on the warming hotplate. He concluded with, *"You have to respect the coffee."*

Wow, there's a new one. It made me smile. This guy was a true coffee aficionado. Me, I just drink the poison. :-)

The funny thing is I didn't start drinking coffee until I was twenty-six. I was a yogi, okay... But, once I did, I was hooked.

I think back to the early 1980s when whole bean coffee grinders first became available to the public. I was one of the first people, at the department store, to pick one up. It seemed so much more poetic to actually grind your coffee before you put it in the coffee pot. This was back when everyone just bought those big metal containers of ground coffee from the supermarket.

When the homebrew espresso machines came on the market, around the same time, I was there. Back when they were stupid expensive. It just seemed so much more...

I remember the words of one of my way back when girlfriend(s), *"If you can afford it, you should do it."* With few exceptions, I have been doing it ever since.

Old meets new in the fact that a while back I was in a thrift shop and I picked up a still new, in-the-box, percolator from the early 1960s. Prior to this, I had never used a percolator. My parents did, but not me. But damn, once I did, the coffee tasted so much better.

All this being as it is, recently, however, I have gotten lazy. ...Lazy, for lack of a better word. I have been picking up the (now) large plastic containers of ground up coffee from the supermarket. I just seems so much easier and less time consuming then grinding my own coffee. :-)

So, that's were I stand: here and now. My coffee grinder still sits on the kitchen counter, awaiting its next usage. My espresso machine next to it. My digital coffee pot is set to go each morning – the mornings I do not decide to percolate.

*"Respect the coffee,"* I don't know... Maybe I do, maybe I don't. But, drinking it has been an interesting ride. The stories I could tell...

re-con-tex-tual-ize

06/Jun/2014 07:48 AM

*"Wow yes strange man screaming "faggot!!" at me from a nasty ass truck thank you so much I'm going to stop being a faggot now, it's over, I can see the demons leaving my body, you've fucking cured me it's a miracle."*

I grabbed this quote from Facebook. It was made by one of my *Zen Filmmaking* friends.

The fact is, this young NYC guy is just seventeen and he has already been rocking the world with Art House filmmaking and he has released tons of music and music videos. He has truly taken advantage of all this digital age has to offer. Yet, here he is, this truly creative guy, contributing to the artistic world, and he gets hassled for being who and what he is.

If I can, again, quote one of my friends, (who shall remain nameless), they stated, *"There's a lot more bible thumpers than butt fuckers out there."* This was a joking comment made in reference to all that was going on about the Duck Dynasty patriarch making homophobic comments several months ago and attributing them to religion. I guess that's why I am not a fan of religion.

The other night I was watching *America's Got Talent* and Howard Stern asked this male dancing duo if they were a couple. One guy was gay; one was not. Though a stupid, unnecessary, question, I thought it was great that you can now state who and what you are on national TV. Think back just a decade or so ago to all the hoopla that occurred when Ellen came out. And, that was probably also the reason for people like Rock Hudson and Raymond Burr never coming out.

This begin said, there is so much reading-in-to everything that a person says. This is the other side of the issue, when somebody says something, and people place their own bias and definition upon it.

Everybody wants to find a reason to criticize. I mean, just this week, Jonah Hill apologized for making a gay comment. Who cares! He made it at paparazzi. We all know these guys say and do all kinds of things to get negative responses out of celebrities. Think how many people have made jokes about Hill's weight and no one apologized.

TMZ did this whole thing last week when Charlize Theron, during an interview, was asked whether she ever Googled herself. She said, *"I don't do that, so that's my saving grace. When you start living in that world, and doing that, you start, I guess, feeling raped."* Yeah, that's true! People write all kinds of lies, distortions, and untruths about a celebrity. Yet, everyone wants an apology from her. They want an apology from a South African woman who has actually made commercials in South Africa telling people to, *"Stop Rapping."* As it is a terrible crisis in that country. I have made a couple of films there and I know every woman fears it and virtually every person has a gun in their house to protect themselves.

This, plus the fact that TMZ is all about slamming whom ever they can by whatever means they can. I remember when Harvey Levin was on the local news here in L.A. and he used to do great investigative reporting. I even remember the night he left and they wished him well. What happened, Harvey?

Jack White just issued an apology on his website about comments he made about the *Black Keys* and his ex Meg White. This came hand-in-hand with the unauthorized release of some of his personal correspondents. Now, here's a guy who changed the landscape of music forever with a two-person band. He's not some flub who has accomplished nothing in life and is spitting out meaningless, opinionated nonsense. He's Jack White! My question is, why can't he say what he thinks and feels? Why does he, or anyone else, have to apologize for who and what they are – for what they think and how they feel?

The fact is, everyone takes everything a person says and recontextualize it to meet their own meaning and definition. Then, in some cases, people reword and restructure what a person actually said, to make it appear the way somebody else wants it to sound. This has happened to me. So, I can tell you, from person experience, that it is all bullshit. If a person has so much time on their hands that they can waste their life writing about someone else, and what they did or did not say, what they did or did not mean, they should really take a long, hard look at themselves.

You know, even as a novelist, I have had my editors want me to reword some of the things I have written. And, in some cases I have. The thing is, when I am writing literature, I am writing from the reference point of a persona. As such, that character is broadcasting what that persona would say. Today, the world has gotten so politically correct that a writer or, for that matter, a filmmaker, a musician or an actor can no longer say what they want to say. Why???

The thing is, you (or me) may like it, we may not. We may think it is funny, we may not. But, at the end of the day who are any of us to judge another person for we have all done things, we have all said things, that others may find offensive. In fact, simply being who and what we are; I am sure, there is someone out there who would find that offensive.

What is the truth of a word? Do you hear it for what it is? Or, do you put your own spin on it?

# Q&A

05/Jun/2014 08:15 AM

A couple of years ago one of my filmmaking buds, Chris Watson, asked me write the introduction for a book he was doing on the great film actor, Joe Estevez, *"Joe Estevez: Wiping off the Sheen."* I was happy to do it as I have the utmost respect for Joe. I also have respect for the guy who put the book together as he came out here to Hollywood and did what few filmmakers have accomplished. He actually made movies with his film idols, like Joe Estevez, Conrad Brooks, William Smith, Robert Z'Dar, Julie Strain, Tom Savini, Brinke Stevens, and the list goes on. He even asked me to be in one of his films but as I always jokingly tell everyone who asks, *"The only bad movies I'm in are my own."* Just a few years before his arrival he would frequently email Donald G. Jackson and myself, from his home in the Midwest, discussing his ideas about filmmaking. Sadly, he never got to actually meet DGJ as he passed away before he arrived.

Anyway, he came out here and he did it, with no help! This is something few can claim – to make movies that receive international distribution. After that he became a published author. Again, something few can claim. So, when he returned to his homebase to go to grad school, (which he has graduated from), and he asked me to write him a *Letter of Recommendation.*

I happily wrote him a glowing recommendation.

Okay, that's the backstory... Now, for the feature article.

The book he wrote on Joe is based on a Q&A format. It works so well as Joe is allowed to tell his story through his own words. When I received the book I had no idea about its format. When I read it I thought, *"This is great!"*

As a journalist, I have interviewed so many people and have written so many articles about martial artists and filmmakers that I cannot even remember how many. And, as a filmmaker and as a martial artist, I too have been interviewed many times, even by Chris a long time ago. The articles that have been written about me have mostly been in the Q&A format. That being said, I virtually never write Q&A articles about other people. From my perspective, I find it much easier to tell the whole story about a person if I write biography immingled with quotations. The problem is, this style of writing takes a lot longer to do.

Maybe ten years ago, my editor called me up and asked me to take over an article that he had assigned to another writer. The writer had sent this Taekwondo Olympic Gold Medalist a list of questions to answer. From this, the writer would have to do nothing, simply submit the completed Q&A to the magazine. The interviewee freaked. When I spoke to him he exclaimed, *"If I wanted to do that then I could just write my own article!"*

Most people aren't that expressive. But, he did have his point.

Oh, and by the way, I had one day to get the interview and write the article... That was a seriously tight deadline. But, I did it.

Anyway... The problem was, the previous writer went about it all-wrong. He simply sent his questions. That is not the best way to do it. The few times I have written a Q&A article, as per my assignment, I always speak with the interviewee and ask them the questions directly. From this, when you put their responses to type, you can portray their intent, even if the content is not there.

The second problem with a Q&A style format is that many people do not know how to be interviewed. As such, when you ask them a question they talk forever and go off onto a million tangents. From this, constructing a Q&A article can become quite difficult.

Now, with the book on Joe, (as it was a book and not an article), there was the time and the space to truly let Joe detail his life and his evolution in the film industry through his own words. This makes it a truly unique reading experience.

A funny story here; as a side note...

A few weeks ago my editor called me up freaking out. One of the producers of the new *Teenage Mutant Ninja Turtles* movie, (that will be coming out this summer), promised to send the magazine a bunch of promo stuff on the film so that I could write an article about the movie. I mean, TMNT did change the martial art landscape forever... But, the guy flaked. He sent nothing and would not return phone calls. The editor was stuck. He was up against deadline and he needed an article immediately. *"Scotty, what am I going to do,"* he exclaimed. *"Hey, I know the Co-Creator of the Teenage Mutant Ninja Turtles, Kevin Eastman,"* I responded. *"You want me to get in touch with him and we can do an article about the source?"* The deal was sealed. I got to get my *Zen Filmmaking* buddy, Kevin Eastman on the cover of the magazine. He deserves it!

How this ties into the Q&A question is that before I went on my quest my editor asked, *"Are you going to do it Q&A?"* *"No, I don't think so. The story is too big to tell in that fashion."* *"Great, I knew you would come through, Scotty."*

Sometimes Q&A just doesn't work, though many journalists instinctively follow that tried and true path. Sometimes the reader deserves to be lead into the story before they dive head first into the questions of why…

Now, as I tend to do here on this blog – I will link all this onto life…

How do you see yourself? How would you define your life if the question(s) were asked? Many people don't know. They would have to fish for an answer. And, here lies the problem with life, if you don't know who you are, if you can't describe what you have done in a few words, in the most direct manner possible, then that means that your life is not defined. If you live a life that his not been defined, then you are simply passing though this existence allowing yourself to be guided by whatever fads and/or desires are out there.

Certainly, we all learn, change, and evolve through time. That being said, the key to living a life that has meaning is knowing who and what you are and then being able to detail that fact in the simplest answer to a Q&A question.

# The Times They Have Changed

04/Jun/2014 07:31 AM

For people like me who have been walking this path of spirituality forever – every now and then I get hit with the fact that no one gets what I am talking about.

...That, yes, there was a time when spirituality and the advancement of human consciousness reigned supreme.

Today, that is not the case. People are all locked-up into SELF. Even those who claim spirituality are lost in advancing them-self, not the overall self.

Now, I must state, as I have stated a million times before, that most people do not even care about rising spirituality. Most people only care about their own personal moment. That being said, I have watched a shift in the consciousness of spirituality. That shift came hand-in-hand with all of the self-orientated self-ism that took place in the 1980s. There/then, it became a time of ME. ME, as opposed to US. Prior to that, those of us with a spiritual nature did not think about personal spiritual advancement, we though about serving the greater good and the bigger WHOLE.

But... The times they did change.

Now, I have never been one to hold onto times gone past. By nature, I am not a nostalgic person. I am what I am, when I am. But, what I have witnessed is that though the trappings of spirituality are all still out there, most people do not see them as a means to raise the overall consciousness of the ALL. Instead, they see them as a way to make the personal self MORE.

I am THIS, you are NOT. Thus, I am MORE than you. False!!!

For example, the physical aspects of yoga have had an expedient increase in modern consciousness over the past two decades. It has amused me that a few of the people that I know feel very proud about they fact that they own a business that teaches yoga. *"I'm really into yoga,"* they state. *"Now, I own a yoga studio."* They brag it everywhere.

What is that? Is yoga for the betterment and the enlightenment of ALL? Or, is yoga for the betterment and the exaggeration of SELF?

When I became certified and began teaching *Hatha Yoga* when I was sixteen or seventeen, I saw it as a means to move people forward into the more refined aspects of the discipline. Now, it is simply a business goal worth obtaining. *"I own a yoga studio! I am good. Look at me."*

For those who may not understand, *Hatha Yoga* and the *Pranayama* that goes hand-in-hand with it, is a GREAT practice. But, it is, and never was, an end-all. *Hatha Yoga* is designed to refine the body and give the practitioner the tools to take the next step in the advancement of human consciousness. It is not something to simply make you feel and look better. In fact, when I spoke to one of my primary teachers, Swami Satchidananda, about the seminal book he created on *Hatha Yoga,* he told me that he had not even performed *Hatha Yoga* for over twenty years at the time he took the photographs for the book. Yet, he still had the knowledge to compose the book and the physical prowess to perform the postures. In other words, his mind had moved foreword to the more refined aspects of yoga, yet he provided the book as a tool to lay the foundations for others to ascend to the higher plateau of universal human consciousness.

For anyone who understands the *Bodhisattva Vow* – that vow is taken in order that the personal self is never in the forefront. Instead, it allows the personal self to leave behind all ego and the ego gratification of being a teacher and, instead, surrender the self so that the personal I, the personal ego, is put on hold until all of humanity reaches enlightenment. Though this is a hard concept for most people to understand, as they are so locked up into SELF, this is the truth comprehended by the true spiritual aspirant; SELF is less, the WHOLE is more.

So, with all this being said, it is time that ALL of us take a look at ourselves and what we are doing. Is, what we are doing benefiting SELF or is it benefiting the Greater Good? If it is only benefiting SELF, then it has no true end-result. If we surrender ourselves, however, for the greater good, then this is where all things in this universe and this life-place get better.

But, be careful... This is a slippery sloop. Many people feel that they are helping, that they are teaching others... This is the wrong place to begin from. For, if a person cannot surrender all realms of the SELF to the service of others. ...If they cannot say I am not a teacher, I am not a knower, I am simply JUST like you – an aspirant on the pathway to higher consciousness, then there is ego involved in the process. With this, all levels of the *Bodhisattva Vow* and all semblance of truth are lost. What comes from this is what is going on now; a spiritual world dominated by ego and self-ism.

But... I remember a time when it was not this way.

The betterment of mankind begins with you. If you are truly spiritual, if you want to truly help humanity, if you want to guide others towards true enlightenment, then let go of self, let go of ego, let go of the I am something and you are not mentality. There/then the truth of the ages will be reborn.

**Learning to Let Go**

03/Jun/2014 08:25 AM

Have you ever watched a bird's feather slowly glide towards the ground? It moves slowly from right to left as gravity causes its passive flow downwards.

Do you ever get caught up in the crunch of your life? You are pulled out of peace, driven by the emotions of frustration, anger, lust, love, and desire. No matter what the cause, your heart is pumping and your blood pressure is surging.

Many write this off with the statement, *"That's life."* Others like the energizing drive of adrenaline. But, as invigorating and/or as stimulating as emotions can be, they keep you from embracing a true inner peace.

In all level of spirituality, psychology, and self-advancement, it is understood that to truly embrace the greater realms of self-realization one must be at peace – a person cannot and should not be defined by emotion. To this end, each of us must find a way of letting go of emotions that keep us from *nirvana*.

Sitting for meditation is easy if your mind is continually at peace. But, for those who live a day-to-day existence, how many can claim that? We are each pulled from one side to the other by all of the things that life has in store for us. This being said, if we hope to find a true inner peace and a means to achieve higher consciousness we must find a way to calm our mind.

There are numerous techniques that have been taught by the various spiritual traditions throughout the centuries. All have validity if they work for you. Many, however, are far too complicated for the average Joe to find acceptable and workable. Therefore, the technique(s) you use to let go and calm your mind should be simplified.

Right now, STOP. Close your eyes. Think about the slow passageway that the feather from the bird makes as it finds its way to the ground.

Mentally, witness that process. See the feather appear in the air and watch it move slowly, passively, towards the ground. Don't rush it. Don't think about it. Simply let it happen.

Witness the movement.

As it moves from low to high let your mind relax, let your thoughts cease, allow your mind to become calm as you let go of all the things that have kept you from embracing true inner peace. As the feather travels feel it/know it: true, passive inner peace.

# Yeah It's Karma

02/Jun/2014 09:55 AM

Let me flash back here a little bit...

When I was a young guy, I had just returned from India and I was living in my first apartment close to where I was going to college. A friend of mine lived downstairs, which is why and how I initially found out about my apartment's availability. My rent was $165.00 a month. Wow, I wish rent was that cheap nowadays. Anyway, my friend and I went back a few years, which are all stories onto themselves but we were both musicians. We would spend hours upon hours playing music.

At home, upstairs, I had my *Dokorder 4-track reel-to-reel* set up with my *Realistic mixer* and my *Marantz cassette recorder* for mix down. There, I would practice, record music, and dream of rock stardom. I was young, okay...

Anyway, there was this old, (retired), guy living downstairs from me. The best way I could describe him is, *"A drunk,"* as he was fine during the day but at night he would come home all liquored up and yell and scream, *"Fuck you's,"* to the surrounding atmosphere in general and/or especially whenever I would plug in to play my Les Paul.

Me, as a person, I have always been super conscious of other people existing in the spaces that surround me. I spent my whole younger life growing up in apartments, at least past the point when my father died, (as I was raised by a single mother, working to make ends meet). As such, I always knew what it was like to have a bad neighbor. I also witnessed what it was like to have a good neighbor. So, even as a late teenager, living in my first apartment, I always tried to be conscious of my neighbors. As such, I never really understood why he would go into a rage every time I would play, as I never jammed loud as we did down in my friend's apartment – which was far away on the other side of the building – a place in the building where no one cared. But, I guess, no matter how softly I played, as I was above him, he would hear the music.

Anyway, his screaming through the floor got me going one night, so I went down to confront him – as I thought that was what you were supposed to do. There he was this old man, just desiring a quiet retirement and there I was this young guy playing electric guitar over his head. Who was to blame, him for being old or me for being young? We concluded that when he came home at night I would not play. Fair enough... But, with this, he started staying out later and later – probably, in his own way, trying to give me space and time to play. This, however, obviously added to his alcoholism. Again, who was to blame? But, it made me feel really-really bad.

Now, if we can switch this to the realms of spirituality... The moment I became aware of all the bullshit that goes hand-in-hand with spirituality, I knew it was NOT true spirituality. Meeting with teachers like Sai Baba whom would do these foolish parlor tricks in India and then witnessing his disciples believing them to be miracles, was just the start. I also saw how many so called, *"Gurus,"* lied and deceived people just to feel like they were MORE. Thus, and as such, I totally rebelled against traditional Eastern spirituality.

Now, I am not saying Eastern (or Western) spirituality is wrong. I am simply saying some of its proponents are fakes. This is why I have always been very clear about who and what I am – what I do and what I have done... I want there to be no mistakes when it comes to the subject of, *"Me."*

About a year and a half ago I had this new neighbor move in next-door to me. This guy is loud! He broadcasts all over the neighborhood whatever form of spirituality that he is propagating and whatever he is speaking about to people on his telephone; which he does insistently. As he is so loud, (and me living next-door to him), he really messed up my life. Before he moved in, everything was fine. But, now... I have had to close my windows and doors and wear noise-canceling headphones just to get work done. As a lot of people, including myself, work predominately from home these days, the other neighbors I have spoken to are effected in much the same way by this guy. But, I am the closest, so I get it the worst.

An interesting side note here is that, just the other day, one of my neighbors stated, *"You better be careful, he speaks with the angels."* As that is what I am told he apparently claims to do. *"Yeah right,"* I exclaimed, *"Is that his prayers, screaming, 'Fuck me over and over again.'"* Which is what he commonly does. *"I wonder what angel he is talking to,"* I concluded.

If I can subtext and paraphrase here... Don't you think that is one of the most bullshit, manipulative things a person can say, that they speak with angels? Aside from a person claiming that they are in personal communication with god, I can think of few more despicable, self-motivated, and deceptive statements. Anyway...

That guy is everything I hate about modern spirituality. There, I said it... But, there are a lot of them out there. He is simply the one who is haunting my life. So, if any of you out there in internet-land know of a better place for me to be, let me know for though where I have lived for the past decade has a nice zip-code, (so I am told), it has become Hotel California for me. ...You know, *"You can check out any time you like but you can never leave."* :-)

Anyway... As I learned a longtime ago, from speaking with my downstairs neighbor, confrontation is never the answer. Consideration is the answer. So, I have let my neighbor live his life, believing that, hopefully, he would stop his inconsiderate behavior. Which never seems to end.

You see, the reason I tell this story is that in life we are all going to encounter people like this; be they spiritual or not – be they musicians or not. There are people who always try to take other people into consideration, and design their life and their living space so that they do not encroach on others. But then, there are people whom only think about themselves. Whether they feel they are talking to the Angels, to the *Devis,* to God, to Satan, to whomever, is unimportant. For if they do not care about their fellow man (or women) first, then who and what are they? I will answer that question; they are selfish. And, at no level of spirituality or human life is selfishness an answer.

Yeah, you may want to be who you think you are. Yeah, you may want to say what you think you have to say. Yeah, you may want to play whatever notes you think you have to play. But, if you damage the life of others around you while you are doing it, what is your *karma?*

And, this is the thing about life, you can be adamant about who you are, you can fight to get your point across – to make yourself RIGHT. But, when you do that, who actually emerges as right? For, *"Right,"* is forever obvious – it is the person who is not damaging the life of another person.

This is why you forever have to rethinking yourself, rethink your space, and rethink the effect you are having. For, at the end of the day, it is only you who will be judged for what you have done and how you have either positively or negatively affected those people who are interactive with your life.

To conclude the story, as for me, soon after the aforementioned confrontation with the older gentleman, I moved out of that apartment building. I did not want my hopes and desires for my life to be defined by having damaged the life, and the remaining few years of life, that my downstairs neighbor had. I hoped a quiet, older person moved in above him. Though I have played music most of my life, I never thought it was appropriate to crank up those amplifiers, kick in the distortion pedal, just to make someone know that I can play louder than them. ℧

This is life… It is defined by you… But, your life is also defined by those who surrounds you. This is where it all gets complicated. This is where *karma* is born. What are you going to do?

# Behind Closed Doors

30/May/2014 01:14 PM

In each of our lives, there is the person we reveal to the world and there is the person who we are inside. In fact, in many cases, we behave differently with the different people that we know. We merge. We become a part of the whole for whatever group we are in.

In life, it is very common that we alter who we truly are the moment we step outside. We have to become what is expected of us. And oftentimes, this is not at all who we truly are. People wear clothing that they do not feel comfortable in, they cut their hair in an acceptable fashion; they walk the walk and they talk the talk of the acceptable.

Inside, where we live, we are supposed to be allowed to be ourselves – to be who we truly are. But, with the ever growing populous of the world, this too has become harder to accomplish.

My friends who have come from apartment life in places New York, Tokyo, Hong Kong, and Delhi have a much smaller expectation of privacy than others. This is due to the fact that they have become accustomed to the fact of listening to their neighbor's conversations and others listening to theirs. Even now, in modern cities like Los Angeles, they build houses closer and closer together in order to maximize living space. Some people I know who live in very expensive homes are no more than a few feet from their neighbor. Thus, privacy is lost.

More than this, there are cameras everywhere. I believe right now London has the most cameras taping everything across the city. But, other big cities like Tokyo, Hong Kong, Taipei, and San Francisco are not far behind. They see you!

Yes, this probably cuts down on crime. It also helps the powers-that-be catch criminals once a crime has been committed. But, all sense of privacy is lost.

When you go into a store or a shopping center, forget about it. You are on camera. Pretty much everywhere, everything you do is seen.

But, back to private space… In recent years we continue to hear stories about how famous people are stalked and video taped via various means. Whether it was that psycho stalker who would rent the hotel room next to the female sportscaster and slide a camera into her room to videotape her naked, the guy who recently lacked the beauty queens computer to get naked pictures of her to blackmail her, or the security guy at the hotel who released the hotel security footage of the pop star's sister fighting with the rap mogul in the elevator, you cannot hide. And, those are just three examples, there have been so many more stories in the news about people getting illegally photographed or videotaped. In fact, there are, *"Spy Stores,"* all over the place where you can easily buy the equipment necessary to photograph anyone. At least these psychos, when they are caught, go to jail. But, your Behind Closed Doors is lost and you must forever be vigilant about what you say and what you do.

The thing about life is most people are fine most of the time. But also, most of us have our moments when we just want to let loose and explode, be it with frustration, anger, utter joy, or eroticism. We expect to be safe in our place. Free from prying eye and ears. Sadly, this is no longer the case. With technology *Behind Closed Doors* may no longer exist. And, this is a sad fact of life that is not going to get better anytime soon.

But, just as people are watching us, we can be watching them. Just a thought to keep in mind. Watch who is watching you and then watch them. :-)

**The Old, The Young, The In-Between
and It Only Makes You Look Bad**

29/May/2014 09:00 AM

When you are young, you have a lot of time on your hands. You don't have to work, you don't have bills to pay, and so you have time to do whatever it is you want to do. When you're old, you also have a lot of time on your hands. You are surviving on your pension and/or your savings, so you have time to do whatever it is you want to do. Some people are somewhere in the middle of life and either by living with their parents, inheriting money, being a trust fund baby, or something like that, they too have time to do whatever it is they want to do.

For all of those who have a means to have time on their hands, there is one commonality. That commonality is: these people set an enormous amount of *karma* (be it good or bad) in motion. With time on their hands and nothing particular to do, people seek out a means to keep their mind occupied.

Many people who exist in this space of life vegetate. They watch TV, they shop, they go to bars and coffee houses, and/or they just hang out. For those who find a calling to go out, at these places they may develop friends with whom they talk and talk and talk. Others find their interaction on the internet. In this case, they are isolated and alone and living in their own head, yet they gravitate towards people of like mind in chat rooms, on various interactive or social media websites. There, they talk and talk and talk. Or, should I say, they type and type and type.

I think, in this modern age, we have all found emotional-stimuli on the internet. We find words written, or someone writing these words, and they give us cause to be adrenalized; be that: happy, joyous, hopeful, angry, frustrated, or unset. This is based in the same mind-things that set us off in real-life. That is: we believe a person to be right, we believe a person to be wrong, or we want to fit in with a crowd as we have no life to call our own and we want to belong to something – anything.

Just as in life, there are those who step to the front of these packs of people. They are the ones who instigate the adrenalizing of others. Then/there, just like a preacher desires to be a preacher so he or she can get the emotional stimuli and ego gratification of guiding people in one direction or the other, so too do these people on the internet find their self-ness by causing others to move in a common direction and to believe what they are saying.

There are those who inhabit these places and these spaces of life who embrace a positive outlook on life. They try to actualize all things GOOD. Then, there are those who do not. They embrace the negative. Though, in some cases, they try to present it as positive. ...Positive, just like the preacher who tells their flock, damnation will follow if they do not abide by his interpretation of the words in his holy book.

Many in these life-spaces take on the mindset of *Schadenfreude* or they spend their time trying to get their point of view out there about people, about places, about things, and about their personal ideologies. If we look to those who speak the loudest, most commonly we will find that their words are based in criticism and negativity. The reason for this is very easy to chart; criticism and negativity cause more people to rally around a cause than does that of positivity.

Then, just as in all the old horror movies, there is the Igor to the Dracula. There are the close followers – those who believe that they are acting upon the desires and the orders of their master. Thus, they set about on a course they believe to be what their master desires.

There reason I discuss this subject and return to the various aspects of it is because many people never take the time to look at their actions and how what they are doing is not only affect their lives but also the lives of those around them who are listening to what they have to say. They are not looking at or thinking about the *karma* they are creating; not only for themselves but for the world around them. Moreover, many people never take the time to think about how they are being influenced by the words and the actions of others. Thus, they are not only becoming unknowing participates in the unleashing of the *karma* instigated by another person but they too will eventually pay the price.

Admittedly, some are simply happy to be able to speak negatively about other people and other things. They feel good about what they have done and how they influenced the thought process of other. They could care less about what *karma* they create. They care less until it comes to call. Then, it is, *"Whoa is me."*

Think about the world around your for a moment and how you take in your information. For example, speaking of bars and/or coffee houses as I did a few moments ago – go to one of those places and take a few minutes and listen to the conversations that are going on around you. In many cases, you will hear all kinds of people, talking about all kinds of things, and they are completely wrong. They are not basing their information upon fact. They are basing their information upon conjecture and what they heard from some other person who heard it from someone else.

Now, we all have our opinions. That's just life. But, do you ever ask yourself, *"What is the basis of my opinion?"* Or, "Where did my opinion come from?" Most people don't think about these things. And, that is where the problem begins. They simply take the lead or they follow and then they do whatever it takes to get their opinion out there.

It's sad. And, at the ends of days, it only makes you look bad if you live your life by these standards.

If you find yourself with time on your hands, this is the question you must ask, *"What am I going to do with it?"* You can sit around and veg. You can hate life and mankind. You can embrace negativity which, admittedly, has a lot of adrenal rush associated with it. You can mess with other people's lives by saying what you personally believe about them and getting it out there. You can tell everyone what you believe is right and what they believe is wrong and then fight to get your opinion validated by cultivating followers. You can spread all kinds of whatever it is you want to spread. Or, you can do and be something bigger. You can put the YOU away and be more than simply that small leader or that small follower and strive for the betterment of all; not hurting, not ego-tripping, not trying to make YOU more. Instead, help the people you hate. Do good for the people that you previous did the opposite to. Never instigate anything that can hurt any-one or any-thing. Let the damage and the negative stop with you. Let the positivity begin with you.

From this, at the end of days, you will find that you did not make YOU look bad, you made YOU look like you cared more about others than you cared about yourself.

What do you think is the best way to be remembered? ... By who you hurt or by who you helped? By the misguide criticism you unleashed or by the positive words you spoke that uplifted instead of bring down?

# The Same Yet Different

28/May/2014 08:58 AM

As an artist, when you are painting a painting, there is always the question, *"Is it done?"* Sometimes you look at a painting that you are working on and you are just not one hundred percent happy with it. Then the choice must be made, do you go back and rework it or do you let it live in its own perfection?

The thing about this question is – yes you can redo it. In some cases, as an artist, you can redo it over and over and over again. But, at the end of the day, it is still what it was; a painting with paint upon a canvas – the same, yet different.

Life and the way you act in life is very similar to this. There are chances for a redo – most of the time. In other cases there are not. But, one way or the other we are left with our life. It can be seen as having been lived within its own perfection, to the best of our ability, or it can be viewed as if something is missing, something is wrong.

You know, the world has changed a lot over the past two decades in terms of art and creativity. For example, what was once very-very expensive to do, like create a movie, is now relatively cheap due to digital technology. I recently read this piece where Quentin Tarantino stated that digital is the death of cinema. He stated this even though his friend and confidant Robert Rodriguez has used it extensively.

I won't go into this debate because I see both sides of it and I have already written extensively about it. I will say that as one of the first people to ever create a film on video that received international distribution, *Samurai Vampire Bikers from Hell,* that I saw the future early. Years before me, look at Frank Zappa's, *200 Motels,* if you want to see a really early contribution to the genre.

Anyway, early in the digital game, everybody wanted their movies, that were shot on tape, to look like film. Enter, Film Look. A very expensive process of adding controlled noise to the video movie. Was it film? No. Did it look like film? A little bit. It was the same, yet different.

When Donald G. Jackson and I created, *Guns of El Chupacabra,* we filmed it with a combination of 35mm, 16mm, and digital videotape for the scenes with the reporter, to change the look and feel of the various elements of the film. One day when we were on the set filming with Julie Strain and her then husband Kevin Eastman, we had our videographer along so we had him shoot the scenes on video that we were shooting on film as a backup. When I edited *Guns of El Chupacabra* I used the footage we shot on film. When I did *Guns of El Chupacabra II: The Unseen,* I used the video footage of the same scenes. Did you notice that? Did anybody? It was the same, yet different.

Now, when digital photography came along, I hated it. Just as with video, gone was the depth of field, that myself, as a filmmaker and photographer, loved to work with. But, just like with filmmaking, digital photography made photography insanely cheaper and easier. So, with the changing winds of time, you have to change or be left behind.

Thankfully, now, many of both the new video cameras and still cameras, (which are pretty much one in the same), achieve really nice depth of field. Case in point, I purchased this new Nikon a little while back and was shooting it as digital had been. I expected everything to be in focus, it was not, there was depth of field that I didn't realize until I looked at the shot later. Though I lost the shot I had in mind, I was happy to see the improvement. The same, yet not different.

This is life. It is all about the availability of your options and what you do with that availability and those options. Options are out there, if you want to work with them. Life is out there, if you want to live it. But ultimately, it is you who must decide when what you are doing is done. Are you making it better by working and reworking it? Or are you simply making it the same, yet different?

# Black and White Movies

27/May/2014 08:34 AM

Over the past Memorial Day Weekend was a great time to catch up and re-watch some great movies filmed in black and white. I love black and white movies. I have filmed a few and there are black and white elements in a number of my other films. Then, there are my films like *Samurai Johnny Frankenstein* that I should have filmed in black and white. Maybe I will do that, re-release that film in B&W.

Anyway... Most of the B&W films that were shown on station like TCM and other nostalgia orientated stations were war related, due to it being Memorial Day Weekend and all. But, I got to watch some great movies. And, there are so many other great B&W films out there!

As a kid, I grew up in an era when most of the movies were filmed in Color but due to budgetary constraints there were still some that were B&W. I always loved those films when we would go to see them in the theater. As time progressed, by the mid 1960s, virtually none of the films, except for a few *Art House* releases, were B&W. Bogdanovich's 1971, *The Last Picture Show*, was probably the first one to make the step backwards on the big screen. Great-great Film!!!

In terms of TV, that was a whole different story. A lot of people didn't have Color TVs until the 1970s, including me, though many of the shows would have, *"In Color,"* written across their title card in order to guide people in that direction. Growing up with a single mother (after my father passed away) who didn't drive did have its disadvantages. We didn't get a color TV until I was fifteen. Before that we had a small portable B&W TV. I remember the first time my mother and I were in San Francisco, staying at this hotel, and the TV show, *MASH* was on. It was the first time I saw it in color and I was blown away. Everything was different. Then, when we finally did get a color TV, I would watch the reruns of shows that I loved from the 1960s and 1970s like *The Mod Squad, Hawaii Five-O, Adam-12, Cannon, It Takes a Thief, The Name of the Game, Mannix,* even *The Monkees, The Partridge Family,* and *Bat Man.* I couldn't believe all that I had missed or maybe better put what I did not know was going on.

All this being said, when something is filmed in color and you see it in B&W, something is lost. But, when it is filmed in B&W everything is devised around that art space. It is created with that vision at its central core. There is simply something beautiful about cinema created in B&W.

All the watching over the weekend has re-inspired me in the B&W direction. I think I will have to do my next film in B&W. So, if any of you out there have a cool location or lo-cal for a B&W shoot let me know...

B&W baby!!!

# What You Do Now

26/May/2014 08:32 AM

What you do now is going to affect you later. Though this seems like a pretty straight-ahead statement that most people would agree with, many people never even take the time to think about the consequences of their actions. They just do what they do and act-out like they act-out.

When we are young, it is a very common thing that a person who is older than us will tell us that we should be careful about the choices that we make. This is their attempt to guide us down a road that will lead to success. Some young people listen. Many do not.

It is very easy to see a person that is going down the wrong road when they are an adolescent. This is due to the fact that adolescence is the time of life that sets the stage for what is to come. It is also the stage of life where a person is most influenced by their peer group and/or drawn to things that may lead them on the road to disaster; both physically and psychologically.

Young people are told not to smoke. Yet, many still develop this addiction. They are told not to take illegal drugs. Yet, many experiment and some fall prey to the addictive qualities of these drugs and the rest of their life is defined by addiction. Young people are told not to over drink, yet binge drinking is at an all time high. This has lead to many deaths either through alcohol poisoning or driving while under the influence. This has also lead to a life defined by alcohol addiction. Many bad things have been done while a person is under the influence of alcohol.

At this stage of life a person may also warn a young girl to not give into the sexual advances of boys, as this has the potential to negativity affect their future through pregnancy, disease, or simply being seen by future possible mates as promiscuous. Some girls listen. Many do not. In fact, at this stage of life many want to be seen as something that is not deemed acceptable by the constraints of society. Thus, this leads to all kinds of things that will negatively affect a person's future.

In youth, young people are also commonly told how they should behave in terms of their interactive behavior towards society. Many find this an easy understanding to master. Others, however, due to the environment in which they grow up may be lead down a negative pathway due to friends or family that are participating in illegal or immoral behavior, while others are simply schooled to be temperamental, ill tempered, and antisocial.

All this being said, it is easy to look back, in retrospect, about what has lead a person to a problematic life once they reach the adult stage of their existence. It is much harder, however, to explain to a person that they are currently damaging their future prospects by veering from the accepted and the straight and narrow.

In youth, one can attribute mistakes that are made to the undeveloped, undisciplined mind. But, there are many adults who follow a similar pathway as the rebellious, disenfranchised youth, and continue down a road that leads to a life defined by uncontrolled, manic behavior. Many youthful people who wander from the straight and narrow end up in jail or under the guidance of a psychiatrist. This may, in fact, be the best thing for them and for society as they are on a pathway that will only continue to damage themselves and others. There are also many adults who follow a pathway, and by whatever excuse and justification they may provide, are not a functioning member of society.

I think it is important to state that in this modern era there has been a certain glamorize image placed upon the rebel, the criminal, and the outsider. They have been depicted in novels and in films. But, these are glamorized images. Ongoing poverty, ongoing physical and mental conflict, ongoing turmoil to one's self and to others may appear artistic, when it is placed upon the words on a page or an image on the silver screen, it is not, however, a life that is well-lived. It is not a life that does not have its ongoing costs and its continued detriment to the people around that person and to the person who is instigating that lifestyle.

It is easy for a person to talk about themselves and discus the reasons why they are the way they are. It is also easy for a person to justify why they have ended up the way they ended up. It is easy for a person to explain away the actions that they have done that have negatively affected those within earshot and lifeshot. But, it is near impossible to do anything that makes anything better once that damage has been done.

To return to the original discussion, it is for this reason that a person, from their youth forward, must continually examine who they are and what they are and then make choices that will lead to the overall good of not only their own personal life but the life or all those around them in this time and this place in history. For it is only then that a person can pass through life and be seen as having made a positive contribution and not having simply lived a life defined by emotion, desire, addiction, and inappropriate behavior.

In other words, no matter where you find yourself in life, live and exist with refined consciousness. Do not let misguided friends, family, or personal desires and emotions guide you down a road where all you leave is regret and destruction.

# The Adventure of Life

24/May/2014 01:27 PM

To begin to tell this story I must go back a year or so ago. I had bought a bunch of acrylic paint from this art store in the OC, (Orange County). They were large jugs of paint. When I got home I realized that they were very watery and hard to work with for my style of painting. I guess I should have taken them back or thrown them away but I hate to be wasteful of time and/or paint, so I just kept them and have used them from time-to-time over the past year or so.

Okay, that's the back-story.

Yesterday, I was painting using those paints. As they are very watery, I poured large amounts of the various colors I was using onto the canvas, mixed them around, and did what I do…

As they are very watery, I had put down my drop cloth and used my dining room table as an easel. I had finished and I was letting the painting dry.

My lady asks, *"Are you sure the cats aren't going to go up there?" No, they never do,"* was my answer.

As if a prediction from the gods, maybe five minutes later we are sitting on the couch watching TV and one of my cats walks towards the table and immediately jumps straight up into the center of the painting. My lady yells and he goes running. …Running with tons of paint all over his paws.

I paint with a lot of paint…

Of course, as he runs he is spreading paint everywhere. He runs through the living room, takes a detour via the bathroom, and ends up in the bedroom under the bed. Paint is everywhere!

In fact, this is not the first time this has happened to us. Maybe twenty years ago we had purchased this new kitten. On the first day she was with us, we weren't looking and she walked through one of my paintings. In that case, she walked through oil paint. A few minutes later, I notice there are red paw prints throughout the living room. What a mess that was… Oil paint… You don't want to know…

Anyway, after the fiasco of yesterday, we get busy. My lady washed down the paws of our cat in the bathtub – while he was screeching like a banshee. (He's a cat; he didn't understand that she was trying to help him out). Me, I go to the store and buy club soda, (which is really good for removing new spills in carpet), and some rug cleaner. A couple of hours later, we are done. My cat still has blue tinted paws but he isn't tracking paint everywhere. The carpet is okay; I'll probably have to give it the once more over. But, it will survive.

The moral of the story... These are the adventures of life. They are all based in Our Self. I set all of this in motion, a long time ago, with the purchase of that paint and the fact that I kept it, even though I didn't like its texture – that is what created this moment.

Good or bad, we set the events of our life in motion. And, good or bad is how we view them. The events of yesterday weren't that bad, at least not in my eyes, though they were a bit of a hassle. But, it was an adventure. ...An adventure that removes the mundane from life and provides a memory worth remembering and a life-lesson worth taking note of.

The memories of our lives, set in motion by our actions, are what defines each of our existences.

## When You Want the Art No More

23/May/2014 09:01 AM

As a lover of art I have been collecting it virtually forever. But, there is a strange condition that goes hand-in-hand with the collecting of art; what do you do with it when you want it no more? But, I will get to that in a moment.

In the modern age, pretty much everyone has a website. Particularly established artists. There have been times when I have found a piece of art and I have wondered something about its creation, so I have contacted the artist. Virtually inevitably, they have all been very pissy with me. Why, I don't know? But, there is always something…

Commonly, the first thing they ask me, before they ever answer my question, (if they ever do), is where did I buy it? Now, I have bought my fair share of art from galleries around the globe, but of late, the majority of the art I have purchased has been found in thrift stores. Though I always preface the, *"Where I bought it,"* answer with a statement to the effect, *"Don't let this weird you out. But…"* And, *"I have found at lot of great art at…"* None-the-less this always seems to turn the conversation sideways.

I guess, I understand. I mean obviously somebody got their work of art somewhere but then wanted it no more. So, they dropped it off at their local thrift shop. I guess that would be an ego shot.

As an artist myself, I have sold my art in galleries, given it away, and donated it for auctions for years upon years. I have never seen one of my pieces in a thrift store but if I did I would probably buy it just to save it from damnation. :-) But, I don't think I would take it as an ego shot. Times change, people change, living environments change, and tastes change…

In fact, maybe eight years ago, I went through all my paintings that had been rolled up and stored away forever and I threw away over one hundred of them. Yep, straight into the trash. There were ones I never liked, no longer liked, or didn't feel had turned out the way I wanted. So… That gives you an idea of mindset about my art.

The other side of the issue is this… As an artist, there have been many times where I have purchased a piece of art at a thrift shop solely because I wanted to paint over the work that was already on the canvas. I did that just today. Stretched canvas is expensive – particularly museum quality canvas. If I can buy a painting (that I don't like) for a few dollar and painted over it upon a canvas that would cost me upwards of one hundred dollars... Well, you see the logic.

I imagine that is how some of the paintings of the great master were over-painted in times gone past – only to be found out generations later. Anyway...

Back to the subject, I am sure a lot of my paintings were purchased or received, one way or the other, and then given away or thrown away. That's just the reality of art... It is so subjective.

Currently, I am in the process of *Spring Cleaning.* It's actually Spring, amazingly... But anyway, every now and then I go through my-everything and clean up and clean out. As I am doing this, I have looked at my walls and removed some of the paintings I no longer like or now feel possess weird vibes. Here's the question, what should I do with them? Many would sell them on eBay or something. But, I'm just not about that these days. Most are too nice and are painted by known artists – as such I would not feel right painting over them. I could just throw them away and let them leave this existence forever – there is a certain emancipating freedom in that. Or, I could give them to a thrift store for someone else to buy for a couple of dollars, (way under market value), and enjoy them for how ever long they choose to enjoy them for.

Art... It was one of those things that you have to question your motives and your actions every step of the way.

## Fighting When You're Injured

22/May/2014 09:04 AM

Recently, there has been this big lawsuit, possibly class action, in the works, set about by former NFL players from being injured on the job. This strikes me as very strange and misguided. What did they think they were getting into when they signed up to play the game? Football is not badminton. It is hardcore and there is no doubt that there will be injuries. Just look at the 1979 film, *North Dallas Forty,* starring Nick Nolte and Mac Davis – they pretty much put what happens to players to film way back then. It is like if a person smokes, they can pretty much be sure of dying from lung cancer or heart disease. But, they chose to do it, so who is to blame?

A few years ago, I wrote a cover story about this guy who was teaching, as he put it, *"A Safe,"* form of martial arts. He thought that way too many martial artists were unnecessarily hurt from their training. Maybe… When I presented the article to my editor, he and I laughed, because we had both come up in the era of very hard style martial arts, where bruises, cuts, sprain, and broken bone were the name of the game. Back then, we just toughed it out and trained though the injuries.

This being said, I know a lot of martial artists who now walk with canes, are in wheel chairs, or have had hip, knee, and ankle replacements. Then, there are many, like myself, whose body is trashed and are in a lot of pain due to the years of training. But, we made a choice to train. There is no one to blame but ourselves.

A person can chose to stop training, (or playing football), if they do not like the possibility of injuries. Through my years of teaching the martial arts, particularly when I operated a school, this occurred all the time. Someone would get hurt and they would never return. That was their choice.

Today, I went to a physical therapy session. My doctor always tries to put me on pain meds when I trash my body in one-way or another. As I live a very active life, this happens more than it should. But, I always turn them done. Drugs are not who I am. Sure, I like a glass of wine, but meds are not good for the body; particularly pain meds. I always feel one should just eat the pain.

Every now and then I will take my doctor up on his suggestion to go and see a physical therapist, however. Sometimes they will give you a little twist or turn or stretching exercise, which you did not think of and that can really help things get better.

So anyway, today I go. I had been to this facility awhile back and each patient had their own room and their own physical therapist doing what they do. Today, I arrive and the facility had all changed. They had pulled down the walls and the patients were now on those physical therapy beds, (or whatever you call them), right next to each other. I mean, like two feet apart. Really-really close. They obviously wanted to maximize their intake like they do in those restaurants were you are sitting just a foot or two away from the person dining at the table next to you. I hate those restaurants! I don't want to listen to people's conversations and don't want prying ears listening to mine.

I am much more old-school – when you go to a restaurant, they sit you in a nice booth, where you can have a nice private conversation and enjoy your meal without someone bumping their butt into you when they leave their seat. This is the same way I feel about things like physical therapy; privacy is key.

Anyway, upon my arrival, my first thought was to just turn around and bail. It is like for any of you have had an MRI, they put you on a table and send you into this tiny-tiny tube with ear plugs in your ears because the pounding is so loud and you have to lay there for a half an hour or more – trapped with no way out, with the top of the tube just a few inches from your nose. Talk about claustrophobia! Many people can't do it. But me, I did the same thing as I did at the physical therapy session today – just lived it for the experience. Even though the experience was not good. But, I won't be going back.

You see, this is the thing about life, there are a lot of situations you are going to be forced into – a lot of things you do not like. You can choose to take them for they are worth and live through them – another experienced chalked up to memory. Or, you can leave.

In many ways, life is like physical combat. If you are not a professional brawler, who likes to fight, you are probably not going to enter into battle by design. Instead, you will be forced into it. But, once in combat, you can turn and run away or fight to the best of your ability. This is why one trains in the fighting arts in the first place, so they will be ready if necessary – including encountering all of the injuries this training entails.

One of the things that the martial arts teaches you is how to fight through your injures. How to fight through the fight even though you don't want to be in the fight and/or your body shouldn't be in the fight. Yes, you may not be one hundred percent, but you are trained how to alter your actions, change the way your body normally behaves, while in the midst of physical combat, in order to maintain your ability to emerge victorious. This, even though you are hurt. These are good lessons to learn for life.

This is also what people who play a sport like football must master. They know they will be injured but they play through those injuries in order to get paid, (large amounts of money), and to emerge victorious from the game.

In life you are handed experiences. In some cases you know what you have set yourself up for. Thus, you must accept the consequences. In other cases, you were expecting something different, these are the things where you have the choice to leave and never look back. But, whatever you do, the definition of your life is defined by what you chose to do. If you look back and try to blame someone else for where you ended up, when you were the one who made the choice to walk down the path in the first place, that only means you were not true to yourself.

Make a choice and live with it. Fight through the after-pain if you must. But, own your choices. This is the way to live a true and honest life.

# Awareness and Impact

21/May/2014 01:39 PM

As one advances through training in the martial arts, the focus shifts solely from developing the physical refinement of the body onto training the more refined elements of the body and the mind. At this stage of training, the martial artist develops skills to make themselves more aware of their environment. The reason awareness training is essential to the martial arts is that it allows the practitioner to assess any environment they find themselves within in order to understand if there is any level of danger or if they can enter into a more passive and meditative mindset.

The fact of the matter is, most martial artists will never need to use the self-defense skills they have learned in actual hand-to-hand physical combat. This is a good thing. Society has become more refined since the time when these ancient art forms were initially developed. But, by having developed these physical skills, which are not possessed by the average person, this is also what allows the martial artists to lift their mind to new and refined levels of understanding.

The average person exists within in his or her own mind. They only think about their own momentary reality, behaving in whatever way they want to behave, and do not study their environment. By encountering life in this fashion, not only do they leave themselves open to unanticipated attack, because they remain in a state of unawareness, but they also invade the space of others. Meaning, as they are only thinking about themselves, they are not taking other living beings into consideration. In times gone past, these unconscious actions would obviously lead to a person's demise, as they would be unaware of oncoming engagement either by human or by animal. In addition, by behaving in this manner, they would invite attack by superior combatants based on their unaware, unconscious, unthinking actions. Thus, people who live in this mind space are always defeated in battle.

Awareness of your environment is the first step in deciding what impact you will have on the world around you. As a martial artist, each practitioner strives to become acutely aware of how what he or she is doing is impacting his or her environment. As martial artists strive to be one with nature, they wish their impact to be as minimal as possible.

In this world, there are many people who speak loudly, walk with a heavy step, and boast of their accomplishments both in the ring and in life. The true martial artist never does this, for the person who behaves in this fashion is only attempting to call attention to themselves based upon a mindset of insecurity. They fell if they speak loudly, others will be forced to hear them. If they walk loudly, others will turn and take notice. If they claim how well they can fight, others will be afraid. This is not the way of the martial arts. As such, the true martial artist walks like a ninja: unheard and unseen. They speak with confidence about what they know but they never try to engage, influence, or impress others with their knowledge, as they realize the true sage is silent.

# Projecting Your Reality

21/May/2014 08:25 AM

I forever find it interesting how people project their own reality onto another person. For example, somebody reads something I have written, somebody reads something that was written about me, somebody sees one of my films, somebody listens to my music, somebody sees the way I am dressed and from this, they immediately decide who and what I am.

Inevitability, they are wrong. Why? Because they are putting their own set of definitions onto my life. They are not taking the time to see me for who I am. They are only viewing the external.

As this is my blog, I write about my life experiences and me. But, this same factor spans the gambit throughout all people and humanity. People see a person and immediately they throw their own set of definitions onto that person. They do this before they even come to know them.

Sometimes when I encounter someone from my past, be they from the 1970s, the 1980s, or the 1990s, they immediately assume I am the same person that I was back then. I am not. Times have changed and I have changed. I have evolved.

The flip side of this is when the last time you saw a person was five, ten, twenty, thirty or more years ago – the image you have of them is based on the back-then. You have not witnessed them grow or age. Due to this fact, your mind is locked in a time gone past. You remember then but you don't know them now.

People change. People become different from what they were. But, at their root-core, people are who they are. The fact is, you can never truly know a person unless you take the time to peer into their mind without casting preconceived definitions.

For example, me, I always tell my stories. I am a very honest person. If you want to know who I am and how I live, read my poetry and novels. If you want to know how I think read my more philosophic writings. Believe me, I know, there is a dichotomy between the two – they are completely yin and yang. But, that is who I am.

All this being said, people can read my writings, they can hear me describe my life experiences, they can listen to my realizations but still all they will do is project their own reality onto me. Just like they will do for you. As such, the truth to life is that there are two true realities: one is the true you, (who you truly are), and the second is the reality projected onto you by others. Which one do you choose to live?

# Immature/Arrogant

20/May/2014 08:03 AM

I have this friend who is in the last year of her teenage years. She was all into this guy. The guy decided to do what young guys do and dump her. She's a young girl and got her heart broken. Remember young love?

Anyway, after he dumped her, he put her on blast on *facebook*, saying all this really cruel, untrue stuff. What an asshole. What happened to chivalry and a gentleman never tells? Obviously, he's not a gentleman.

You know, I really hate this backstabbing sort of thing. I believe if a person has something to say to you, they should say it to you – resolve the issue or not, and then move on. It is nobody else's business. I've had assholes do stuff like that to me both on the internet and in the real world. Maybe you have too? And, what does it prove? The guy's friends find ammunition to dislike his ex, based on altered truths and lies. Her friends have a reason to know the guy is an asshole. But, what does all that equal? A relationship ended, a person was hurt, and the guy who ended the relationship did after-damage just to get over one more time on this very nice girl.

As you grow older you get to see people evolve through their life. I have known, (and known of), a few people who have acted like this and in some cases based their whole life around this type of behavior. They are the ones that though they get momentarily fulfilled, as they performed these ego-based negative actions, are the ones who end up out in the cold.

I hate to use the term *karma*, but I guess it best describes what occurs... They talk shit about other people, to other people, based on them trying to get over and though they may experience a moment of elation, over time, they are the ones who's lives end up empty and lost.

It is really simple: if you do bad things to people, if you say bad things about people, if you alter the truth about people to stroke your own ego, if you make up lies about people, *karma* is set in motion. If you don't stop doing that kind of stuff. If you don't fix the *karma* you created, it will, through time, hunt you down. And, you will pay the price.

I know, I know... You can't explain that to a nineteen year old for his life is in front of him. But, it was like today when I was sitting back for a moment and having brown rice for lunch. I was watching CNN as I ate and they did this piece on this guy who was giving a graduation speech at a university. Instead of being all hopeful and praising of the students, like they generally do, this guy instead told the students that many of them were, *"Immature and arrogant."*

It is something to think about... Who and what are you. And, where will you be, who will you be, when you are middle aged. Your then is created by your now.

**He Doesn't Want To Get Better**

19/May/2014 09:16 AM

Over the past weekend I decided to re-watch the Paul Thomas Anderson movie, *The Master,* on HBO OD. I had seen it in the theaters when it first came out but I was left wondering a few questions about the story and its conclusion; which, I suppose, is exactly what Anderson had intended.

There were a couple of poignant things that were stated in this film that held my attention and drove me to thought. At one point, the son of Philip Seymour Hoffman's character, states, *"He's just making it up as he goes along."*

Hoffman's character was a teacher of refined consciousness in this film and was guiding people towards a better self. Though this statement was given as an insult, it was exactly what all modern teachers have done as they have chartered a new course of refining a person's consciousness. Whether it was L. Ron Hubbard, (who some people claim Hoffman's character was based upon), Maharishi Mahesh Yogi or Osho, Bhagwan Shree Rajneesh, (who I spent time with in India), each of these teachers were teaching a new and revolutionary path of consciousness. As such, they were expanding and refining their teachings as they went along.

The second point came near the end of the film when Amy Adams' character stated, *"He doesn't want to get better,"* in regard to the on going drinking and debauchery of Joaquin Phoenix's character.

I think this is what truly sets a person's course of human evolution and rising consciousness on the path moving forward. First and foremost, a person needs to be aware that there is a higher and better self. Then, they need to decide to pursuit that path of refining their consciousness. For it is only when the individual decides to observe what they are doing, study why they are doing it, and then choose to change their behavior if it is negatively affecting themselves or others that a person can rise to a new higher state of Self.

Finally, at the end of the film, when Phoenix's character walked away from the path and the teacher, we find him in bed with a girl, using some of the mental mind manipulation techniques he had learned from Hoffman on the girl he is in bed with. Here, again, we find an interesting and common practice of the person who does not choose to live a path of true consciousness but none-the-less decides to take what he has learned from another person and use these techniques to play mind games with others – for whatever end goal he may desire.

This is one of the dangerous points on the path of consciousness and it is one of the main reasons I always warn others, who enter the path, to be careful of whom they are listening to. For there are so many people out there who are truly lost in the realms of the lower self but they have learned a few techniques as they have experimented with consciousness rising and then use these words to manipulate others.

It has long been the inside-joke in psychological circles, that the reason a person desires to become a psychologists is because they are messed up. We have all heard stories of some of the bad things psychologists do to people. But, a practicing psychologist must earn an advanced degree. They must be licensed. In spiritual circles it is not like that, any person can claim any thing. So, where does their certification come from? Where is your protection? Be careful!

Overall the film was a nice watch. And, just like other films on the subject, it does provide interesting food of thought.

Rising human consciousness is there. There... If you chose to pursuit it.

# Old Man/ Young Woman

17/May/2014 05:01 PM

I was in *The Last Bookstore* today. For those of you who may not know, *The Last Bookstore* is a downtown bookshop that pretty much is just that, the last really good bookstore in L.A. I think this is very sad. L.A. used to have some great bookstores spread all over the city. Now, they are all gone. Times change...

Anyway, when I was in line, waiting to check out, there was this old guy behind me. He was probably in his eighties. As he stood there he started to do that finger-framing thing; you know where artists, photographers, and filmmakers make a frame with their hands to see what an image will look like isolated. He was doing this towards this young girl behind the counter. She noticed his actions and asked, *"Do you want to take a photograph of me?" "No, I want to paint you,"* he replied. But, it was obvious he wanted much more than that. She smiled, totally playing into his fantasy.

Youth is beautiful, that is just the way it is. In most cases, age is not. As such, the old are always attracted to the young – especially in the case of men to women. I see this all the time when I am eating in a restaurant. The funky old-guy will be smiling and all-playing up to the young waitresses thinking he has a chance. They go back time-and-time again, to the same restaurant, hoping for the same waitress, living in the daydream that they will get a date.

I think it's sad to waste life in the pursuit of an unhaveable illusion. Dude, just because they are nice to you and smile at you doesn't mean they want to be with you! They are just doing their job and they want a tip.

I have always said, *"Leave the young to the young."* Sure, I am just like every other guy, when I see a pretty young girl who looks my direction; it sets my mind to dreaming. But, all an old dude would do is mess up the life of a young girl if they were to get with her. I mean, their life is in front of them. The older you get, the farther your life is behind you. Old to young only equals eventual disaster.

I know, when guys are out there and they are not in a relationship, it is simply a natural thing to be looking for someone. Nothing wrong with that... But, dudes set your dreams in the right direction.

I think back to this time a single friend and I were in a bar, throwing back a few, a couple of years ago. This guy was single and was constantly on the prowl. A lady walks into the bar and his eyes immediately go to her. I immediately see that she is pretty haggard and is noticeably missing several teeth. He got all excited and was ready to pounce. But, before he could make his move, some other (older guy) snatched her and was buying her a drink. *"Damn, we missed out,"* he exclaims. *"She doesn't even have all her teeth,"* I reply.

This is just an example; guys – single guys are always looking, always trying to fill the lack of relationship hole that it is their life. I have no answer for this. It is simply the way it is. I will say, again, if you are and old guy out there on the prowl, *"Leave the young to the young."* Not only do you have very little chance of being anything more than a friend (if even that) to them, but you shouldn't embarrass them and yourself by trying to be more. Would they want to take you to a nightclub? Would you want to go?

If I can quote myself one more time, from one of my previous writings, *"Nobody wants to see an old person dance."* Anyway...

All this being as it is, mostly, I say, it is sad that the internet killed the bookshop businesses. A truly important part of our society and culture is now gone – probably forever.

# The Scream Queens Get Old

17/May/2014 08:36 AM

Though there have been *Scream Queens* in each era since film upon the silver screen occurred, there was no greater era for *Scream Queens,* at least in my opinion, than during the 1980s into the 1990s. At least not yet...

The women who inhabited this era were the stunningly beautiful Brinke Stevens, Linnea Quigley, who is such a sweet person that I have worked with, and then it spreads out to actresses like Michelle Bauer and Monique Gabrielle, and even onto actresses who went mainstream like Jamie Lee Curtis. If you want to expand upon this inner circle just a bit further, there are actresses like, Jewel Shepard and certainly the incomparable: friend, former-filmmaking partner, and force to be reckoned with, Julie Strain. (And, this is just to name of few). Filmmakers like Fred Olen Ray, Jim Wynorski, and David DeCoteau took this this film genre, in this era, to the max.

*"Youth is beautiful."* That is true. There is a beauty in the look and the innocence of youth. That, *"Youth,"* truly feed into the roles these women played. But, time ticks on for all of us – as it has for these actresses.

Now, this is not a criticism at any level for all of these actresses are still beautiful in this stage of their life. (I am in the same age group). But, with these actresses moving on in time and in space, there has been a vacuum created. It has come in combination with the changing of the independent film industry in general and the lack of emerging talent. Though there is a never ending supply of beautiful, young actress out there – but with the combination of no filmmakers, in the indie industry, truly addressing this genre, and none of the new actresses moving up to the forefront, all we are left with is what once was.

Times change; that's just life. People get older, that too is life. Many try to hold onto youth, as they get older, that is very understandable. But, I forever find it sad when, in life, a great era comes to an end and nothing better replaces it. This, at least so far, is the case with, *"The Golden Age of Scream Queens."*

## Would Your Ever Make Another Roller Blade Seven?
16/May/2014 10:08 AM

*"Would you ever make another Roller Blade Seven?"* I get asked this question fairly frequently. In fact, as RB7 was just named number twenty-seven of, *"The One-Hundred Best B-Movies of All Time,"* at *Pulse Magazine,* (thanks guys), I have been asked that question several times this week. Last year the question was asked a lot when I was named number ten on the list, *The Best Movie Trash Creators* on imdb.com.

To answer, *"Yes, I would."* In fact, I would love to make another film of that caliber. The problem is, what we did then for relatively little money would be very-very expensive to do today.

Don Jackson and I made *Roller Blade Seven* and *Return of the Roller Blade Seven* for about thirty-thousand dollars. We shot it on 16mm and doing that, in itself, is not cheap. During the production, our executive producer had us add extra, *"Name Talent,"* which wasn't in the original deal. We had set the Name Talent standard at two: Don Stroud and William Smith. But, she kept getting new ideas so the money went out: Karen Black (RIP) was $3,000.00 and Frank Stallone was $6,000.00. Now, I was happy to work with both of these people, as they are both very talented actor, but they did cost money.

More than that though, when we made RB7 it was a different time in the film industry. People wanted to be a part of something. So, virtually every person who was in the film, including myself, was paid no money for his or her participation. But, they were happy to do it. I mean if you look at some of the scenes, there were upwards of over fifty people in one shot. They were all great and very nice people.

Also, we shot RB7 with no filming permits. We would simply go to the locations we had picked and film.

It was a different time. You could do things like that. At one point, when we were shooting out in the desert, a sheriff's helicopter landed to check us out. As long as we had no guns, which we didn't, they were all good. They flew off and filming continued...

Since 911, everything has gotten sketchy. It is much harder, if not impossible, to shoot with that many people with out getting filming permits, renting the location, and all that entails... Hell, it's hard to shoot with even a couple of people nowadays. Which means, it would cost a lot of money to bring a film like RB7 up again

Now, RB7 was not without its problems. Though I wrote a long chapter about the production of the film in my book, *Zen Filmmaking,* I plan to write another article, *"Roller Blade Seven: Darkness in the Light,"* on the subject about all the negative and bad things that took place during filming and post production; including the fact, I was totally broke by the end of the production, so much so that I had to sell my *1934 D'Angelico New Yorker,* just to survive. A guitar I have never been able to replace. And, that's just one story... A lot of shit went down.

But... All this being said, people still watch and talk about the film and that is great! Many hate it. Calling it one of the worst films ever made. Maybe... But, many also like it. They love the bizarre, psychedelic, abstract nature of the first *Zen Film.*

In closing, I would love to do another *Roller Blade Seven.* In fact, Don and I planned to do the next chapter as, *Wheelzone Rangers.* But, we got distracted and made other films; both individually and as a team and never got back to doing it. Then, he passed away and all that is left of the *Zen Filmmaking* team is me.

All this being said, if someone out there has the money, (I know I don't), and would like to finance another bizarre wild ride into the *Wheelzone,* give me a call. I am willing and I am available. :-)

# Acting for the Camera

15/May/2014 12:29 PM

Unless you are creating non-narrative films, like I have been focusing on for the past few years, acting is at the heart of any film. It is the actor who gets your story told. But actors are also, many times, the thing that makes a film hard to watch; as they are the central focus, their performances are the first thing that is commonly judged about a film.

Acting has evolved over the years. If you like to watch older films from the 1930s and 1940s like I do, you will immediately notice that the acting was much bigger back then. The performances where much more exaggerated. This is due to the fact that most of the actor's of that era were schooled on the stage. In the theatre their performances needed to be bigger. From this, they took this same acting style with them to the silver screen.

This is one of the reasons that I so much like working with my friend Conrad Brooks. He came from that era and he acts like he is still in that era. I love his performances.

In independent filmmaking, particularly the low to no budget genre, acting is what generally makes a film watchable or not. Now, this is a doubled edged sword because most people working at this level of the film industry are inexperienced actors – at least in terms of on-camera experience. If a person can remain natural in their performance then there is no problem. But, most people can't. Most people, at least the inexperienced, when they act, they are acting. And, this is what may kill the believability of their performance.

Also, particularly when people are attempting to make a spoof film, they intentionally overact. They believe this is how it was done. But, in actually, this is not the case. Bad acting is just that; bad acting. It is a whole onto itself. Therefore, by attempting to recreate it, defeats the entire purpose.

Now, there have been some great performances based upon spoofing an actor or an acting era. Billy Zane did a great job in the last of the Ed Wood scripts, *I Woke Up Early the Day I Died.* This film had no dialogue but the performances were great. And, of course, the spoof-based performances of talented actors like Johnny Depp have been great. But, these are very intentional performances given by highly talented actors. When one is inexperienced and doing this, it does not translate well to the screen.

If we look to the Republic Serial from the 1930s, 1940s, on into the 1950s, there was some great programing made in that era – whether it was for TV or the big screen. Series like *Commando Cody* and *The Adventures of Fu Manchu* truly defined an era and were the first to bring comic book type heroes to the screen. If we watch the acting in these serials, it was over the top. But, it was over the top, specific to that era. Just as when we watch Capt. James T. Kirk, (William Shatner), on the original *Star Trek* series, his acting is over the top but believable in its era.

To try to emulate these performances never really translates well to screen. I know, because we did this in *Roller Blade Seven.* Though the style of acting we employed did set the stage for the overall vibe of the film, most people didn't get it and did not understand the influences we were harkening back to, as times had changed and most who watched the RB7 film(s) were not aware of that era gone past or were not yet even born when it took place.

To this end, and through the years upon years I have been making films, I find it is far better to simply be natural in all onscreen performances – natural to your era. Even if your film is a spoof, by being true to yourself, by being who you are on screen, while wrapped in the cloak of a character, the audience will find your performance far more enjoyable to watch than if you try to be something you are not and perform as those people did in times gone past.

# Feeding the Dragon

15/May/2014 08:03 AM

A while ago this guy wrote this piece about me completely distorting reality and posted it on a website. He based his op-ed upon something somebody else had said and written, which also distorted reality. It was a well-written piece and I told him so. I also told him, in a personal message, why he was wrong and how he had drawn incorrect conclusions. The same night I sent him this message I get a raging email telling me what an asshole I am. It was sent to an email address that only could have been had via the message I sent to this guy – though a different person supposedly penned it. Funny, I thought…

Maybe a year later, I get a message from this same guy telling me that he is a grad student. And, as such, doesn't have much money. Okay, I get it… He wanted to review my movie *Max Hell Frog Warrior* but he had only seen it via illegal download and didn't feel it was right to review a movie after watching it in that fashion. He asked if I would send him a copy. He also asked if I would send him copies of my other films so he could review them, as well. This made me smile…

You know, here is a guy who has already made his opinion about me and my films abundantly clear. So much so that he posted a completely defamatory and false written work about me and never altered it or took it down after I explained the truth to him. (I hope his university papers are more accurate than his op-ed's). Now, he wants me to send him movies so he can slam me some more. Awh, people… They make me laugh.

I have heard that some people claim I don't like bad reviews about my films. Again, here is the case how anybody can say anything they want about a person, be it true or not. The fact is, that is completely wrong. In fact, when a review is well written and not based upon untruths, I think that they are fun, even if they are a total slam on one of my *Zen Films*. Now, Don Jackson, he hated bad reviews. He never understood why people called him the Ed Wood of the video age. Really Don??? But, that's not me. Believe me, I know, if you weren't there – weren't on the set with us, if you weren't having the fun we were having making the movies, if you don't understand our motivation for making them, if you're comparing them to bigger budget films, then yeah, some of them can be pretty terrible to the untrained eye. Why do you think I rarely watch no-budget films, because in many cases they are just too painful to watch. ...Not all, but some...

I've spoken and written a lot about how in this world of the *Wild Wild West* of the internet anything goes. And how, when people download things for free, (from offshore websites that are actually making money by posting stuff), these people are really damaging the overall good. Would you work for free at your job? This is especially the case for filmmakers like myself who pay for their movies to be made out of their own pockets. Yet, as studies have been done many-many times, in classes on ethics, most students don't see illegal downloads as a crime. I don't know... You need to think about what you're doing and the implications it has... Your choice, your *karma*.

All this being said, pretty much everybody wants to become famous out there. And, if you take the time, and do it right, you can become famous on the internet. And, who knows where that will lead?

Also, like I have said many-many times before, reviewing movies is an easy way to get your name out there, as all you have to do is talk about the good or the bad aspects of what somebody else has created. So, in fact, it is pretty easy – it doesn't take much effort.

But, I believe you, (meaning each of us), really have to look at the bigger picture of what you are doing before you do anything; be it reviewing movies, writing op-ed pieces, or simply projecting your reality, (what you believe), onto others. For in each of these cases, what you are doing is based upon you wanting to be more, you wanting to critique and judge others, you wanting to be viewed as intelligent or all-knowing, you wanting to become famous, or whatever... The key word here is, *"You."* YOU becoming more. YOU getting YOUR thoughts and ideas out there. YOU getting over on somebody. YOU being seen as something bigger and greater. YOU...

Whenever life is solely based upon YOU – YOU are not thinking about the impact you are having. You are only caring about YOU. If you live in this space, this is a very sad place of existence. For just as the drug addict will always need more and more, you will always need more YOU. More YOU projected out to the world.

This is difference between people that are ultimately seen as making a positive contribution to the world and those seen as ego-filled. Are you adding to the greater good? Or, are you only adding to the YOU of this world?

Anyway... I choose not to send the guy any of my films. Why feed the dragon?

# Talk and Talk and Talk and Talk

13/May/2014 09:26 PM

Have you every noticed how some people love to converse about another person. They discuss this and that about him or her. They know this happened... They assume that happened... They make all kinds of claims, but they were not there. So, in actuality, they don't known anything. Even if they were at the location where an incident took place, they are not inside the head of the person that they are discussing, so they do not understand the person's true motivation.

The fact is, in many cases, people who talk about people have never even met the person they are discussing; yet they talk and talk and talk.

Is this the purpose of life? For some, maybe it is.

Like I long ago said, *"You know you're famous when people you never met say things about you that aren't true."* And, you don't even have to be famous in the traditional sense, because people will talk about you anyway.

Since the birth of the internet people have had carte blanche to say whatever is on their mind. The fact is, most people who have a life and are doing something with it do not have the time, energy, or desire to waste their time writing about others; based on things they do not even know to be true. The people who are out there doing – don't waste their time. But, those who have no life or a lot of time on their hands, and nothing better to do, spend an enormous amount of time in cyberspace believe that it is in someway living life. Sooner or later (perhaps) they will realize that it is not. But, in the process many have nothing better to do than to embrace negativity.

There was a study done at Yale about how a negative statement made on the internet spreads out at an exponentially faster rate than that of a positive statement. Personally, I find this very sad. But, it is very telling of the world we live in.

All we have to do is look at how many young people have committed suicide over internet attacks. In 2012 I wrote an article for a magazine about a young martial artist, with *Asperger Syndrome,* who killed himself after being bullied at high school. The article was titled, *"The Tragic Story of Bully Victim Tyler Long."* And, that is just one example. It is obvious that there are a lot more people out there who have been hurt, injured, or have even taken their own life due to cyber attacks. Yet, those who unleashed these attacks are, in many cases, proud of themselves. This is a very dark glimpse into human psychology.

Hurting someone is easy when you can do it from a far. Try doing it face-to-face and the outcome is generally quite different.

What this says is that the people who attack people in cyberspace are cowards. People who talk about people behind their back are cowards. But, what does that mean, because the damage that they do is still done? Sure, you can say the person who unleashed the cyber attack will get their *karma*. But, that is just wishful thinking. Reality is reality. If someone hurts you or your life, you are hurt and that is your reality – that is real reality. And, in many cases, on-line, you don't even know who it is and/or you have no way of defending yourself. Though a coward performed these actions, it is still you who is left with the results, not them.

This is why many people attack via the internet. This is why so many people talk about people when they are not around. They are protected. This makes them no less a coward but they can embrace all the negativity they feel like and go forward without getting their ass kicked.

Have you been talked about behind your back? Have you been attacked on the internet? It doesn't feel good, does it?

The cause and the effect are left in your hands. It all starts and ends with you.

We really need to study what we are doing to other people. We really need to take the time to consider others before we say or do anything that could negatively affect another person's life. If we have said or done something to hurt someone, we need to undo it and stop the negativity from spreading further. This is what is the defining factor between being a better, more conscious person, and being an asshole.

Life cannot only be about you. Meaning, it cannot only be about the, *"I."* We need to step beyond the limitations of Personal Self and care about others – even if we don't like a person or are mad at another person. We need to care instead of attack. We need to stop invading a person's space on the internet and in life – behind their backs. We need to stop discussing and criticizing when an individual has no way to respond. We need to stop attacking when there is no method of personal self-defense. We need to step away and not embrace negativity. Why? Because this makes us more, this makes us better. Plus, it makes life better. It leaves one less person hurt or damaged, which makes everything better.

Ask yourself, *"What is the benefit of saying bad things about another person?" "How does that make them any less or you any more?"*

If we look to the way Magic Johnson responded tonight on Anderson Cooper's show to the comments made about him the night before by Donald Sterling – there we see the way a person should behave. I am sure, deep down inside, he was not happy with what Sterling said, but he responded with dignity, grace, understanding, and forgiveness. This is the model for the way we all should behave. Ego, vengeance, retaliation, or personal attacks should never be something that we employee. For in the end, though we may sugarcoat these exhibitions of force, all they are is a deception not based upon the truth. All this does is to diminish the person who is making these deceptive and misguided comments own integrity and validity. We should each be like Magic and discourse with forgiveness and grace.

Who do you want to be? Do you want to be someone who always has to cast the first stone or throw in their two-cents – no matter how much your two-cents hurts another person? Or, do you want to care more about the betterment of humanity than your own momentary emotions?

The world is made by you. Your words, your deeds, and your actions spread out across humanity. Yes, you may gain ego gratifications and momentary empowerment by hurting or retaliating against someone else. But, is that who you are? Is that who you want to be?

Stop being negative. Stop instigating negativity and everything becomes better. If you are one of the ones helping to create a positive life-scape then you will be so much more rewarded with a sense of accomplishment than you ever were by unleashing negativity.

Negativity breeds fear, hatred, and emotional imbalance. Positivity breeds a better world.

Choose good over evil.

# There Is No Rank In Yoga

13/May/2014 07:54 AM

The world is full of people who struggle to survive and become. You can only become, once you have found a way to survive. For without the necessities of life: food, water, shelter, and family – little else matters.

All one has to do is watch the news and they can see the life of many of the world's people out there who live through hell and struggle simply to find a means to exist. And, this is not only in the developing regions of the world – though those regions were the first to host human life. Look at the countries in the Eastern Europe and the Middle East, once thriving, now lost to the realms of devastation and war. We can say, *"This is not right."* But, this is simply the way of man (or woman). This is how people extend their hands post their ability to survive as they guide themselves toward, becoming.

When things are well in a person's life: when they have food, shelter, income, and an ongoing means of survival, they shift their attention to the more refined aspects of life. Various people are drawn to different things, but all people are defined by what is available to them. ...*Life is defined by availability.*

Though *Hatha Yoga*, (the physical aspects), and the martial arts have been around since time immemorial, they are two of the key focuses of human advancement and improvement being propagated across western society since the mid-twentieth century. Though these both have risen and fallen in popularity, to varying degrees, through the years, they each provide a person with a pathway to human betterment.

Yoga is very popular right now. Yoga businesses are thriving. The martial arts have maintained their place in modern society and people are constantly drawn to them for various reason. Though both of these physical activities offer an individual a pathway to becoming, in actuality very few people ever spend any time engulfed in these roads to betterment.

People speak about the martial arts. They may watch the films and respect the techniques when they are demonstrated on a television series. They may discuss who is better; who is worse, and state, *"That guy could kick this other guy's ass."* But, it is all talk. Very few people put on the gi, step on the mat, and train. And, when I say, *"Train,"* I am not talking about talking a self-defense course or going to a dojo for a few months. *"Training,"* equals years.

As is understood in the martial arts, simply because a person has earned a black belt does not make them a master. A *1st dan black belt* is still a student. It is not until a person has earned a *4th dan black belt* that they are truly considered a teacher. And, that takes year. But, people don't devote their time to it. Yet, the talk on the subject but have no true basis of understanding. They are really missing out...

*Hatha Yoga,* (by various names and new concoctions), is the yoga that people are drawn to these days. It is the physical aspects of yoga: the stretching and the breathing. Though it is very popular, few people spend more than a few hours of their life doing it.

Whereas the martial arts are orientated towards rank and advancement, yoga has no rank. It is simply a personal pathway to human betterment; which like the martial arts takes time – it does not happen overnight.

Though these two physical activities can truly set the course for the evolution of a person's life, few walk down these roads. As has been the case since the dawning of humanity, people would rather converse, discus, critique, and criticize, rather than take the time to advance their own inner-being.

So, this is the question you have to ask yourself, once you look around and realize that you are surviving in a stable manner, *"Who and what do I want to become?" "I am surviving – who am I becoming?"*

In times past, people would discuss how people wasted their life watching TV. Now, people say the same thing about the internet. In time, there will be something else. All this is true to a certain degree. All of these things: movies, TV, radio, books, the internet, are there and we can partake and learn from them. But, at the end of the day, it is who we become that defines our life not what we watch, listen to, or read.

Becoming is the ultimate goal of life. ...Whatever that becoming is. It is you who can talk, discuss, love, hate, criticize, and critique. It is also you who get up, take the time, and actually DO something with your life. You can actually,

*"Become,"* something. But, it isn't easy. It takes time and focused energy.

Are you going to talk or are you going to become?

# Talking Pictures of Other People

12/May/2014 08:05 AM

I just finished up the filming of a music video this past Saturday. We did this whole Bollywood thing at this Hindu temple set. It was cool. I love Bollywood productions!

Every now and then I get brought on to direct one of those real high-end union music videos. It's great. I don't have to do much but just sit around and guide the ship. The crew does everything else. Not like *Zen Filmmaking* where my hands are on and in everything from directing the actors, to doing the lighting, to shooting the camera, to whatever...

At one point on Saturday, I had a vision. I wanted to go handheld in amongst the dancers. My cameraman freaked. That wasn't in the schedule or on the storyboards. A cameraman can give me his opinion but he can't try to overrule me or he's off the set. This is the thing about filmmaking. The D.P. or cameraman can be your biggest asset or your worst curse. They can make your vision look great or they can totally fuck you over. Most are cool and are happy to work with you. They get the art. Some, however, particularly film school geeks, get the idea that it is their show and they are the one in control. Wrong!

This guy almost got to that level. He was a newly graduated USC film school guy. Nice enough. But, full of all the bullshit film school teaches you.

Now, I must preface this with the statement, I've had some good experiences with USC film school guys. One of my first films, *Samurai Ballet,* was filmed by me, (of course), and this guy in his last semester at USC. Good guy, great job! Hell, probably one of my first starring roles was for a USC student film, *The Funky Cuts Barber Shop.* Fun and great experience. I saw it on the big screen at USC, at their end of the semester fest, but never got a copy as 16mm transfer was big money back then. If any of you people out there have an in at USC, hook me up with a copy; I am sure it is their archives.

But, back to the point... Cameramen are really your lifeline to film production. If they mess you up, they can really kill a picture. I've had bad cameramen that shot on autofocus and, as such, the walls behind my characters looked great and in focus, but the characters were totally out of focus. One of the most poignant stories I like to tell is when I was helping this one friend put his first film together and on the first day of production the cameraman back-loaded my *Arri,* meaning the emulsion of the film was on the wrong side. That obviously killed all the footage, which killed the film. A lot of money, gone to nothing. He was a film school grad. And, these are just a couple of examples. I've done a lot of films and music videos; I've got a lot of stories…

Taking pictures of people is an art and an art form onto itself. And, in most cases, photographing people is at the heart of any film production. Now, I'm not talking about taking headshots, that's just mindless bullshit. Any monkey with a digital camera can do that. I am talking about capturing your subject(s) with art attached. And, the more people in the shot, the harder that is to do with vision and with art.

It was like I was at the *Rose Bowl Flea Market* yesterday. There are always thousands of people there. As we were walking, up ahead I notice this guy taking a photo of my lady and me with a long lens. Now, this obviously pissed me off, but what can you do about it? It's a public place and as much as you want to raise a stink and kick their ass, the law is the law. They can do it. But, *"Why,"* is my question? What is a photo of my lady and me in a crowd going to mean to the photographer?

This is the same up in Santa Barbara. Everywhere you go on State Street there is always someone talking pictures of people. I was up there a little while back and there was this older guy with a camera around his neck, high up on his chest. I could see he was snapping photos with a remote control that he had in his pocket. Most people don't know cameras; so most people didn't even know it was happening. But why? You can take all these shots but what is it going to prove? There is no art in them. Simply a mishmash of images.

Just like the paparazzi at places like, *The Grove.* Like I always jokingly tell them when they take my photo, *"I doubt you'll make any money trying to sell a photo of me to TMZ or Radar Online."*

This is the thing. There is art everywhere. There is art, if you have the eye for it. But, most people do not. They just want to take snapshots. This is true of many cameramen in the film game, as well.

Sometimes in restaurants or bars or clubs there will be a person etched in perfect lighting. It would make the perfect photograph. But, even though I carry a camera with me everywhere, that image I see probably would not translate to the captured image, especially in this digital age. As digital camera are well... They just have their own mind of image interpretation. Meaning, taking that photo would not only encroach on a person's privacy but it would also, most likely, not be what is seen by the human eye. ...I've written a lot about, *"Seeing What the Camera Sees."*

Anyway, what all this equals is that, first of all, you have to have the artistic vision to see the vision. Then, you have to have the skills and the tools to recreate what you saw, when you saw that perfect vision of a person in some place and some time and then capture it in it's orchestrated perfection instead of invading a person's space and not getting it anyway. Mostly, if you have art in your blood, you need to remain free to change and adapt as necessary to capture that art. You cannot let yourself be held back by what they taught you in school or your ego, as this will only keep you from capturing that perfect image.

That is art. That is what the reason to take pictures of other people, to make that art.

# Empty Life

10/May/2014 07:46 AM

    In the modern world we are constantly bombarded with the fact that we MUST be doing something. Life is all about *Being and Doing; Believing and Achieving.* Though this is all well and good, it has left the modern person with the inability to simply let go and do nothing.

    We each want to do. Me, I love to fill my brain with information. Though I, of course, love music, when I drive I generally listen to the various NPR stations and news radio to keep myself informed and expanding.

    But, driving is a doing. Driving is not an undoing. So, I justify my experience there as a learning process.

    Ever since the dawning of the small portable radio and earphones era, people have taken their entertainment with them. Whether it was sports or music it could be wherever they were.

    At one point, in the later 80s, I was very into the afternoon radio show of Dr. David Viscot. He was one of those cutting edge psychiatrists and talked with people, telling them to let go of the bullshit and get straight with life. Every now and then I would take my portable radio and earphones and listen to him when I knew I would be doing something, like waiting, that I didn't want to be doing.

    The psychoanalytical system he designed promised to change your life in one session. Me, dealing with chronic anxiety, due to having one of those childhoods you never quite get over, set up an appointment. The shrink they put me in with was this pretty young blonde woman who the moment I walked in fell in love with me. But, all that's a different story… The one session promise didn't really work. But, I still liked listening to him on the radio as I drove in the afternoons. Sadly, his show got cancelled. He did late night TV for a little while. But, what he spoke about and the way he said it didn't translate well to TV. He passed away a few years later.

    Portability continued… Giving birth to the *Sony Walkman* for cassettes, which was great for long flights. And, a bit later came the very small, battery operated, portable TV's.

People could watch their local stations anywhere they could get reception. I bought one of those but never really used it.

Now, it's your phone. You can get and do pretty much everything on it. All this to keep you occupied.

When people are at home and not doing, they are watching TV, reading, listening to music, cooking, and cleaning. What they are not doing is nothing.

Now, consciously doing nothing is much different from unconscious doing nothing. Each of us sits around letting our thoughts run wild as we space-out from time-to-time. That's all good. But, what few people do is to embracing the nothing, the no-thing of life and consciously moves their mind to the cosmos.

The thing about this is, it takes no effort. Yet, people find embracing emptiness almost impossible.

The reason they find this to be a problem is the societal programing we all have received, telling us that we must be scampering around and doing something at all times. Our brains must be filled. We must be doing or life will pass us by.

Now, I love TV. I watch TV all the time. But, the fact is, most TV is a complete brain fuck. You are not doing anything, yet you believe that you are. Listening to music may make you feel a certain way but it too is achieving nothing. If you read books and magazines that expand your brain, that is one thing, but most novels are not like that. So, reading also does not lead you to overall good. Yes-yes, you are doing something, but in essence you are doing nothing. Not the good, *"Cosmic Nothing,"* but instead, you are doing the, *"Doesn't mean anything nothing."*

In Zen we often speak of the *Zero Experience.* What this mean is that you turn off. You become the conscious nothing. Many spend years in meditation forcing their mind to embrace this space. But, that is not necessary. Simply release. In fact, do it right now. STOP. CLOSE YOUR EYES. TURN OFF.

Immediately, you will realize that you can do this. It may last only for a few seconds but you will feel the difference. You will have experienced that space of emptiness, of empty life.

Once you understand that this can happen, your whole life will be changed because you will realize in that space of profound emptiness new realizations are born. You are not looking for them, you are not trying to find them, you are not thinking about them; they simply exist.

This is the space, known in Zen as, *"No mind,"* or, *"Mushin No Shin."*

It is from emptiness that you experience the truth. You don't have to look for it – it is already there. You don't have to be anything; you don't have to do anything. Just STOP and cosmic truth will find you.

Stop seeking something to do when you have nothing to do. Instead, embrace Empty Life.

# Discipline and Penance

09/May/2014 08:30 AM

In the life-realms of spirituality and the martial arts, the ideology of discipline is often discusses and self-imposed. The spiritual person refrains from things like lust, sex, and immoral thoughts in order to become closer to god and reach cosmic consciousness. In the martial arts, the martial artist focuses their body and the mind by performing prescribed practices in order to become more in tune in order to cause themselves to become more perfect in their physical and mental actions. Though these two groups of people choose to impose a set of disciplines on themselves, most people are not like that.

Once a person is an adult, they decide that they can do whatever it is that they want to do. They set about on a course of doing. If they want money, power, sex, or fame, they go after it. And, they do not care who they hurt or the damage they leave in their wake.

As a child, when you did something that your parents or your teachers deemed was wrong, they would punish you. For example in Korean culture they do, *"Goo dan juh son doo duh."* Which basically means, *"Kneel down with your hands straight up in the air."* Imagine doing that for more than a few minutes. In western culture, at the time when I was raised, my parents would just hit me with a belt if they decided I did something wrong. In fact, in my junior high school the vice-principal, if you did something wrong, would take you into his office, take out this big paddle, and hit you in the butt with it. Pretty hard-core! Things have thankfully changed a bit by this point in history.

These things and more were done in order to instill a defined sense of what is right and what happens when you do something wrong. But, the moment a person reaches an age when they can question authority; many immediately run in the completely opposite direction and chart their own course. And, in doing so, some walk down the road of doing evil.

In the west, we see the martial arts as a good thing. But this is not the case through out the world. Many cultures look down on the martial arts as animalistic. And, in fact, fighting is one of the lowest levels of consciousness. This being said, many a martial artist hopes to gain a deeper sense of self through the practice of these ancient physical art forms. As such, they do all kinds of things to force mental discipline on their physical body. For example, standing in a low horse stance is one of the common practices. I know as a young martial artist of twelve or thirteen I would go to the studio early just to stand in the horse stance for a hour before class. I have had many students over the years, young and old alike, who do the same thing. Though this practice does little to enhance the body, it does cause one to focus their mind and force their body to do something that is not natural. As such, mental discipline is born.

As stated, most people don't care about any of this. They don't want to sit and learn to meditate. They don't give the years of time and refined focus it takes to become a proficient martial artist; they just want to do what they want to do.

This is one of the big problems with people in life and this is where all the chaos and conflict of human existence is born. It comes from people thinking first about themselves: what they want and how they want it, before they think about the person next to them or the person on the other side of the world.

As most people don't care about any one but themselves, and/or the people and things that they care about, they never set about on a course of penance when they do something that harms another person or place. They just dismiss their responsible and move forward with their life. But, just as when you were punished as a child when you did something wrong, many people do what they do, not caring until they can do it no longer – until a higher authority catches them and they are punished.

Certainly, the concept of penance draws up religious connotations. But, it should be more than that. It should be the ideology that we each embrace. Meaning, that if we hope to be more, if we want to be a whole person, if we want to make this earth-place better not worse, we must take everyone and everything into consideration as we move through life. If we do something wrong or negative, if we do something that hurts another person, we should take it upon our self to right that wrong. We should not need to be taken into the vice-principal's office and paddled. Through mental discipline, we need to stretch our consciousness out from simply being trapped in our own brain and embrace the world while we consciously refine ourselves to the degree that we become more and better. Then, if and when we damage the life of another person or another thing it is us that should consciously moves forward to right that wrong.

It is you who chooses to be more or less.

# Portable Sushi

07/May/2014 07:07 AM

    For those of us who like Asian food, it has been a great boon to now be able to get things like sushi and sashimi at the local supermarket. It wasn't always that way...

    My local *Ralph's* supermarket has an in-house sushi chef and he makes some good stuff. You can buy his creations just a few minutes up to a few hours after they have been created. Or, he will do stuff for you on the spot.

    *Trader Joe's* also has sushi to-go. For those of you who are not West Coast, *Trader Joe's* is a boutique supermarket originated here in So. Cal. Now, it has expanded and spread to a lot of stores. They have unique food items and a great wine selection.

    Last night, I grabbed some of their sushi for dinner. Damn, it was terrible! Now, this has been a problem of late. Their portable sushi has just gotten very-very bad. (This kind of sounds like a review on Yelp). I can't even tell you what's wrong with it but, even though they now have brown rice sushi, it is just soggy and terrible. I couldn't even eat it all, it made me sick.

    Now, I am no stranger to fast food sushi. I kind of played with this fact in the title of one of my books, *Sake in a Glass, Sushi With Your Fingers, Fifteen Minutes in Tokyo.* I wrote the poems that make up that collection at a time when I was constantly traveling in Asia. In fact, the year I composed the book, I believe I was in and out of NRT, Tokyo's Narita airport over forty times.

    This being said, the food I ate there was always well prepared. I never had a problem with it.

    And, this is the point of all this. Life is all about content, preparation, and presentation. The matter of the fact is, most people in life may start out caring about something they are doing but then their interest wanes, and they care no longer. They start doing a crappy job. Though the job may get done, it is done with no level of excellence.

    This is something that we all have to watch out for. Because if we don't, what we present to the world becomes diluted and people began to turn away from our creations and us.

If we choose to do something, we really need to do it right. We really need to remain focused and present our presentation with excellence. Otherwise, people write stuff like this about our very bad sushi. :-)

# Racist and Repressive

06/May/2014 09:09 AM

In the past few weeks there has been a lot of call-outs on people being SOMETHING. ...The NBA owner who was secretly tapped has been called a racist. This, even though his girlfriend is mixed race: Black and Mexican. The Beverly Hills hotel owner, who represses gays in his country, yet owns one of the premier hotels in the city that caters to everyone. And, this list goes on. I was watching the new episode of the HBO show *Silicone Valley* a couple of days ago and one of the Caucasian characters was dancing all around what he was saying to not be racist, yet he came off as racists. Of course, that's just a T.V. show... But, it ideally depicts how tippy-toed everyone must be these days.

Everyone is something defined by someone else. But, nobody knows what is really in the mind of the person they are defining. Nor do they care to find out. They just want to throw out judgments.

Everybody defines everybody by their race. This fact, in itself, would seem to make everybody racists. But, does it?

When you met a person, you notice their age, their hair color, what they are wearing, and their skin tone. Does that make you racist?

If you provide a complete description of the person to someone else, you probably will mention their race. Does that make you racist?

Each of us is defined by our culture and our religion. Though we here in big cities, with open minds, do not think twice about whether a person is gay or not, that is not the case for much of the world – especially if a person is very religions. Many religions are not gay friendly. That's not good but that is the way it is. So, is the hotel owning Sultan repressive or simply religious?

Oftentimes when people get into confrontations, the first thing they will say is, *"You whatever..."* That, *"Whatever,"* is generally made up of what is most noticeable about a person. It may be race, style, or sexual orientation. Do you think the African-American ball players would not call out a person's race if they were in the early stages of a fight?

When I was a kid growing up in Southcentral L.A., I was called racially derogatory terms everyday. But, that was okay, right? Because the African-American children that surrounded me had been repressed by my race. Not by me but by my race.

When I am in Asia, or here in the States, because I am fairly fluent in a few Asian languages, I hear racial comments all the time coming out of the mouths of Asia people. But, because they think I don't understand, they talk away. And, because nobody else can understand them, they don't know what is being said. Racism or culture?

People want to find definitions. People want to be judgmental. People want to find a reason not to like a person who is richer, more successful, or simply different. Thus, the minute anyone finds out anything about any person they have ammunition. This is not good, but it is the way it is.

It is not racism, it is not repression; it is simply the way the small-minded person operates. What can you do about it? Don't join in the conversation. Be bigger. Be more. Don't waste your time.

# Do Something Nice

05/May/2014 07:43 AM

    Most people wake up in the morning and perhaps they think about the dream they were having, for a moment or two, as that was the last reality they were living. Once this has concluded they immediately shift their thought patterns to themselves. They check what condition their condition is in: how they are feeling, what they are thinking, whom they are loving, whom they are hating. The thoughts then commonly go to the day in front of them. They get up; think about what they will have for breakfast and what they are going to wear. The men shave, the women put on their makeup and out the door they go. The one pattern that never changes in all this is that all thoughts are about self and how that self is going to encounter the world; what that self wants, how it wants to be perceived, and how it will obtain its desires.

    This pattern of constantly focusing on the personal self is embedded into an individual throughout their life. We are constantly bombarded by what society deems acceptable in terms of beauty, faith, occupation, and level of affluence. Virtually everyone attempts to achieve these levels. Thus, all thoughts are on self and how to get that self to where and what that self wants to be.

    But, let's change this up – at least for a moment. Instead of thinking about your self and what you want, why not take a day and do something for someone else. Why don't you take today and go out of your way to do something for someone else – do something nice.

    It is really not that hard. And, you can always go back to thinking about yourself tomorrow.

    Just do something nice for someone and everything and everyone will become just a little bit better.

# Spiritual = Special

04/May/2014 02:25 PM

From the time I was about sixteen into my early twenties I was very close with this one Swami. One day she told me the story of how, as she put it, *"I was a terrible liar. I lied about everything."* Then, she entered the spiritual path and all that ceased. Immediately, I understood why. Before she had entered the spiritual path she had no sense of self and nothing to claim as her own. Once on the path, she entered the novice stage, known as *Bramacharya,* and later became *Sanyass.* As such, she WAS. She had BECOME. As she was now something, she no longer had to lie about being nothing.

The primary reason a person lies is that they are not whole and true onto themselves. They wish to present an image of themselves to the world of being a person they wish they were but are not.

The spiritual path, by whatever name or form, provides a person with the sense of belonging and being SOMETHING. They belong, because they are part of whatever group they are a part of: be it a church, a temple, a *sanga,* or whatever. They are something, because they are, *"Spiritual."* They can claim it to the world and this sets them apart from you. They believe they are more than the person who is not spiritual. Moreover, even if someone walks a different spiritual path, they feel that they are more than them because they know they are on the right path and any other person is on the wrong path.

This is one of the biggest illusions about being spiritual. Though spirituality is based in a sense of becoming part of the god-movement, becoming selfless, moving towards enlightenment, removing the self from the constraints of the material world, in many ways it does just the opposite, for it provides the individual with a sense of SELF, a sense of, *"I am."* It provides them with a basis for ego.

This is why so many people enter the path of teaching spirituality. By teaching, it makes them feel supremely superior. They know the truth. They are passing the truth on to those below them who are questioning and in need of guidance.

Though I can say this over and over again, it will make little difference, because people always seem to miss the point, but if you are basing your spirituality upon SELF, if you are using it as a tool to fix something that is missing in you, while deceiving others, your spirituality is not spiritual at all. It is just a way for you to stroke your ego.

True spirituality is about you removing YOU from the equation. True spirituality is about BEING as opposed to, *"Being Something."* True spirituality has no room for YOU to claim that you are anything.

Be spiritual while embracing these simple explanations and not only will you but the entire world will become free from walking down the road of *maya,* (illusion).

Spiritual should not equal Special. Spiritual should equal Selfless.

## Important to You. Important to No One Else.
03/May/2014 08:17 AM

We each have moments in our life when what we are thinking, what we are feeling, is so overwhelmingly important; we become fixated. We are living in a space where nothing else matters.

Most people, when they are in this space can think of nothing else. This is the mind-space that causes frustration, anger, depression, rage, suicide, and all other levels of uncontrolled emotions – all simply because the importance of what is in our mind is so overwhelming.

In life, most people never learn that what is important this moment will not be important the next. Thus, their actions and their emotional responses become dominated by the emotion(s) present in whatever moment of desire they are living.

What is important this moment will not be important the next. This fact is easily charted simply by thinking back to one of those all-encompassing moments when you were controlled by what was on your mind. Though in that moment it was all you cared about – what happened to that desire? Where did all those emotions go? They left with the passing time of life.

Emotions, desires, wants, must-haves, they last only as long as they last. If you get them, you lose interest and a whole new set of life desires are set in motion. If you don't get them, you eventually forget the desire and move on.

Understanding that the frustration and the emotions of the moment are only that, the frustration and the emotions of the moment, frees a person. For you then can observe what you are feeling but you are not overpowered by these emotions.

Think how many stupid mistakes you have made while engulfed in the wanting. Think how many things you have done and said, that made you look really foolish, solely based on what was important to you in a specific moment of time. If you want to remove further foolish actions, based on your momentary desires from your life, stop allowing your emotions of wanting something to be different to control you.

Most importantly, we must all realize that what is important to us means nothing to the person sitting next to us. They have their own set of wants, desires, and needs. So, why would they even care about ours? Therefore, if we project our desires in their direction, expecting them to have the same wants, all that does is make us look ridiculous.

You can go through life pursuing, and then becoming frustrated, angry, sad, and depressed when what you want to happen does not happen. But, this is a low level of human consciousness. As interpersonal human consciousness is defined by we the individual, we have the power to be more than our desires and, thereby, not let them control us.

Yes, we may want. Yes, it, (whatever it is), may be important to us. But, we can choose to see through the illusion of this specific want, know this want will not last forever, understand this want matters to no on else, and emerge as a better/bigger person for controlling it as opposed to letting it control us.

**Bad Advice from Bad People**

02/May/2014 01:14 PM

 There has been a record-breaking heat wave in L.A. over the past few days. I was driving and got stuck in a massive traffic jam, in all the heat, on the freeway a couple of days ago near Chinatown. I was listening to KCRW and Kai Ryssdal. He had a guest on his Marketplace show, Zac Bisonnette speaking about his new book, *Good Advice from Bad People: Selected Wisdom from Murders, Stock Swindlers, and Lance Armstrong.* It was a great interview. I bought the book.

 In brief, the book views how we, the modern populace, spend literally billions of dollars on self-improvement and self-help products. The book then details how we, the modern populace, willingly take advice from unscrupulous people. ... People who have done a lot of wrong and lied about who and what they are. It was a good read.

 Now certainly, it is no secret that I have a big problem with this kind of a person. The person who puts themselves out there to the public, but is not truthful about who they are. They do this for ego gratifications and to fill whatever hole of insecurity and insignificance they feel. And, they do it to make money. Bad, Bad, Bad!

 As I dance around spiritual circles a lot, I see this all the time. And, the reason I have a problem with this kind of person is because I have seen the damage, both monetarily and psychologically, they cause in people who are seeking a better life and a deeper understanding, only to be guided down the road to nowhere by a deceitful lair. Yet, since time immemorial people like this keep stepping up to the pulpit.

 As I have stated in the past, I believe I was lucky to come up in time where those of us who were seeking a deeper understanding of the truth could actually spend time with true teachers who did not base their teaching(s) upon the bottom line. Krishnamurti never charged a dime for his lectures. Baba Hari Dass never charged for his *satsangs*. In all the years I was with Swami Satchidananda the only money I ever spent was ten dollars that I donated due to the fact that we were buying him a new quilt for his room at the *Los Angeles Integral Yoga Institute.* While I was in the *ashrams* in India, they never asked for anything. I returned back to America with virtually the same amount of money I left with.

There are still true-teachers out there. But, they are a bit harder to find.

Today, there are all these people claiming to have some sort of truth or knowledge, while attempting to attract disciples or as I like to call them, *"Customers,"* in order to enhance their bank accounts. If they are charging you, they are a fake! True spirituality is not about business.

I think back to when Wayne Dyer was first breaking through in the 1970s. (As Wayne Dyer and Tony Robbins are pretty much at the top of the self-help game). Anyway, on a morning talk show here in the L.A., Dyer stated in essence, *"I've made more money in the past year than I previously made my entire life."* Okay, but how does that help humanity?

From this statement and others, Dyer has cloned many a person who has attempted to follow in his footsteps. None of them have had the impact he has had, however. Most, were only were poor imitation, as they do not possess the Ph.D. in psychology earned by Dyer.

Now, I am not singing his praises. I am simply stating facts.

A few years back I had a page/article on this website devoted to an interaction I had with Dyer in the early 1990s, complete with his hand written letters to me. I will say, I respect him for personally writing, in his own hand. But, as I presented in the piece, I do not believe he is what he seems. Though I suppose he is trying to be...

Overall, I am not about negativity at any level, so I eventually took the page down as it may have come off as such. But, as I stated in that piece, when he was simply attempting to move forward the understandings of Maslow, he had the credentials. But, beyond that, it became a bank-game.

Now, from his own words, Dyer had a pretty hard childhood. As we each are formed by our childhood, I certainly do not fault him for trying to climb to the top of the heap. Which, in many ways, he did. That being said, every time a word is spoken without pure-intent, every time an action is taken with out focused-consciousness, people's lives become damaged. If you claim spirituality, at any level, and you are not

TRUE, you leave in your wake a damaged public who is then fearful of moving onto other more pure teachings. So, one really needs to be careful what they say and do and how they do it.

As stated, I move in spiritual circles. Frequently, I meet people who make their living from, *"Being spiritual."* I often question them about their livelihood. They commonly respond, *"How else can I make my money?"* I frequently exclaim, *"Get a fucking job!"*

Just for the record here, all the money I make from my books goes to the *Tibetan Children's Fund* and *The Tibet Fund*. And, I have never charged for teaching the martial arts in all the years I have been teaching them. I believe that making the martial arts a business robs their true essence. So, I base what I am saying on the reality I am living.

In closing, if you get a chance read the book, *Good Advice from Bad People: Selected Wisdom from Murders, Stock Swindlers, and Lance Armstrong,* as it provides a pretty good, insightful, and fun insight into what is going on in the modern mind. But, moreover, *"Physician, heal thyself."* For all you self-proclaimed gurus and teachers out there get your own shit together before you mess with the lives of other people.

**Self-Reflection**

01/May/2014 10:22 AM

People, whether they walk upon the spiritual path or not, rarely take the time to truly delve deeply into their being and find out what is really going on inside of them – why they are the way they are.

Life is filled with constant distractions. The biggest, of course, is desire and the pursuit of what we all want. But, the distractions of life are much more sublet than that. Simply living a day-to-day existence takes the mind away from studying ourselves. Whether it is the trials and tribulations of school, work, driving from one location to the next, or riding your bike along the beach, all things draw us out and away from looking in.

Most people never even take a moment to think about looking inside themselves. They are too busy being whomever it is they have become. They are so wrapped up in THEM – what or who they love or hate and what they are currently experiencing, that they never STOP and question the WHY of how they ended up where they are and/or who they truly are.

I don't tweet but two passages I wrote that I am told are frequently posted on Twitter are, *"How much of life do you let pass by without a thought?"* and *"Take the time to just do nothing. It will open up a completely new world of insight for you."*

I think those aphorisms are from my book, Zen O'clock: Time To Be.

Ask yourself, *"How much of life do you let pass by without a thought?"* For most people, their entire life goes by motivated only by the prevailing desires of the moment. Love, hate, happiness, anger, wanting, needing, sadness, and the list goes on. What they never question is, *"Why?"*

Why are you feeling what you are feeling and what brought you to the YOU that is feeling it? And, are you going to control IT or is IT going to control you? The latter is the way most people live their lives.

I've said this before, but this is where the big problem with the concept of living in the NOW that is constantly taught in New Age circles falters. The NOW is fine. But, the NOW of most people is absent from the NOW of consciousness. It is simply the NOW of the NOW. So, in essence, most people have already reached the ultimate pinnacle of higher consciousness, simply by being absent from a formalized sense of SELF. They are already dancing in the NOW. They are happy, they are sad, they are whatever and they do not possess the mental facilities to even begin to understand why.

This is where it gets tricky. On the path of consciousness, the refined NOW is based on an acute sense of SELF that is then released into the conscious NOW. It is not the NOW of I am in love so I feel really good or I pissed off so I am screaming about something or someone. That is the unconscious NOW. Sadly, most people who claim to be spiritual teachers live only at that level of realization. Then, at best, they make excuses for their actions. They have not step into the more refined levels of consciousness where they can actually be in the NOW of full consciousness.

This brings me to the next quote of me quoting me :-), *"Take the time to just do nothing. It will open up a completely new world of insight for you."*

Life, even life on the spiritual path, is commonly based upon doing. We all are told we must DO. Whether this means going to school, going to work, or even meditating – all that is about DOING. But ultimately, doing will only equal so much. If you want to know yourself, you have to STOP. And initially, this also means you have to stop thinking. For all thinking does is provided you with a long list of programmed thoughts and justifications for you making excuses about who and what you are. You need to freeze this common thought pattern if you hope to emerge in a space of True-Knowledge.

And, this is the sourcepoint for YOU, if you desire to truly gain a deep understanding of YOU and YOUR place in the universe. First, you have stop thinking that you know anything. STOP! Next, you have to let your mind release.

Now, this is not like meditation where you attempt to force your mind to stop thinking. You simply must STOP all formality, all former beliefs in who and what you believe yourself to be. STOP thinking you must have this or you must have that. ...That you must be this or that. Just STOP! Take some time to do this. And, from this, the self-realized YOU may emerge.

Self-Reflection... It is not a technique of you forcing yourself to more deeply believe the self-proclaimed or programmed nonsense that it is already in your brain. It is the process of letting go of all you know. From this, the true you is presented.

**Is That All You Have to Offer?**

30/Apr/2014 09:05 AM

Not everyone in the world is a philosopher, author, musician, filmmaker, artist, chef, really good car mechanic, or whatever. Not everyone in the world is wired to have a creative or analytic mind. In fact, most people are happy to simply pass through life, living their existence to the best of their ability.

As I long ago wrote, a specific person may not make a substantial contribution to the world, but if they are a good person, they set good things in motions. From this, perhaps the next generation or the next or the next, in their biological line, will be born the one who changes the world for the betterment of all humanity.

To be good, to do good, does not take much effort. You simply have to live in a space of niceness. Most people do. Some people do not.

I think we have all encountered those people who set about on a course of disruption. Whether this is in school, work, or a social environment, or is on the more abstract realms of the reality like cyberspace, these people come in and mess things up. Maybe they feel that is their duty. Who can say? But, the result is the same, unleashing discontent and unhappiness.

What are the results of that? The further deterioration of time, space, and the life of all those around them and all those they encounter.

Some of these people grow large in their sphere of influence. Most, however, remain small as small is all that type of behavior requires. Meaning, it takes much more to make an actual contribution to society, to this world, and to this existence than it does to tear something down.

Think about this... You can easily go to your cupboard, take out a drinking glass, and smash it on the floor, breaking it into a million pieces. Can you make a glass? Can you recreate that glass you broke? Probably not.

From this example it is clear to see that breaking is easy, creating is much more difficult.

For the people that break – for the people that try to hurt, try to destroy, I question, *"Is that all you have to offer?"*

Take the time, put away misplaced ego, put away anger, and put away hurtful thoughts and actions. Be good and learn to create. From this, your contribution to this life place will then be respected and not scorned.

# Invasion of Space

29/Apr/2014 09:27 PM

I am sitting here this evening listing to a dog. ...A dog belonging to one of my neighbors. He barks and barks and barks. (That's why I like cats). It is a warm evening, so the windows must remain open.

I have a neighbor in the other direction who's teenage son frequently practices his saxophone; badly. Though I am all for music, man this kid just cannot play. When he plays it is hell to the ears.

I had to take my car into the shop today. As I was discussing what condition my car's condition was in, I notice that somewhere/someplace recently someone smacked his or her car door into my door leaving a big ding.

I have this other neighbor who is prone to screaming obscenities like, *"Fuck me,"* over and over again.

This is life. People WILL invade your space. Why do they do it? Either because they do not care, feel there are entitled to do so, or are so wrapped up into their own head that they cannot see beyond their own illusion. No matter what the case, what they do messes with your life. In fact, with each occurrence your life will never be the same.

There is this whole thing going on right now, big in the news, where this NBA team owner didn't want his multiracial girlfriend posing with ballers and posting it on twitter. Okay, sounds like a jealous boyfriend to me. But, they have made this whole racial thing out of it. Maybe it is, I don't know? What I do know is that someone secretly tape-recorded their private conversation and then released it to TMZ. That is illegal in California yet no one is speaking about that. They are just on a witch-hunt, wanting the head of a racist. No matter what the root truth is about what he did or did not mean with his words, his space was invaded for someone else's gain.

Sometime good people and good things invade your space. A positive person, a positive occurrence, or help when you need it arrives. That is great. I believe we are all thankful when we encounter that type of situation in life. But, what is more dominant is the pain we encounter at the rude, unthinking hands of others, when there unconscious/unthinking actions invade our space.

We have to strive to be more than that. We must always try to be conscious of the space of others and never damage or hurt the life of others by the *Invasion of their Space.*

# Nothing Will Give You That Time Back

29/Apr/2014 08:20 AM

There are situations in all of our lives when we wish we could get back the time we lost. Maybe it was at the end of a bad relationship. Maybe it was when we saw through a person or a cause that we believed in and then realized that the person lied to us or the cause was a fake. Maybe it was even when we had reached out our hand to help someone. Then, we realized that they didn't appreciate or deserve our help. From all of these things and more all we are left with is the realization that it was a waste of time.

All life is based on interaction. All life is based on interacting with people. All life is based on belief. Our belief system may be large; like believing in a religion or a cause. Or, it may be small; like the emotions of like or love for a person or a thing. But, at the end of all that – all that exists is what you are left with: time well spent or a waste of time.

The fact of the matter is, in life nothing will give you that time back. Be the time spent: bad or good.

We can have memories that make us happy. We can look back to what was and remember the good times: the emotions of love and happiness. But, that is just a memory. The time is gone. We can also look back to bad times. We can think of the people who made us angry and/or the situations that robbed our life. Those times are also gone. One kind of memory fills us with joy, the other with anger. But, no matter what we are thinking, all that memory gives us is a remembrance of what was. It is not now. We cannot be there again.

Some memories make us want to go back, relive what we lived. Though we can try, it can't really be accomplished. Even if we have another good time, it will never be the time that was. At best, all we are left with is another memory of a time that cannot be lived again.

Many years ago I returned to South Korea after having been gone for a few months. I had returned to see this girl that I had spent some very good times with. Back then, I used to bounce in and out of South Korea quite frequently.

A few months the previous, the girl and I had traveled the entire country, from north to south: from Seorak San to Jeju

Do. It was great but I had a gig in Japan, so I had to bail. Then, I went back to the States for a month or so to oversee what was going on at my martial art studio. But, the whole time I was gone I could not help but think about returning. So, I did. Hoping for another time in perfection.

I get back, all was as expected. I questioned what should we do. Though I had no real plans or desires, she suggested we go back to Seorak San. Okay... I rented a car.

As hotel rooms were at a premium in Seoul at that time of year, I decide to hang onto mine – pay for it even though I wasn't going to use it, just so I would have a place to return to.

The next morning we headed out on the road. Maybe fifty miles deep, bam, a truck smashes into us. We were okay but the Hyundai I had rented was destroyed. We took the bus back to Seoul. Luckily, I had the hotel room waiting. My lady friend called up the rental company and they, being a South Korean business, wanted me to pay for the whole car – meaning they wanted me to buy them a new one even though I had paid for insurance. Word to the wise, never-ever do business with a Korean. The stories I could tell you... Anyway, I wasn't going to do that, so the next day I bailed the country. My lady friend went and gave them the keys, told them where the car was.

This is just one example, but as you can see, attempting to relive a perfect time equaled living a not so perfect time. And, that is just life. A moment, the feelings of a specific moment, can never be relived. It can be remember, you can attempt to reenacted it, but it can never be relived.

This is the fact of life; we are all trapped in a continuum from birth to death. All we have is the time in between. Some people want to spend that time filled with adrenaline – based upon anger and frustration. Many people create that in their life simply so that they can experience the rush. Most of us are not like that, however. We want the feelings of joy, happiness, and love.

But, no matter what we set our life up to experience, we will all sooner or later be seduced by the darkness. There will be times when all we wish is that we could have the time back.

Good or bad, this is life. We can try to make this life good but we must accept the bad, for it will come to all of us. In those moments, all we can do is set a new course and hope to spend more moments of happiness and peace than those lived in the bad – left regretting the negativity of the past, wishing we had our time back.

Just like in the martial arts we set a course for combat. We must learn the foundational techniques then we must adapt them to answer the needs of a specific confrontation. See, move, define, and refine. Your life, try to live it well.

# Living in the Wasteland

28/Apr/2014 01:04 PM

I know of this one young lady who is dealing with a pretty serious bout of cancer right now. Whether she will make it through or not is anybody's guess. But, she frequently states, *"My lifespan will be less than yours."* It is very sad because she is a very nice person.

Due to her cancer and her cancer treatments she must have quality health insurance. To facilitate this, she has a job. The problem is, with all the meds she must take, plus her various chemo treatments, it leaves her not with her best foot forward.

Recently, she has been given a number of new duties at her job. Though she performs them, she does not believe that she does so with her normal level of excellence. And, she understands that her mental state is not up to par.

I think it is very sad that in this day and age, in the wealthiest country on the planet, that we cannot take better care of our people. ...That if a person is sick and possibly dying that instead of adding to the stress already abundant in their life, due to their illness, that they cannot be given the time and the space to relax and possibly heal and become better. Or, if they are going to die, at least give them the time to spend their last days on this earth in peace.

Yes, yes, I know, there have been way too many people who have taken advantage of the medical and financial benefits we have in place in this country. And yes, I understand that most of the people receiving the various forms of state and governmental aid should get off their ass and get a job. That being said, there are those, who have played by the rules their whole life and our government is not there when they need help.

As I have said in many places before, I am a supporter of Obama but this is one of the ideal examples of where the Affordable Care Act falls very short. We, the people, are now forced to have health care. If a person can't afford to pay for quality health care, they must get it through their job. (Because health care designated for the impoverished is just terrible).

But a job forced on a dying person simply so they can get quality health insurance is very-very wrong.

We, the U.S., needs to stop buying friendships around the world so pseudo dictators, (who claim that they are our allies), can live in the lap of luxury in McMansions and start refocusing on us.

U.S. should equal us.

## I Continue to Believe in People but They Continue to Let Me Down

27/Apr/2014 07:59 AM

I am an eternal optimist. I always believe in people. I always believe that they are going to do the right thing. But, more often than not, they don't.

I believe we each have had people spread false rumors about us, say things that aren't true, take our words and turn them around to suit they own point of view, and lie to us. Those actions and more have happened to all of us but I just don't understand why people can't choose to be more than that?

Why do people only care about themselves? Why do they not care whom they hurt?

I realize there is no absolute answer to that question. It is a bit rhetorical. And, it can and will be debated in psychological circles forever. But, what is the motivation for these people and what is their end game? For if they distort reality about other people, if they lie to other people, how does that make them or their life any better?

It is really obvious when somebody is doing or saying something bad. If it is based on attacking and/or damaging anyone or anything, it is bad. Yet, people thrive on this level of reality. And, in fact, they relish in the positive response they receive from unleashing negativity. That is just strange to me.

Instead of doing, saying, and writing bad things, why can't people do the opposite? Why can't they make the commitment to do, say, and write only good things? Doesn't that just seem better? Doesn't that seem like it would make all of life better?

Nobody is perfect. We all do things that are not right. But, for many of us, when we do something that is not right, we set about on a course to fix it, not embellish it. We attempt to remove any negativity we may have set in motion.

It is you and it is me who chooses to set a course of life positivity in motion. This is done simply by consciously gearing our actions towards the betterment of all.

Sure, we all get mad at this or at that, at this person or that person, but it is we who can choose to rise above it. It is we who can choose to not let our dissatisfaction grow exponentially by expanding negatively upon those feelings.

As we all know, what we feel today will not be what we feel tomorrow. And, if we do something negative based on what we feel today it can only resonate into further negativity in our lives tomorrow.

Life is based in us – we the people. If you've done something negative it is far better to undo it than to let it linger in the world and create more negativity. Undo it. That is better. Let positivity flow.

# Insanity Brewing

25/Apr/2014 04:30 PM

Mental illness is one of those things that though it is much more openly talked about these days, there is still a lot of stigma attached to it.

Some mental illnesses are self-treatable. Like anxiety and panic disorders where diet, exercise, and human interaction can really change the game once a person is directed down that road.

I've known more than a couple of people with undiagnosed *bipolar disorder* and though they could function in society pretty well, they were very prone to complete freaking out sessions. But, as they were functional, (more of less), they survived.

Other, more serious, mental illnesses are not like that, however. There is the next level of mental illness where no self-cure can help. I first witnessed this level of mental illness when I was in forth grade. This one kid in my class, whenever he didn't like something, would put one of his fingers in his mouth, bite it, as he pounded on the top of his head with his fist, and made this loud, *"Rurrrrr,"* sound. He eventually left or was asked to leave the school. What was going with him, I don't know. But, I do know it was serious.

A bit later in life, when I was in my later teens, I was hanging out with this sweet girl who lived up Isla Vista, Goleta way. She would come down to L.A. or I would go up there. We went to bluegrass festivals and did stuff like that. In any case, she was the first person I came to personally know who admitted had a mental illness. She never hid the truth about herself – that she had done some time in an institution. Being considerate, I never pushed the issue too deeply, however. But, I believe what she suffered from was *Schizophrenia*. As within her and her behavior there was something going on that was just a little different.

I believe it must be one of the most terrible punishments to have to pass through life with a mental illness like *Schizophrenia*. Though, there are certainly medicines, in this day and age, that can help to control it, none-the-less the person is left different and constantly battling accepted reality; especially if they do not take their meds.

Just a side note here... In India, the crazier you are the holier you are. I am sure many of the people who are considered saints of the past like Sri Ramakrishna and even some of those I met and interacted with were quite mentally ill. But, being in India, as long as they directed their mental illness towards spirituality, they were seen as being holy.

I have known other people who also became engulfed with *Schizophrenia*. As is commonly the case, it presents when a person is a young adult. One person I knew ended up dancing around on the docks in Redondo Beach thinking he was Jesus.

I don't know why so many people with mental illness go towards becoming a being like Jesus. I mean, though he changed the world forever, he had a pretty messed up death. Anyway, that's just a thought.

Another case was a girl I met in San Francisco, which I detail the story of in a couple of my novels and poems. I thought the girl was just duped up on Acid when I met her. But, she went nuts all over me and did this whole, crazy staking me all the way to L.A. thing. Scary...

There have also been a few people I have met via the film industry who either let me know of their condition or, through time, I begin to observe it.

After being around these various people, throughout the years, and me, being who I am, (I tend to study people and their actions), I have come to notice a similarity in the behavior of those with diagnosed and undiagnosed mental illness. They all possess a similar difference from those without mental illness. From this observation, I sometimes get a hint of what is to come a little bit further down the line in the life of a person I have met. I recently met this one girl, which has caused me to ponder all of this.

Now, one of the hardest things that a person with mental illness must confront is coming to terms with who they are and then explaining it to the world – which will ultimately culminate in them gaining treatment. As stated, mental illness is now much more openly talked about, but a person who exists in that mind frame must find it very difficult to seek out help. ...To let people know what's going on with them. And perhaps, if they are suffering from *Schizophrenia*, they may not even realize that they are living in a completely different reality. All of this equals very unique and troublesome life complications.

There has been a lot of talk in spiritual circles about simply letting people be who and what they are. …Let them live their abstract reality if that is what they choose to do. I believe this is very counterproductive to a functioning and a fulfilled life. Look at the people on the street who are lost in some different space and time. They are not in India, so they are not seen as holy. They are trapped on the outskirt of society forced into a short-lived and highly troubled existence.

In this case, drugs are good. And, it may provide them with a way to maintain a functional existence.

Whatever the cosmic reasoning for handing a person the ticket of mental illness – that person should be able to seek out help. We really need to care more about other people than we care about ourselves. We need to step beyond the image that may be portrayed if we find out that a friend or a family member is suffering and actually reach out and try to get them help.

Why would you want anyone to suffer? Yet, so many people still lie and hide the fact that a friend, a family member, or even themselves, is suffering from mental illness.

Now, this is a double-edged sword and you have to be careful. Like the case of the girl I met in SF. She wasn't on meds and she went nuts. For her, the rules of life were all different. Most people are not like that, however. They will take the help if you guide them to the help.

Ultimately, never try to pretend that you know, because you don't know what is really going on with a person. At best, just point them in a direction where they can find some help and let them know that you will not judge them for seeking it.

# What Do I Want?

25/Apr/2014 08:51 AM

*"What do I want?"* That sounds kinds of like the title of a country western song, I think. But, anyway…

*"Everybody wants something from me but nobody ever gives me anything."* That is a statement I semi-jokingly make when asked about my personal realization about my life. I say that tongue-in-cheek, of course, but in many ways it is true.

People wanting to be in one of my films constantly contact me. Great! Thanks! I am always happy to give people the chance to live their dreams and to be on the silver screen. But, a lot of these people are not nice people.

The film industry is one of the most ego-based conglomerates of people anywhere on this planet. Many actors, actresses, and even crew people come on board and show up on set full of self-worth and wanting to be treated like stars even though most of them are very-very far from it.

Making a movie is not easy and nobody wants to help me to do anything. They just believe that their presence on the set and them spitting a few lines in front of the camera is all they should offer.

I've said this before, but from the moment I got in the film industry, I was always willing to get my hands dirty. I was always happy to help out and make things happen. But, most people are not like that. They just want to show up and not do anything in regard to preproduction, production, or post. Thus, it is all just left to me.

The editors of the magazines I write for always expect everything done yesterday. And, they want to pay me chump-change to get it done. This is because, (I guess), I am a competent writer and I can do the interviews and write the articles very quickly. As such, that is what I am constantly expected to do.

In reality, that's fine. I would rather get an article over and done with than to have it on my mind. But, I never set-out to be a journalist! That was not what I wanted to be. It was simply a way for me to make a living. Moreover, there is never any thanks involved. In fact, there has been so many cases where the person I am writing a cover story about questions,

*"Why aren't you on the cover?"* Because, let's face facts, I have done a lot. But, that can't happen because I am just the guy who can write professional articles really fast. So, none of the editors think about throwing me a bone.

Now, I don't mean this all to sound self-serving and/or whoa is me, because that is not what I'm about. It is simply that so many people out there in the great-beyond of cyber space have some warped opinion about me, that everything is easy, I have all this bank, and I am, *Living the Life of Riley.* I know this, because they contact me and tell me what they believe all the time. (I got a note just this morning that inspired this piece). But, as much as I wish my life were that way; that is not what is going on. I too have to struggle to survive. And, there is only me doing everything and that is not easy.

So, *"What do I want?"* I would like all the things I am doing for other people to be done for me. And, I would like everyone to quit assuming that what I am doing is free or easy.

And, hey... Give a brother a hand. :-)

## Bringing Back What Wasn't Good in the First Place
25/Apr/2014 07:59 AM

As a musician and a lover of fine string instruments I have been buying, selling, trading, collecting, and even giving away, guitars forever. (By-the-way, if you have a line on a Gibson L5-S and want to buy me a gift I gave mine away at the Montreal Jazz Festival a few years ago and have not been able to find a suitable replacement since).

Anyway... When I first started in the world of guitars it was great. Nobody really cared. You could go and find really-really good instruments in pawnshops and used guitars stores all over the place. Then came the mid to later part of the 1980s and everyone jumped on the bandwagon. They all wanted to buy vintage guitars. But, most of these people did not truly appreciating the difference between new and vintage. They didn't understand or care about how wood that has aged sounds different then new wood. They didn't study how the instrument construction process was so much more refined and precise in times gone past. They just wanted to own something. Or, they wanted to buy to sell.

By the later part of the 1990s and into the new millennium eBay killed the vintage market. It became a seller's market and prices became insane. I guess to countermand these trends and fulfill the desires and needs of musicians who wanted a piece of history, but couldn't afford it, companies like Fender and Gibson began producing reproductions of their own creations. Some of them were and are pretty good. Some are not.

As this process has continued what I have noticed happening, more and more, is these guitar manufactures are recreating some of the guitars and basses that were just really looked down upon, way back in the way back when. I mean guitars like the RD Artist, and basses like *The Ripper* or the *EBO,* which they now call, *The SG Bass,* were bad, bad, bad. (And, that is just three examples). But, they look vintage, right? And, vintage is always good, right? No.

I guess this is one of the paradoxes of life, if you weren't there, you don't know. From this, not only guitar manufactures but businesses across the business spectrum have cashed in on the unknowing people who don't know what they couldn't know, because they weren't there.

Sure, sure, any good guitar player can make magic with even the most basic of instruments. But, creating music is more than that. It is about having a relationship with your instrument. It is about making music with a friend.

For you musicians out there... Well, maybe I don't have to say this. But, if you haven't experienced it, check this out. Go pick up a used guitar. Especially one that was played a lot by its previous owner. When you start to play it, I bet that instrument will affect your playing style. Though it will be still be you playing, you will notice you taking on the style of music that was previously played on that instrument.

If you buy it, this effect will obviously go away in time. But, all things have an energy. This is especially the case with sometime as responsive to human energy as a musical instrument.

All this being said, if you want to embrace the past, do it. That's all good. But, if you are going to embrace the past, at least first study the what was and the what was not cool before you dive in too deep.

# Negativity and Where it is Born

24/Apr/2014 08:53 AM

I was working on an article for a magazine with a tight deadline today but I though I would take a moment and go and hit *Starbucks* for an afternoon break. I cruised over, ordered a latte, (non-fat, of course), and picked up one of their very good popcorns. I sat back on the patio.

A moment or two into my sit, I hear the only other guy out there raising his voice to the person on the other end of his phone. Apparently, he had purchased some new internet item, he didn't say what it was. But, as his conversation went on, he got louder and louder.

What had happened was that he had purchased the item and they didn't turn on its internet access after he had paid for it. They apparently wanted to run a credit check and do all that kind of stuff after the guy had already bought the item and had been with the company for years.

Now, I always have to preface the writings that involve other people with the statement, *"I don't want to know."* I just wanted to go and have a *Cup of the Joe,* sit back for a moment, give my eyes a rest, and ponder the realities of life. But, this guy dragged me into his world.

He was mad. And, I don't blame him.

I think that we all have had experiences with banks, credit card companies, and various service providers where they have really messed with our lives. I remember I was buying this lens for my camera a few years back. I had forgotten my ATM/Credit Card at home so I pulled out one of my hand-dandy checks that I keep in my wallet for emergencies. I wrote a check for the two-thousand whatever dollars it was. Though I had tons of cash in my account, the service that this store used to approve their checks would accept it, as none of my checks had ever gone through them. I mean, who writes checks anymore anyway? In any case, I couldn't get the lens, which cost me loads of time and energy and did make me a bit annoyed. I had to come back the next day with the cash just to be sure I would have no further problems. Big hassle for no reason!

And, that is just one example. I know we each have our own. I certainly have a number of other ones.

So, this guy was yelling, *"Wait till I tell everybody what happened to me..."* Like the person on the other end of the phone would even care.

It is like I have long said, *"It's all about who answers the phone."* One person will know their stuff and can fix anything. The next person knows nothing and just doesn't care. If that person answers your call, you're screwed. Which probably is what happened to this guy.

*"What! I'm supposed to call you back in twenty-four hours! You're customer service. That means you are supposed to provide me with a service!"*

As interesting as this all was... Or, was not... Man, the negativity was just swirling. I could almost feel it. And, nobody wants to be in the presence of that kind of negativity. It is just... Yucky.

Now, the source of this negativity was not the guy. It was what had been done to him. But, it was how he reacted to this action that caused the negativity to transcend into a new realm; namely, *Starbuck's* patio.

So, this is the question we all have to ask ourselves when we are encountering something that we don't like and we become angry. Are we going to allow the negativity, which is sourced elsewhere, to express itself in our lives? And, are we going to transmit that negativity to the world around us?

I mean, we all get mad when we are screwed over by somebody or something. But personally, I would not have had that conversation on the patio of *Starbucks*. But, that's just me.

We all are defined by desire. We want what we want. We buy what we want. Then, all the problems with that achieved desire begin. So, where is the root and the sourcepoint for negativity? Is it our desire? Or, is it what happens to us after we achieve our desire?

Once we get what we want, shit may happen. That is just the action and the reactions of life. What you do with the reaction is your choice and that is what sets the definition for you and your life.

Me, I finished my popcorn and left – took my latte' with me. I just didn't want to experience any more of that guy's negativity.

# Time Will Catch Up With You

23/Apr/2014 09:45 AM

I was speaking to this normally very upbeat lady yesterday and I could see she was feeling kind of down. She stated, *"The time is just going by. You must know how it feels?"* She then went on to reference how she had recently seen her grandkids and they had turned thirteen. She remembered them when they were just born...

Tick, tock time catches up to all of us. It is the single most defining reality of life. The thing is, most people do not realize this until it is too late. They let their life pass by and then, all of sudden, wake up to the fact that much of it has gone by.

In life, we are all supposed to do something... Jobs, to make money, are a big part of it. But, jobs rob so much of our life.

Some people really love their jobs. To them, that is where they want to be. And, this is all good. Most are not like that, however. A job is something they simply must do to survive. Survive... While it takes all of their life-time and they hate much of the time they are spending at their place of employment. If nothing else, most people want to be doing something else...

This is the point where a complicated mess is born. ... Because we all must make money to survive. Yet, by surviving we oftentimes are kept from doing what we really want to do.

There are tons of people and programs out there that teach you how to think your way past this. ...How to program your mind into a state of denial that this, doing what you are forced into doing, is okay – losing your life-time while you are at your job. But, all this mind junk is just that; junk.

Like so many areas of life, people and programs teach you ways to be indoctrinated into the mind fuck of believing that it is okay to do what you are forced into doing. The programs, if you buy into them, are like taking a painkiller for the realities of life. ...A life that you do not want to accept. Yet, life goes on and your life-time is gone.

Back in the 60s Dr. Tim Leary would say, *"Turn on, tune in, and drop out."* Though culture was much more open to that mindset in that era, I always wondered how someone was supposed to survive if they dropped out. Where were they going to sleep? What were they going to eat?

When you are young you have a lot more options. This is due to the fact you can grab a few extra bucks from your parents if you need it, you can live under your parent's roof and not be forced to make it on your own. In recent years it seems that there have been an inordinate amount of people who are stretching their dependent-youth out way longer than it should be. Why? People don't want to step-up, be an adult, and take on the responsibility of life and many parents allow this to occur.

Yet, in doing this, their life-time is passing by, as well. It is just passing by at a different frequency; that of dependency – which equals *karma* creation.

And, this is where it all begins. This is what sets the stage for the living of your life-time – the spending of your life-time and the defining of you and what it means to be alive.

The true test of life and the definition of who you truly are comes by you supporting yourself, not taking from others, while contributing to the overall good of this life-space. All this, as you embrace your time in this existence.

Now, here comes the kicker... What does it mean for you to be alive?

Alive, you are defined by you. Alive, you are defined by whatever society you find yourself in. Alive, you are defined by how you live your life, where you live your life, and what you do or do not take – what you do or do not contribute.

Your life-time will go by. Do you see your time ticking?

Your life-time will go by. One day you will be no more.

Your life-time will go by. All you will be is a memory to those who knew you and a possible of source of discussion for those who did not.

Your life-time will go by. How are the people that met you and those who did not going to remember you? What words and what actions will be your defining factor? Are you going to help or hurt people?

We are all tapped by the confines of life. We all have a limited life-time. We all must survive during that short period of time.

Your life will be gone. Your life will soon be over. Get used to that fact. You have from now until then, (wherever that then is), to hurt or to help, to do what you are going to do.

What are you going to do? And, how will it define the life-time you lived?

# All in Your Mind

22/Apr/2014 08:01 AM

Have you ever had an upcoming event, a meeting, or a date scheduled with someone and you played out what you thought was going to happen in your mind: what you were going to say, how you were going to act? I believe that all of us have done that in one way or the other.

Much of life happens in an instant. We are doing what we are doing and we are confronted with a situation or we bump into a person that we did not anticipate happening. In these moments we live and we react naturally, in the now.

There is another world, however, one that is lived in our minds. A world where we want something to happen, we hope it will happen. In this imaginary world we practice the words we will say and the moves we will make.

The problem is, this is life. What is lived in your mind virtually never happens once the anticipated set of circumstances comes to be played out. The reason for this is that there is another person, maybe a whole lot of people involved. Each of them brings their own personality, their own *karma*, their own mind into the equation. You are just one small part of it. And, they too have a reality that they hope to project.

It is for this reason that the teachings of Zen and Yoga teach the practitioner to silence their mind. For if you have a silenced mind then you are not wasting your life-time anticipating a reality that will never come to be.

All this being as it is, in life, most of us think about and anticipate what will occur when we see or met this person or that. ...What we will do when we step in front of a group. ...What we hope to happen when we arrive at our desired location. This is simply how most people react to life. It is not bad or good. But, living in this mind space is what defines a lot of people. On the downside, it is also what sends a lot of people into depression, (because they continually encounter situations that do not turn out the way they dreamed), and it also send many people to the hospitable because they mind play scenarios that are upsetting, thus they cause their blood pressure to rise.

Have you even been in a store or a supermarket and you see a person talking to himself or herself about what they see in front of them or what they think about what they see. This does not necessarily mean they are mentally ill, it simply means that they have lived way too much of their life in their own mind.

If you live an active, interactive life with people, you will be less prone to this mental masturbation. You will be less prone to it due to the fact that you are out there, living your life. But, if you spend a lot of time alone, you will be much more prone to dancing around your own mind, maybe way too much.

So, as in always the case, your life is defined by you. You can choose to be out and living. You can choose to be meditative and forcefully silencing your mind. You can also choose to live, *"All in your mind."* Life is about lifestyle choices. How do you choose to live?

**I Didn't Know**

21/Apr/2014 08:13 AM

How many times has somebody hurt you or did something to hurt your life and when you told them what they had done or they finally figured it out they exclaimed, *"I didn't know?"*

When somebody says, *"I didn't know,"* what they are actually saying is, "I didn't care." Or, *"I didn't care enough about you to know."*

Let's turn this around. How many times have you, all of sudden, realized that you had done something that hurt someone or you finally realized that you were doing something that was hurting someone else's life? Did the thought, *"I didn't know,"* come to your mind? Maybe it did.

Here is the point where your life comes to be defined. Ask yourself, *"Why didn't I know?"* Almost universally the answer will be, *"I was thinking too much about myself to care."*

Life is an interactive playground. Many people pass through it concentrating only on themselves. Though this is obviously the case, it does not make this mindset right. Whether you are a spiritually based person or not is unimportant. What is important is the impact you are making on this life space.

Everywhere we go people surround us. Each of these people has their own set of desires for what will occur in the space they find themselves in. Some of these people do not, "Know," or care what impact they are having on the space around them, some push the boundaries of their space in order to make their ideas, thoughts, and desires known to all that surround them, while others pass through the space, not invading the physical or the mind-space of others, and leave little impact. Still others, enter whatever life space they find themselves in, study their surroundings, and then move forward very consciously on a path of consciously never hurting anyone. Which do you think is the superior path?

Life is complicated. There is no denying that. People are a selfish breed. That is very obvious. But, if you want to live in a space where people actually like you and care about you, you need to stop making excuses for your hurtful, unconscious actions. This is the first step on the path to self-actualization. The next step is to care. Care more about them, (other people), than you care about yourself. From this, not only will your life become better but all of this world will be a better place. It starts with you.

# Who Stands By You?

20/Apr/2014 08:17 PM

Most people have no interest in spirituality – especially the more esoteric realms of spirituality. I am sure that the majority of the people who read this blog have no interest in it. And, when I go off onto some metaphysical tangent they question if I am wack. That's all good with me. They're probably right. :-)

For whatever reason, I have forever been drawn to the eastern realms of metaphysical knowledge. Though I was raised a Christian, like many of you, and had to go to *Sunday School* and all that, the religion never called out to me. I only saw it as some formalized ploy of mental indoctrination and manipulation. Eastern spirituality, held deeper meaning to me.

Due to this fact, by the time I was young teenager I was very active in the circles of eastern spirituality around L.A. My close friends, however, had no interest. They were more into getting high and drunk. No matter how hard I tried to bring them along for the ride, none had any interest. But, that was fine with me. I have always let people be who they are. I'm not a Christian who believes you will end up in this overpowering Hell if you don't follow Christian dogma to the letter of the law.

I also had, what I believed, were very close friends in the spiritual circles that I associated with, as well. I mean, I knew some of these people for years. We traveled together, sang *kirtan,* did *karma yoga,* meditated, and all of that. But, when other things took over my life, when it was time for me to go in another direction – my own direction, and leave the fray, they were all gone.

My non-spiritual friends never left my side, however. No matter how weird they may have thought I was. But, I cannot say the same thing about my spiritual friends.

And, this is an important thing to think about as you chart your way through life, particularity if you are walking the spiritual path – whatever that spiritual path may be. ...Your spiritual friends will, most likely, only be your friends as long as you are believing in what they are believing in and living a life that they find acceptable. Once you veer to the left or to the right, they will be gone.

In fact, most spiritual groups teach this. They state, *"Associate only with those of like mind."*

Again, I find this an ideal example of religious brainwashing. But, it is a common practice across the entire religious spectrum.

Throughout your life, people are going to come and go. That is just the name of the game. But, if a person is choosing not to associate with you because of what you do or do not believe in, there is something wrong in that relationship from the get-go.

## Asian Culture in the Modern Western Mind
19/Apr/2014 09:25 AM

In the modern mental makeup of the western mind, Asian culture is looked to with a sense of reverence for its meditative, martial arts, philosophical, and cultural influences. But, why is that? If we initially look to one example, just a few decades ago, the Japanese peoples were highly looked down upon for their seemingly unprovoked attack on *Pearl Harbor* during the *World War II* era.

It is very important for me to paraphrase any of this discussion with the fact that the American-Japanese were wrongly persecuted during that same timeframe by the United States after this attack took place. They were sent to interment camps simply because of their racial origin. That is just wrong. I knew several people who lived in those internment camps and a couple of people who were born there. Their experience, at the hands of the U.S. government, was simply wrong. We Americans should have been more that. The land of the free and the home of the brave.

But, here again, if we are looking for the truth, (the big picture, if you will), the Japanese (of Japan) also were very wrong in their actions. What they did to the culture and the people of the Korean Peninsula and Eastern China was horrific. Plus, what they did to the people and the captives in places like the Philippines, Burma, Singapore, and Indonesia was also unconscionable.

At the core of this behavior is ideology and religion. Ideology because people believed they were fighting for a just and righteous cause. Religion because they believe their emperor was an embodiment of the divine. Thus, they were fighting for, (and instituted groups such as the kamikaze), were dying for god.

There is very little difference in the actions of the Islamic suicide bombers that are currently taking place. They are doing what they are doing for a belief in their action's righteousness and that by doing it they will earn god's favor.

But, all of us who actually ponders the right and the wrong and the realities of this universe understand that these types of actions, no matter what their motivation, are wrong as they hurt and injure innocent people. Thus, they are not righteous or godlike at all. No god would ask for this type of action to be performed.

So, this is where we come to the question, *"Why are these cultures looked to with such reverence, especially after all of the dastardly deeds they have unleashed?"* The answer is, they offer a pathway to an illusive desired reality. Meaning, they have for centuries, charted documented pathways to enlightenment, *god realization,* and becoming one with the all.

Whether or not people ever reach these goals is unimportant. Because there have been documented cases of people that have. Thus, those who do not achieve the universal oneness simply feel they were not worthy. And, the writing of these Asian cultures also proclaims this. ...Keep being reincarnated until you finally reach *nirvana...*

Now, I too have been accused of glamorizing Asian in culture in my books. But, that is not what I am doing. What I write about is a historical perspective for the zealot and the interested to gain the foundational understanding of these cultures and these techniques in order, if desired, to take the next step towards higher consciousness.

In all of my works, I state it is the individual who must consciously release themselves from all forms of definition to find the, *"Ultimate I."*

If you lay your foundations upon what was presented before you, you can then study, learn, and then leave it all behind. From this, you avoid many of the obstacles on the path of rising consciousness, as you have learned where they exist.

Just like all things in life, the information is out there. What you do with it is your choice. Various aspects of Asian cultures, for millenniums, have focused on the pathway to achieve enlightenment. As such, the doctrines have been devised to guide you to achieving this end goal. But, as in all cases, if you stick to your books, you may memorize the text, but without letting go of the known, you can never truly understand the source.

Look to Asia for a pathway if you want. Don't, if you don't want. But, if you want a truer, deeper understanding of reality, you must do something. Sitting and talking is not doing anything. Meditating without a sourcepoint equals zero.

Praying to the gods may get you what you want, but what you want today will not what you want tomorrow. Thus, wanting is a never-ending cycle.

Only letting go once you know is the pathway to the ultimate truth of reality. Know, let go, or don't. Your choice, your reality.

# Paying For Your Sin

19/Apr/2014 08:56 AM

We all do bad things in life. Even when we are doing something that is right for us, that action may, in fact, be hurting another person.

A conscious individual is constantly studying their life and their life-effect in order to balance their doing right from their doing wrong. And, doing wrong to others, no matter what the cause or the motivation, is forever wrong. This is where the person of consciousness is willing to put their own self on-hold – put their own wants and desires on-hold in order to make the good of others more important than the fulfillment of their own needs. Most people are not like this, however. But, from all selfish, thoughtless actions, no matter what the motivation, if a person or this life-place is hurt, *karma* and/or sinning is put into play.

Many people tie the word, *"Sin,"* to more biblical proportions. They think of *Cardinal, Mortal, Venial Sins,* or the *Seven Deadly Sins.* But, what is a sin? A sin is as an action performed, whether knowingly or not, against another individual or against humanity or this life-place that hurts or damages the greater whole. Hurting someone or something is very easily done. Thus, sin is very easily created.

How many people have you known that when they have done something bad to you actually come up and say, *"I'm sorry,"* and set about on path to fix what they have broken? Very few, I would imagine.

Most people do all kinds of wrong in their life, and due to their unconscious existence never even know or care. Or, if they do acknowledge their actions, they try to hide from them, they try to lie about them, they try to make excuses for them. But, even if they do try to fix them, their fix-mode is short-lived and their fix-actions are half-assed at best. But, damage to anything... A person, this earth, or this life-place is a sin. So, what happens next?

Most people are in a constant state of wondering, *"Why me?"* The answer is sins. Most people are in a constant state of wanting what they do not currently have. Why don't they have it? Sin. Most people are in a constant state of lack of fulfillment and dissatisfaction. Why is that? Sin.

I have talked and written a lot recently about New Age, Self Help and similar techniques. All of these programs are designed to make people feel better about themselves and to answer the needs that they are not embracing. But, at the root of all of these programs is nothing more than a mask for people to hide from their sins.

People do not want to take responsibility for their actions. People do not want to own their actions. People do not want to fix their actions. People want to dance around the truth. Yet, they sit in a constant state of desire, questioning why their life is not full and they are not fulfilled.

Are you unfulfilled? Are you desireful? Are you unhappy? You are paying for your sins.

If you want to stop paying for them. Stop creating them. And, fix the ones you have unleashed.

## What the Fuck is Going On?

18/Apr/2014 08:18 AM

I was pulling into a shopping center parking lot off of *Pacific Coast Highway* this morning. As I began to enter, an elderly lady in a mini van decides to rapidly back out of the parking spot she's in without looking. In doing so, she almost hits me. I swung wide and missed her attack. But, her rapidly and unconsciously backing out also almost hit the car progressing down her lane of traffic. The car slammed on its brakes and honked – stopping in just the nick of time. The lady in the minivan sat there, doing nothing. The car she almost hit tried to back up but the car behind him was in too close, so no movement could be made.

By the lady in the minivan's actions, she massively tied up the traffic behind her. Yet, she refused to give in and pull back into her parking space.

I cautiously proceed forward. Just then, another minivan pulls out of its parking spot, also without looking. Thus, tying up traffic in that lane further. I travel a few more feet, another older lady, not paying attention, tries to cut me off to pull into the jammed lane of traffic next to me. Finally, at the last moment she sees me. I swerve out and around her and continue moving forward. Just a few feet further I hear a guy from the window of his truck screaming, *"What the fuck is going on?"*

Me too. I wondered the same thing.

Some days in places like L.A. and Tokyo you drive with no problems. As if the Red Sea has parted you make your way to your destination with little incident. Most days are not like that, however. Not anymore anyway... There are way-way too many cars on the road and way-way too much traffic.

But, who is behind the wheels of these cars? People. They are what sets the whole driving melodrama into motion. Drivers who are so locked into themselves that they do not care.

I had a Production Meeting scheduled for noon. I didn't really have too much to do at home this morning so I took off a little early to be in the out-and-about before I had to make it to my meeting. I went and hit up my favorite bagel shop for breakfast. All good. It is right by my post office so I walked over there after my bagels to check my mail. As I was crossing the street, en route back to my car, this asshole steps on the gas and speeds up as he passes me by. I guess, in order to give me a fright. In earlier days, I may have flipped him off, yelled, *"Fuck you,"* or just went and kicked his ass, but as the saying I recently read goes, *"I don't like myself in prison strips so I let assholes be assholes and just walk away."* Remember the Elvis movie, *Jailhouse Rock,* and how he ended up in prison?

Anyway, so that's how it all began today...

After I navigated my way through the aforementioned parking lot and hit up one of my favorite thrift shops, where I picked up a cool old LP, I still had some time on my hands before my meeting so I continued my cruise down PCH and stopped at the water, looking out onto Torrance Beach.

The day was cloudy; there were two surfers in the water and a pod of dolphins playing just beyond the surf. It made me think back to the first time that I surfed Torrance Beach. It was a cool and cloudy day, just like today. I was still in high school and the movie, *Jaws,* was all the rage. My friend and I were in the water on our boards. All of a sudden my friend freaked out, *"Sharks!"* With my heart pumping and my adrenaline surging I rapidly paddled my way back to shore. Once on the shore my friend was relaying our adventure to one of the locals. *"Oh, that was just dolphins."* I laugh even now at our folly.

As I looked out watching the beauty of the sea, the cloudy day, the surfers catching their waves, and the pod of dolphin rising in and out of the water, I wondered if any of those dolphins in the pod were there, all those years ago. As some of them do live for many-many years. Mostly, I just realized that this is what life is all about, these few moments of perfection, framed by all the bullshit of the world that each of us has to live through. These perfect moments are what make us understand the ultimate beauty and essence of existence. With this, we can forget all the nonsense of the world – at least for a moment.

**Compression**

17/Apr/2014 09:00 AM

Compress or Compression can loosely be defined as, *"To press together or to be forced into a smaller space."* Compression has become the key to all of modern life.

People want things fast. People want things now. People want things portable and they do not care about the quality of what they are receiving as long as they are receiving it.

This is one of the biggest problems musicians and audiophiles have with music released on formats such as MP3. Yes, the music is there. But, it is so different, so far removed from the way it sounded when it was created, that if you actually know what it sounded like, it would be impossible to listen to. This too is the problem with CD and or any other digital recording and archiving technology, at least to date. Much of the quality of the music is gone. Combine this with the fact that now many people play music from poorly designed and constructed speakers powered by their computer, much is lost.

It is compressed. It is not whole. It is not complete.

In today's world, people constantly walk around with earphones plugged into their ears, power by their phones, blasting music in their ears. The basis of the songs are there but gone is all of the quality. That, plus the fact, I can help but be concerned about the fact that with all this unregulated sound blasting into young people's ears, many are going to end up having damaged their hearing.

Compression makes things small but it also robs the true quality of anything and everything.

Compression is not only left to music. Pretty much everything is now compressed so that it will fit into modern society.

Schools... Many schools and particularly colleges and universities now offer online education. But, for those of us who actually did our time in universities, the learning experience, though it did take time, was all about the interactive reality of being there.

Spirituality... Having watched spirituality expand over the past fifty years, I have seen, *"The Trying," "The Doing," "The*

*Achieving,"* be replaced by watered downed metaphysics being handed out to the masses, over the internet, via online courses, via DVDs, etc., leaving no one more whole, only more craving of true knowledge. This is all based on the fact of compression and people handing out, *"Smaller,"* watered downed versions of the true pathway to enlightenment. ...You need the experience of personally interacting with a teacher to truly grow.

Compression is a fact of life. Life is becoming more and more compressed. Though it is a fact of life, it does not make it a better, more complete life.

If you want to live a full, more complete life, live behind the compression and embrace the expansion.

# Let's Change Our Pants

15/Apr/2014 12:31 PM

The actions of humanity forever amuse me...

I was in North Redondo Beach today, walking between a few of the cool thrift stores that exist on *Aviation Blvd.* There is a bus stop on the corner that separates the four of them: two on one side of the street, two on the other.

As I passed by the bus stop, I could not help but notice... There was a man, changing his pants as he sat there.

Now, this is a busy street and there are a lot of cars driving by and a number of people walking by. He was not isolated. Yet, he knew it was time... It was time to change his pants.

As I stood waiting for the light to change, so I could continue my quest, I noticed that the man, once he had completed the change was then neatly folding the other pair of pants. The ones he original was wearing. Folded, he lay them down on the bench next to him. Perfect Zen!

In life, we can question reality all that we want. We can discuss the finer points of philosophy and consciousness till our ears turn blue. But, at the end of the day, life is just what life is. And sometimes, you need to change your pants. :-)

# Rocks on the Road

15/Apr/2014 08:40 AM

When I was sixteen and driving my first car, my friend and I left San Francisco in the evening. We were driving down *Highway 1.* It was a cold and rainy night. We were listening to *The Doors* on the 8-Track player.

We had entered Big Sur and as is commonly the case when it rains in Big Sur, boulders were rolling off the hills. I was in a curve and there it came out of nowhere – a boulder rolling onto the roadway. I saw it, but I didn't have the ability to get out of its way. Bam, we hit it. It flattened my tire and dented my rim.

My friend and I got out, changed the tire, and we were back on our way. But, instead of just driving home, we had a new mission. Every boulder we saw on the road, we stopped, picked it up, and moved it to the side of the highway. We did this so no other cars would suffer the same fate as us.

It took us most of the night to get through Big Sur. But, we felt we had accomplished something.

This is thing about life; rocks are going to find their way onto the roadway of your life. Out of nowhere, bam, there they will be. And, they can really mess you up.

When this occurs, you have two choices: one, you can let the damage done by the unexpected boulder ruin your everything or two, you can fix the damage and get on your way.

Sometimes, the hands of fate create these rocks on the road. In other cases, people instigate them.

In life, there are people who are going to throw boulders on your roadway. Whether they do this consciously or unconsciously is unimportant. It is going to happen. Just as whether or not they care about what they have done is unimportant. Because once it is done, it is done. All you can do is decide the next course of action on your pathway.

You can choose to be stopped by the rock and choose to move no further. You can also choose to get yourself back on the road. If this is the case, you have two choices. One, you can choose to put up your guard and attempt to protect yourself from allowing any more rocks to enter your pathway. Two, you can accept the rocks on the road as a condition of life, move forward, and try to clear the path for others as you move down the roadway of life.

Everything is you. What road do you leave in your wake?

# Your Actions Define Who You Are

15/Apr/2014 08:31 AM

Understanding a person is very easy, as their actions define who they are. You can see through a person's persona very quickly, simply by studying their actions.

People pretend. It is a simple fact of life. People lie. That too is a fact of life. People pretend to be something they are not. Whether that is based on wanting to gain control over a specific person or situation or if it is because that personified image of a person is who they hope to become, is irrelevant. Pretending to be something you are not, is false.

If a person is erratic, prone to fits or anger, prone to ego-centric behavior, prone to trying to hurt other people, prone to *schadenfreude,* prone to holier-than-thou-ness, prone to lying about who they are, that is whom they are. No matter how many excuses an individual makes, no matter how many times they say they are sorry; who and what a person truly is and what they truly are is exhibited in their day-to-day behavior.

If you think back to a time in your life when you were experiencing young love. You met a person, you were infatuated with them, and you tried to impress them. This may have equaled spending money on them so you look wealthy or cultured, taking them to places that you though were trendy, fun, nice, or impressive. Or, it may also have involved you lying to them to impress them. This is a common condition and experience in life. That being said, it does not make it right.

Oftentimes this type of behavior is assigned to the young and the infatuated. As such, it is written off and it can be excused. Many people as they move through life, however, have found that they can maintain this style of deceptive behavior. They can paint themselves as being something they are not. But, just as a new love soon comes to find out the true nature of their mate, so too should you study the nature of those you associate with before you are ever taken in by their deceptive behavior.

People are, who people are. And, that is fine. If you choose to associate with a specific type of person, that too is fine. Life is your choice. But, whatever you choose to do and whomever you choose to do it with – for all action there is reaction. What you do, who you associate with, sets the stage for the next set of events in your life.

There was a time in my life when all I wanted to do was go to India and be a monk, forever. Even before I arrived there, however, I began to see the folly in this. Once I spent time there, I saw through to the fact that no matter what title a person held, they too were human, with all the personality flaws of humanity. Though some people buy into the god-man complex of their guru – that is only because they have never gotten close enough to their guru to study their character assets and/or flaws.

This is primary reason I am so against *gurudom* and so for *humandom*. I have lived it. I have known these people. I have seen how they are worshiped. I have also witnessed how the people that worshiped them were never close enough to truly see them for who they truly were. And, moreover, I have witnessed how these gurus allow the personified image of themselves, as a deity, to be propagated.

Simply being a human BEING, one does not have this problem. A human is who they are. Thus, they do not have to claim to be anything but that. They do not have to personify any lie about themselves.

So, the next time a person tells you that they are a priest, swami, medium, psychic, guru, soothsayer, witch, whatever, ask them to explain how they became what they claim to be. Ask them how that makes them different from you. Then, ask them do they actually live the life that is associated with what they are claiming. If they say, *"Yes,"* that is their first lie, which all other lies will be based upon. For no one lives the true meaning of the exalted positions they claim. They simply want to have their ego stroked by telling people that is who they are and via their title they want people to come to them in order to seek their knowledge and wisdom. All this is just the lie of ego.

For me, I hate titles. That is why I always have the students I am teaching call me, Scott. That's my name. Leave the sir, the mister, the master, and the professor behind. I'm just me. Nothing more than them. Perhaps I have walked down the road a little bit further, so I can illustrate the path and some of its pitfalls to them. But, that's it. Nothing more... I claim nothing!

If you claim to be something, you can never live up to people's expectations of that claim. If you are simply you, you are free to be everything, which is ultimately nothing. And, nothing is the ultimate essence of Zen. If you seek no admiration, than no criticism will come your way. If you do not desire to be anything more than what you are, *Right Here, Right Now,* then you cannot be temped to lie about yourself.

Ultimately, a good life is based upon doing good things and helping other people. You don't need fame or a title to do that. Simply be the best essence of you and stop hiding who you truly are.

Be you. Claim nothing. That is the pathway to true spiritual freedom.

## Everybody Sings Their Own Praises
## But Nobody Exclaims Their Faults

15/Apr/2014 08:13 AM

Have you noticed how virtually every person you meet will tell you all about how good he or she is at this or at that. *"I am great at this." "I am an expert of that." "I can teach you." "I can show you the way." I can show you the truth."*

Even on the day-to-day level of reality everyone proclaims his or her excellence. In fact, most Self-Help programs teach their practitioners to accentuate their positive points to people at every opportunity. Okay...

But, let's look at this from a different angle. How many people ever tell you that they are not good? How many people ever tell you they are wrong? How many people ever say, *"I'm sorry?"* Virtually never. Everybody is so locked into their own space of, *"I am-ness,"* that they never even consider the effect of what they are saying or what they are doing is creating in the world around them.

The, *"I-am,"* mentality is the source for most of the problems of this world. Particularly on the interpersonal scale. The, "I am good," mentality is a mask so a person does not have to look into the depth of their own flaws. This is why so many people are drawn to the Self-Help techniques that proclaim the, *"I am good,"* reality. For by stating this, a person no longer has to study what is actually wrong with them and attempt to fix it. They simply by-pass this level of consciousness evolution and move directly onto the, *"All is right."*

Now, Self-Help teachers will proclaim that by accentuating the positive one overcomes the negative. But, if the negative elements of your being are not truly understood, then how can you be a truly whole person? If you don't fix the bad, you are never truly good.

# Pathway to Transcendence

14/Apr/2014 09:45 AM

At the root of the inner-being of all those who walk the spiritual path is the desire to know. We want to know the truth about life, interpersonal reality, god, and enlightenment.

But, the desire to know is not left only to those whom are consciously upon the spiritual path. Even those who claim to not care about the truth – allow something negative to happen to them and then they immediately question, *"Why?"*

Whether the desire to know is brought about by the death of a loved one, the loss of something loved, or simply a question that has been reverberating within a person since their birth, to find the answer they must first find the pathway to that answer.

There has never been a shortage of people who claim to know the truth and are willing to teach their version of reality. People love to step up to the pulpit for then they are believed to be the true knowers. Like I have discussed a thousand times before, those who claim to know, never know. It is only those who run from the fanfare of talking and teaching that have anything worth saying.

When we look to the life of modern teachers like J. Krishnamurti. A man who was picked as a child to be Maitreya but he refused the trappings and left it all behind. Did he teach? Yes. But, it did it from a position of humbleness and purity.

Westerners like Alan Watts, a chain smoker and an unapologetic alcoholic. He took eastern knowledge at a time when it was far too abstract for many westerners to truly understand and presented it in a cohesive, practicable, philosophy.

Forming a pathway to, *"Knowing,"* understandably is the sign of a true teacher. The problem that currently exists is that so many people have taken the teachings of east and west and merged them with modern self-help and personal empowerment ideologies. With this, though they claim that they have the key, that key is so convoluted that it is of little help to anyone.

Think about this... Have you turned to a teacher or a teaching – particularly one of the modern teachers who has offered a pathway to knowing and to happiness? Perhaps they inspired you for a moment. But, how long did you practice what they taught? Has it remained an integral part of the path of your life? Did it give you the knowing you desired?

This is why so many people love a guru one moment but then speak badly about them the next. They thought the person knew but realized they did not. They saw through their illusion. Or, they thought the person knew but the knowledge they possessed could not be consciously and correctly passed along.

The primary reason why so many modern teachers fail is that they never embraced true, *"Disciple Consciousness."* Meaning, they never actually did the time, (they never took the time), to truly be a student and learn the essence of one system before they stepped up believing that they were a teacher.

The fact is, the process of truly learning a system of metaphysical knowledge takes a long time. And, it is never the student who decides when they are ready to teach; it is their teacher who tells them when they are ready.

But, most modern teachers grabbed a little here and a little there, packed it up and called it a, *"Teaching."* It is not. It is just their own version of their own pathway to being considered a teacher of knowledge. But, they do not teach true knowledge. They only teach their own idealized version of what they think to be true.

I am not saying that there are not modern teachers who do possess knowledge. I am saying that there is way too many of them who instead of taking the time to actually learn a tradition, they decide they have the understanding to make their own hodgepodge of a conglomerated spirituality and then attempt to feed it to the masses.

In each era, there are movements that move forward defined by modern culture. Of late, many of these have been about how people can feel better and become more successful. All good. But, how many books have people purchased, how much money have they spent on attending lectures attempting to fulfill this desire. But, this desire was never fulfilled. The fact is, there is no quick fix to you. There is no quick fix to knowing. There is no quick fix to happiness. No teacher or teachings can offer you this.

Some people are born into a space of understanding, some people are lucky enough to have the desire to move with an established teaching and through time after embracing, *"Disciple Consciousness,"* for a long period move away and are, for lack of a better word, *"Fixed."*

Knowing takes time. Knowing takes understanding. Knowing does not take worshiping a person's personality. Nor does it take worshiping your own personality.

Let go of looking for someone who has no knowledge but claims that they do. Let go of listening to the false teachers. Let go of thinking you know, and then the true knowing may enter. This is the pathway of transcendence.

# People Want

11/Apr/2014 09:52 AM

I used to live in this small apartment right on the sand in Hermosa Beach. The building was actually in Redondo Beach but that was simply a city boundaries sort of thing, as I looked out onto Hermosa.

I enjoyed living there. The place was small and jammed with all my books, guitars, keyboards, LPs, Italian racing bikes, (I was really into bike riding back then), and the etc. But, it had a great vibe. And, it was a very creative time in my life. I did a lot of living and did a lot of writing while living there.

Back then, I had a large amount of disposable income. The time frame was just at the beginning of the whole ATM thing. So, getting cash out of your bank was not yet super-simple. As such, I would sometimes thumb tack several hundred dollar bills to my message board incase I needed some cash.

I was very trusting back then. So, when I needed the maintenance crew to come in and fix something, I didn't even think about the hundred dollar bills hanging there in plain sight.

One day, I found a guitar in *The Recycler* that I wanted to buy. *(The Recycler* was a newspaper that was the best source for used and vintage guitars and other stuff like that in that era.) I knew I had enough money up on my clipboard. When I went to grab it, however, I realized that I was couple hundred dollars short. Two hundred less than I knew that I had up there. Instantly, I knew what happened. But, it was one of those things. I also knew the response if I brought it up to the management. The maintenance crew would deny it.

This is the thing about life. It doesn't matter how much faith you have in people, a person, an organization, or a whatever. Each entity is in it for themselves and will do what it takes to get them over and get them through life. I could question the people who took my monies motivation, I could focus on their culture or their socioeconomic status, but all that is nothing more than Mind-Stuff. They did what they did. And, there was nothing I could do about it.

Back in the 70s I had more car radios, 8-Track and cassette players stolen out of my car than I can even count. In the later 80s I bought a new jeep, drove it home, parked in front of the place I was living at in Hermosa, and went inside. I came out about a half hour later and my radio/cassette deck was gone. ...This is back when those items actually held value.

The motivation for all of life is that people want. To achieve their wants, they need money – they need money to survive and money to buy the things they want; whether those things are material objects, drugs, or whatever... If they cannot get the money by the means deemed acceptable by society, they steal it.

Many get away with this type of lifestyle – at least for a long period of time. Most eventually get caught; then they lie, cry for help, blame everything and everyone but themselves. But, they still stole what they stole and did what they did, leaving the victim of the crime less in their own existence.

I have been around the world many times and I have seen this type of behavior go on everywhere. I have had people try to jack me for money in what are considered holy places. I have had so many things stolen; even small, ridiculous things like the identification card holder on my *Ralph Lauren* suitcase that was stolen while entering Tibet. I had a large *Body Glove* sticker removed from my suitcase somewhere at the airport(s) between L.A. and Taipei. I can ask, *"Why?"* But, the answer(s) would all be the same. People want.

People want and they are not human or conscious enough to either realize that wanting is just wanting or that ultimately wanting is just, *"Momentary reality."* Meaning, you want what you want for this moment but you won't care about it in the next. Think about how many times that has been the case with your life. You wanted it, you sat in pure desire until you received it, and then once it was in your possession for a time, you no longer cared about it.

The other option is that most of us, if we desire something, will set about on a course to get it. We earn, we save, we buy. But, a lot of people do not live at this level. They simply take.

When something is stolen from you, it is a good time to look at your life. It is a good time to look at you. The questions to ask yourself are: *"If I didn't own it, it would not have been stolen. Is what that object is, is what those things are, me?"* And, *"Do I really need them?" "Can I live without them?"* The answer is yours…

Moreover, what are you willing to do to keep an object or a thing from being stolen? Will you live your life in a constant fear that it will be taken? Or, when it is gone will you simply realize that you no longer needed it? Again, the answer is yours to provide…

One way or the other, the truth is clear. People want. People take what they want. What do you want? And, what are you willing to do to get it and keep it?

The reason all this came to mind is that I had the thought/desire to maybe move back to that building in Redondo. It was a cool place to live. Though now, it is insanely expensive to live there. But, if nothing else, I can look back to the literature I created while living there and the loves and life I embraced there. They will be with me forever… But, the two-hundred dollars it is long gone. All that is left is the memory and the thoughts about life that the stealing of it purchased. :-)

# Interpretation

11/Apr/2014 08:15 AM

Life is defined by interpretation.

From the moment we are born, our life is in a constant state of interpretation. When we are very young our brains are attempting to translate the words and the actions that are going on around us. Once we have a basic understanding of these, we begin to look for the subtle meanings of both the words and the actions of other people. As we come to know ourselves, (as human beings), we decide what we want to say, how we want to say it, and how we will act when we are saying it. From this, other people are forced to interpret our intellectual disbursements.

Religion is interpretation.

Religion is a translation. You are not reading the religious texts you believe in either in their original form or via their original language. *The Torah, the Bible, The Pali Canon, The Dhammapada, The Vedic Texts, The Bhagavada Gita, The Ramayana, The Tao Te Ching*, you name it... What you read is not the original text. It has been edited, translated, altered, and interpreted to suit the editor and whatever religious body is in charge of the edition that they are producing. Over time these texts have been altered more times than can be counted and have become quite convoluted. (Don't believe me? Read your religious history books). Then, after all this, individual ministers add their own understandings and interpretations to the words and the teachings presented in these books.

If we look at this from a modern perspective, the Christian Bible went through a long period until it was formalized as a prescribed text. For all Christians this book then became dogma. Then, *The Dead Sea Scrolls* were discovered and the various testaments that had been removed from *The Bible*, known as *The Apocrypha*, were released. More recently, *The Gospel of Judah* and *The Gospel of Jesus' Wife* have been proven to be historically valid. From these new texts, a new realm of Christianity was unveiled. Yet many, due to their ridged indoctrination, refuse to accept them.

The boundaries of an individual's interpretation are formed by what they have been exposed to.

Your interpretations are based upon what you choose to believe or not believe.

I once had a friend who said to me one day, *"I always have to go home and think about what you have said."* With this, he pulls out a small notebook with a list of questions, trying to be sure of the true meaning of my various statements. I laughingly said, *"I didn't mean anything..."*

Some people seek to understand the true meaning in both the words of others and in life. But, these people are few and far between. Most people pass between birth and death simply trying to maintain a feeling of okay.

Ultimately, you can seek deeply. You can attempt to penetrate the deeper meaning of written words, the exact comprehension of what a person did or did not say, and attempt to discern the ultimate meaning of the universe. You can do this. You can attempt to know. But, at the end of the day, understanding words, understanding life, understanding *nirvana* is only your interpretation and your belief in believing that what you know is right.

Ultimately, nobody knows anything. Every person, every mind, every everything is different. As such, my interpretation is not your interpretation and yours is not mine. If you accept this, you are free.

# See It For What It Is

10/Apr/2014 08:59 AM

People are *yin and yang:* good and bad. Just as is understood in the concept of yin and yang, there is a bit of bad in the good and some good in the bad.

Most of us base our lives on trying to be good and do good. But, in each of us, there is an underlying element of evil. Just as in people who knowingly set out to do bad things, somewhere deep down inside they hope to be good.

Most of us want to hang out with nice people. We want to do good and fun things with these nice people. But, as explained in the theory of yin and yang: nice, fun, and good are defined by what is bad. ...We only know good because we know what is bad.

In life, we are going to see obviously bad things done by bad people. We are also going to see obviously good things done by good people. Most actions are not that obvious, however. Therefore, the questions has to be raised, of all those things that are done in life where the borderline, between what is actually good and what is actually bad, is not all that clear, who can and should prescribe the definition?

Let's take a little bit deeper view of this... Why do you want to do good things? It makes you feel good; right? Why do you want to do bad things? It makes you feel good; right? Therefore, from an internal perspective, at an emotional level, your response to the doing of good or bad is the same. It is simply the repercussions of your actions that comes to define you as a human being. And, it is simply your level of conscience that makes you feel good or bad about what you have done.

It is important to keep in mind that some people have little or no conscience and feel no guilt. Thus, defining reality by their actions is very difficult.

In physical life on this physical plane, the definitions of good and bad are fairly obvious. Helping is good. Hurting is bad. In the interactive ethereal internet reality we now embrace, things get much more complicated. This is because of the fact that the normally in-place checks and balances of common reality are lifted. No one is who they are. At best, they are simply a projection of themselves or how they wish to be seen. At worst, they are a hidden entity, projecting a substrata of consciousness defined by the darkest parts of their being.

So... In all of life, you need to be conscious enough to lift the veil of illusion. See bad for bad, but question the motivation. See good for good, but question the motivation.

In the ethereal internet world, never fall under the illusion that anything is what it claims to be for most likely it will not be. Thus, any concept of good or bad is lost due to the structure of its environment. See it for what it is.

# Bumper Stickers

09/Apr/2014 01:14 PM

I was cruising home today after teaching a class and I saw what could only be described as a gigantic bumper sticker. It said… Well, I will get to that in a moment.

A lot of people rock their bumper stickers. Particularly when they are young. You see a lot of stickers for a person's favorite band or favorite radio station. As someone gets older and they still want to put bumper stickers on their car it is usually in support of a political candidate or something like, *"Think Peace,"* or *"Coexist."* All good…

On my first car I had an *om* symbol. I also came upon a bumper sticker from the band Parliament, *"God Bless Chocolate City and Its Vanilla Suburbs."* I thought that was pretty amusing, so I had that on my car for a minute. But, I guess I should get to the point…

So today, I'm driving home and a car in front of me had the driver's words of choice precisely cut and plastered across his entire rear window. They read, *"If you have divorced and have remarried you are committing adultery."* This, of course, put a smile on my face.

I drove up next to the guy and he was maybe in this later thirties. He had one of those long beards with no mustache, the kind attributed to the Amish or the Mormons.

You know… Everybody is motivated by what they are motivated by. Everybody believes what everybody believes. But, I cannot help but wonder why this guy cared so much about divorced people remarrying that he would go to all the trouble of writing it across his rear window.

I don't know… Maybe he wanted me to write about it in my blog. :-)

Sometimes life and this world are strange.

# Feeling the Energy

09/Apr/2014 09:54 AM

Have you ever noticed how some people you encounter have a very positive energy: they are smiling, laughing, and make you feel good simply to be around them. Then, there are others that the moment you are in their presence, make you feel weird. For people like that I always like to grab a term from the film, Ghostbusters, *"I got gooped."*

Energy is all around us. This is life. Everything vibrates with energy. And, this is not some weird hippie mumbo-jumbo; it is science.

People too radiate energy. Some are very positive. Others are very negative. The positive people you want to be around. The negative ones you do not.

You know, I've spoken and written a lot about personal energy over the years and I have told the tale of how one time when I was walking down the street in Bangkok, minding my own business, I walked past a lady and, BAM, I was hit with some of the most intense negative energy I have ever felt. It was actually palpable. Maybe you have had a similar experience.

Most energy transfer is not that decisive, however. More commonly, it is very subtle.

I think back to one of the first times I took notice of how some people embrace negative energy and come to be defined by it. I had a teenage student at the martial art studio I ran many-many years ago. He would come in and everything was, *"Woe is me."* He couldn't do this. Didn't like that. He simply was embellished in negativity. Wherever he was, negativity spread because that was all he was about – that was all he spoke about. Obviously, he didn't stay at the school very long.

One would think that it is so obvious in life that embracing negative energy only leads to negative ends and a life defined by misery. This being said, many people don't even notice how they are behaving or do not even care. In fact, I've had really negative people tell me, *"That's just who I am."* But why? Why be like that?

See this is one of the tricky things in life. People surround us. Whether or not we are friends with them, whether or not we know them, whether or not they are coworker, students, neighbors, or someone just sitting next to us at the movie theatre – we must interact with them. ...This, whether they are a negative or a positive person.

People choose to be who they are. Some chose to embrace negativity. Some, for whatever unknown reason, simply become controlled by it.

You can argue forever, why? But, it doesn't matter. Like I was told, *"That's just who I am."* Saying anything to a person like that will not change their life attitude. It will just wear you out trying.

So, what are you going to do with this energy when it presents itself?

Some people get really paranoid. *"That person is so negative! I just can't take it. They are really affecting my life."* Then I would ask, *"Why are you letting them do that?"*

The ultimate truth is, negative energy is forever negative. If a person embraces it, whether knowingly or not, they experience the consequences of it in their own life. This is also true of the individual who pretends to be positive but is actually negative. ...A lot of people lie about who they are; both to others and themselves. But, the proof is in the pudding. Look at their life and see who a person truly is.

If you question how to protect yourself from the effects of a negative individual – what you can do is to choose to set up a barrier between you and negativity. You can do this, even if you have to deal with it on a daily basis. How? Let someone else's negativity motivate you to become more positive. Let it drive you towards becoming a more whole and complete expression of you. Don't let their negativity infiltrate your mind. You are more than that. You can control it and control them by never letting their energy define any part of your life. Instead, simply exude positivity. From this, all the life spaces that you are interactive with become more joyous and positive.

Wherever you find yourself. Whatever mood you are in. Be positive. Life will be better.

**When Things Go Away**

09/Apr/2014 08:06 AM

Don't you hate it when places that you really like go away? For example, when a restaurant that you really love closes and it is gone forever…

In the early 1990s there was a movie theater in Santa Monica that used to play Hong Kong Kung Fu movies at midnight. For me, it was the total thing to do. My lady and I would go and grab a hot dog at this GREAT hot dog cart on the *Promenade,* walk around a bit, then go and watch the show.

I was writing a lot of martial art articles at the time and doing films. Also in attendance were a lot of the Asian actors and stuntmen of the period. So, there were a lot of, *"Faces,"* in the crowd. It was great! But, then the crowds begin to diminish. By the end, at one midnight showing, my lady and myself were the only people in attendance. They stopped showing the films. Gone was an era.

Speaking of movies, when I was living in Berlin, there was this little, small-screened, English language movie house. It was great. They played some very abstract Art House films. Time went along and I became the only person showing up. They went out of business.

One of my favorite restaurants ever was *Hamburger Henrys.* They were on Wilshire in Santa Monica. They had the best Caviar Burgers. Great French Onion Soup. And, a gigantic Salad Bar. They actually launched about the same time as *Madame Wong's, West;* which was a nightclub across the street. This too was a great place in its time. Very small inside. Very intimate. But, everybody from the era played there: *X, Oingo Boingo, The Motels, The Plimsouls, 20/20, The Knack,* you name it. Even a couple of my bands did shows there. But, times changed. Metal came along. Nobody wanted Caviar Burgers anymore and both went by the wayside.

More recently, a great restaurant and art space named *Royal/T* closed. The food there was really good. And, the space was amazing. The owners did a whole theme thing. The waitresses dressed up in Japanese style waitress outfits, etc. *Royal/T* got a lot of press for a moment but then, everybody stopped coming. Gone…

Like, *Numero Uno Pizza* on Ventura Blvd. I discovered that place in the 70s when I was going to CSUN and living in the Val. It never changed, the interior, the music on the sound system, it was like stepping back into the late 70s/early 80s. Recently, however, it closed its doors. Gone forever...

A funny story... Just before *Royal/T* and *Numero Uno* closed, my lady and I took her sister and her family to these two restaurants. Soon after, each of them went out of business. Now, this has become a joke among us, if she goes, they will close.

In life, things come and go. Some last for a long time. Others do not. The only defining factor for the comings-and-goings of life is if we care. For it is only us, the ones who care about whatever we care about that sets the stage for memory. But, just like the comings-and-goings of businesses when they are dead, they are gone. When we are dead, we are gone. Then, all we cared about passes into nothing.

# Space Invaders

09/Apr/2014 07:29 AM

I think it is very interesting how in certain periods of our life we continually encounter the same time of person or a similar type of situation. I don't know if this is based upon our *karma*, personal projection, or being tested by the powers from the great beyond. None-the-less, in certain times we interact with a certain type of person over-and-over again. This is why people move to religious community, I suppose. So, they will only interact with people of like mind.

Recently, I have been forced into interaction(s) with a type of person that I would call a, *Space Invader*. Meaning, they come into an environment and take it over either knowingly or unknowingly via their unconscious actions – messing with the lives of all those around them. I have written about a few of these situations in recent blogs.

Today, I was speaking with a smoker. He believes it is his right to smoke anywhere he sees fit. Thankfully, laws have been put into place, and are continuing to be put in place, to curb this type of activity. But, these laws leave him unfazed.

I asked, *"What about the damage you cause to others with your second-hand smoke?"* His answer, "What if I don't believe in that?" I said, *"It doesn't matter if you believe in it or not; facts are facts!"*

I remember when *Starbucks* instigated their no smoking policy a couple of years ago. I saw some customers literally throwing fits when the staff, (who mostly smoked themselves), would go out there and tell these people they couldn't smoke on their property. *"It is my right!" "This is public property!"* Well actually, no it isn't. It is private property.

For those of us who don't smoke, I think we can each remember times when we were enjoying a cappuccino, a cocktail, or a meal somewhere outdoors and then somebody lighted up and ruined it for us. *Space Invader!*

Now, I am a sinner too, (in more ways than I can count). I mean, back in the '80s and '90s we rode our Harleys with straight-pipes. Meaning, they had no mufflers. This really added to noise pollution. This is probably one of the primary factors that lead to the tinnitus I suffer from. ...That, and standing in front of one too many blasting *Marshall* amplifiers. (That's my *karma*, I guess). Of course, I ride with a muffler now.

Anyway, I remember I was cast for an *Orange Crush* commercial back in '90 or '91. My Harley and me. Also cast was this blonde girl who also had her own Harley.

The commercial was for South America and I guess they wanted to present the whole long blonde hair California thing. Anyway, after we drank our *Orange Crush(s)* and did our dialogue, we rode around Hollywood behind a camera truck while they filmed us. Every time we would set off a car alarm with our tailpipes, the girl, (I forget her name), would get all excited and give me the thumbs up. Man, bikes were loud back then and some of them still are. When I saw the commercial they had edited in a lot of her thumbs up but made it look like it was all about the *Orange Crush*. Funny... Very *Zen Filmmaking*.

From a psychological perspective, the modern proponents talk a lot about owning yourself and owning your space. But, owning your space does not mean invading the space of others. I think this is something we each have to be cautious of. Because, not only do we not want to create negative *karma* for ourselves, but we want to be thought well of. If we mess with people's space, either via things like smoking, noise, or whatever, then negative thoughts are directed towards us. And, nobody wants this, because negative thoughts are the sourcepoint for negative actions.

We, as conscious individuals, want to be good. We want to do good things. We want to think good thoughts and have good thoughts thought about us.

Don't Space Invade!

# All the Swagger

08/Apr/2014 11:52 PM

As someone who teaches the martial arts virtually every day of my life, I forever find it amusing when I encounter someone who walks with, *"All the Swagger."* They walk in like they should be feared, should be respected, should be something...

Whenever I witness someone behaving in this manner, I think back to one of my friends... This guy looks tough. I mean, this guy looks scary. He's the kind of guy you don't want to mess with. But, this guy can't fight.

A funny story came to me about him a year or two after an incident took place. He and a few of his friends were at some car rally. He got drunk and was walking, full of swagger. Some guy bumped into him and my friend got all up in this guy's business – attempting to intimidate him and drive him away with his fierce looks. The guy who bumped into him, in turn, began to kick his ass. He took the fight to the ground and was pounding the crap out of my friend. It was only when the thirteen-year-old son of one of my friend's friends smashed the attacker in the head with a watermelon that the fight concluded.

That's the thing about swagger, it means nothing.

Way back in the way back when, back when I had my first martial arts schools, the aforementioned friend would come by on his vacations and his days off. I tried to train him on a one-on-one basis. But, he just didn't care. He had the looks, right? That was all he needed. Or was it?

Personally, when I first began training in the martial arts, they were quite revered. I mean, there were very few schools and the idealized image of a martial artist was perpetuated in the media. But then, an influx of so-called, *"Masters,"* began arriving from Asia.

It was at this point that some boxer would step up to the, *"Martial Artists,"* and knock them flat.

That's the thing... If you can't take a punch, you can't fight. And, trained boxers are some of the fiercest opponents that exist.

In the late 1980s and early 1990s *Brazilian Jujitsu* hit our shores. Then, it wasn't all about being able to take a punch, it became about being able to defend against the takedown and the chokehold. But, in either of these cases, trained fighters knew how to fight. It wasn't swagger. It was technique.

Now, if you want to take this to a more refined and spiritual level – fighting is barbaric. So, don't do it. Moreover, don't pretend that you have game, when you have none – for the first trained person you step up to is going to knock you out.

All this being said, swagger is for the unenlightened. It is for the criminals. It is for the person who can't truly fight. For, if they could, they would not need to perpetuate a lie, based in a projected reality, housed in their own mind, in order to try to make themselves feel and look tougher than they actually are.

People who known how to fight, don't fight. Because they do not need to fight for they have already won the contest. Thus, they need no swagger.

## Do Dreams Know the Stories That They Tell?
08/Apr/2014 07:28 AM

I believe for all of us dreams are a unique element of our life. It is us in there, yet it is a different life. *"You only live twice,"* as the lyrics to the James Bond movie theme go.

Dreams have been debated forever. A person's dreams are investigated when they go into psychotherapy. They are discussed in religious and philosophic texts. And, there have been tons of books written about the interpretation of dreams and what a dream actually means.

When I was around ten or eleven my mother and I purchased a book that, like a dictionary, supposedly broke down what each element of each dream meant. Every morning I would wake up and look to the book to see what the definition of my dream was and what I could expect for the day ahead. I did that until I realized that the book was generally wrong in its interpretations. :-)

Some people, in the morning, write all of their dreams in a journal. That's chill if you can do it, I guess? But me, I have too much going on. When I wake up I like to jump out of bed and get busy.

Some people base novels, poems, and screenplays upon a dream they had. I tired to do that, but dragging myself out of bed in the middle of the night just to write down the storyline from a cool dream I had became too counterproductive to my life.

But overall, the writing down of your dreams is a good thing, I suppose... Good, if you desire to keep documentation for that part of your life – because, as stated, it is another completely different life that you live in there. And, as we all know, dreams are generally quickly forgotten.

For me, dreams were always a curious reality. From the time I was a very young boy forward, I began to have dreams of the future. I would be living my life and then, all of a sudden, I would be experiencing what I had previous witnessed in a dream. I would know exactly what was about to happen next. It was like watching a rerun of a T.V. show.

Many times, when I would encounter this experience, the outcome or certain actions of the participants would be slightly different from what I witnessed in my dream. Eventually, I begin to understand that this was do to the *karmic* life actions and personal choices that had taken place between the time of my dream and the now.

As I got older, I consciously stopped my mind from doing this. Me, I don't want to know the future. I want to live the now, in the now.

But, all of this begs the question, *"Do dreams know the stories they tell?"* For if you can see the future in your dreams, if dreams are an integral and orchestrated part of your reality and your psychology, if dreams foretell things to come in your life, then they must serve some higher, more rational purpose, than simply a dance in a different reality.

No one really knows the answer. So, the question I ask is moot. Some people claim to know. But, as we have all witnessed, those who claim knowledge rarely, if ever, truly possess it. But, if nothing else, dreams are fun and I am sure they have some other purpose than just to live a new, different, strange, bizarre, limitless, reality.

**Forced Order, In-Order**

08/Apr/2014 07:14 AM

For anyone who knows me, they know I am a fan of *Starbucks*. Wherever I am in the world, (by this point in time), I can pretty much hit one up. At home, here in L.A., it is certainly no different.

I first was introduced to *Starbucks* when they hit L.A. in about '91. Don Jackson and I were editing *Roller Blade Seven* at an editing suite in a building connected to the *Beverly Connection* in West Hollywood. This is a plaza across the street from the *Beverly Center*.

This sweet young Chinese via Hawaii lady I was hanging with at the time came by the suite and hung for most of one of our days of editing. She mentioned the place to me and I was all about it. Ever since then... Well, I was hooked.

*Starbucks* has changed over the years. Once upon a time it was only the cool and the trendy who worked there. Now, well... That is not necessary the case.

Way back, in the way back when, it was also only the artsy and the interesting that hung at the few locations they had. Now, it is grandmas, grandpas, the homeless, and way too many people sitting there for hours-upon-hours writing their scripts that will never be produced.

How *Starbucks* handles their employees is also different. There was a time when I would hit my, (then), preferred location over at the *Crossroads Shopping Center* in Torrance and I would virtually never pay. The staff knew me, I knew them, and that was that.

A few weeks ago I was heading up the coast and I hit one of my local *Starbucks* en route to the freeway North. I noticed that the barista at the bar was calling out the drinks and exclaiming, *"Out of order."* Strange... But, I didn't give it much thought.

Yesterday, I found out why. I was at my now preferred *Starbucks* here in PV (Palos Verdes) and one of the baristas I know saw me enter and immediately made my drink before I passed through the order line. When I got to the pick up counter, the drink was done but he couldn't hand it to me. He had to make and pass out the orders that were placed before mine. He explained that he could get in trouble if he were to give me mine first; even though it was already complete.

Now, this was no real issue to me, just an amusing wake up call to how times have changed and how times continue to change. There are now cameras on the employees at *Starbucks,* monitoring their (and yours and mine) every action. ...Monitored by the secret forces that are in control of this organization that rose out of a small shop in Seattle and now dominates the world.

Forced order, in-order... It is scary how what was once cool and free is now dominated by a ridiculously rigid structure.

Welcome to the New World.

# They're All Rednecks

07/Apr/2014 01:35 PM

I was kickin' it this AM, getting my bagel and coffee on at *Noah's*. I was sitting at one of the outside tables (of course) when a group of young high school girls came and sat down. Personally, I avoid listening to people conversations. Like I continually state, *"I don't want to know."* But, these girls were loud and joyous and I could not help but hear what they were saying.

These girls were off to college in the fall. One had been accepted at the University of Montana. My first thought went to the Frank Zappa song, *"Moving to Montana soon..."* In any case, she had already been set up with a roommate for the dorms, whom she had checked out on facebook. The roommate to be is a Local/Yokel. *"She looks kinda weird,"* the girl proclaimed. The other girls chime in, *"Everybody who isn't from L.A. is weird..."*

The conversation continued... *"People from Florida, they suck." "Oregon, Washington, way too grungy. And, they take too much dope."* With this everybody laughs. *"Arizona, that school likes to party." "Yeah, but they're all rednecks."*

All of this made me smile. Young, with the world in front of them, and all the answers and definitions already in place.

Life is like this/that. We each are from where we are from. We either love our place of origin or we desire nothing more than to leave it behind.

I have told this story before but my father died when I was ten years old just before Christmas, 1968. On Christmas Day I was sent to live with some relatives in my mother's hometown in the Midwest. As my mother wanted time to get the family things in order. At least, so she said. Anyway, I get there, they cut my hair, refuse to let me wear love beads – no more Nehru shirts, etc. (Remember, this was 1968). Anyway, all I knew was gone and I was thrown into a completely alien environment. All the kids were of a completely different brain space than me. I lived there until June, when my mother came to retrieve me – which is a lifetime for a kid. So, I understand the radical-ness of life and lifestyle changes that can take place just a few thousand miles away.

By the time I went to India, I was ready. I had already traveled extensively. Plus, I was several years older. And, it was by my choice. But, in truth, there is nothing that can prepare you for your first glimpses of India. The sights, the sounds, the smells, it is radical.

Ultimately, definitions are what make us who we are. (As amusing as some of them are when viewed through the eyes of another person). The environment we are born into also defines us. Combine this with the places we either knowingly or undesirefully inhabit. But mostly, we are defined by our choices based upon our definitions and environmental determinants.

Change happens to all of us. We are thrown into the grand abyss of this life and it is then us who must choose how to deal with each life situation. Many times, these choices are not fun or desired. But, they do occur. So, we must make a choice defined by our life definitions.

Life, from birth to death, is a continuum of experiences based upon our available set of choices: both bad and good. The decisions we make, based upon the choice we are given, ultimately defines who we become and who we ultimately are as individuals.

Personally, I would not have even applied to the University of Montana. But, that's just me.

# The Damage You Cause

07/Apr/2014 08:20 AM

  I have recently been thinking a lot about *karma* and its interrelationship to life. How, when you are all caught up on your personal *karmic* debt, yet you are encountering some negative experience brought on by the mind, attitude, and/or actions and lifestyle of another person.

  Certainly, the reason we are driven to think about and ponder a certain subject is brought on by our life experiences. And, this is the case with me.

  Me... Someone who goes out of their way to be conscious of the space of other people. Me... Someone who goes out of their way to help other people. Yet, I have been encountering life and lifestyle-damaging actions brought about the hands of others. Why is that?

  Now, I have detailed the origins and understandings of *karma* in many of my previous lectures, books, and writings. So, I won't go into that here. But, we all know what *karma* is. And, each of us, in various times in our lives, begins to encounter weird realms of *karma* and we cannot help but wonder why?

  Let's investigate...

  At the root of all instigated bad *karma* is that a specific individual does not care about what affect they are having on other people. They only think about themselves – how they feel and what they want. From a perspective of consciousness, I forever wonder why people encounter life like this. Why do they live their life in that pattern? For then, all that can befall them is chaos and unhappiness. Yet, people continue to behave in this manner.

  The second instigator and root cause of a person instigating bad *karma* for himself or herself is that they do not study their circumstances. This is one of the first things that a student is taught in the martial arts, once they have moved past the basics – that you must always study your environment. Not only does this make you more in-tune with the elements of nature that are around you but also, if you must defend yourself, you are aware of your options.

Most people do not do this, however. They enter into whatever space they are in, and once inside either try to own it or do not care about what damage they cause to it – thinking only of themselves. This is simply wrong. This is not only against the ways of nature but it is also against the ways of humanity.

Finally, some people do bad, simply to do bad. Most of us our not like that, however. Though, a various stage of my life I have met a few individuals who thrive on the negative energy they encounter by hurting or damaging the lives of other people. This gives them a distorted sense of power. These people have always eventually fallen prey to their own actions and deeds, however, and have lived and left this life-place very-very broken and destroyed.

So, what is it? Why do people damage the life and life-space of other people and do not care? Moreover, why do they not try to fix what they have broken, if and when, (if ever), they realize they have been messing with the life of another? Ultimately, I believe it is probably base on self-worth, ego, and the, *"I am,"* morality.

Many people don't care. Most people are not spiritual, even though many claim to be. In fact, living in the world I live in, I have even seen people go so far as to cast spells and do prayer and invocation sessions to further damage those they hit with their thoughtless, negative actions in the first place. ... All this, to protect themselves from taking any responsibility for what they have done. This is very sad.

Life is really up to you. It is you who defines you and it is you who defines what *karma* is set in motion.

If you care about reducing your interactive *karma*... If you actually care about people, nature, humanity, spirituality and making this life journey better for all, (not just yourself), then the first step to achieving this is you need to study your actions, and ponder how they affect this life-space. You must think about what you are about to do before you do it. This then will keep you from unleashing *karma* onto others. Then, if you have wronged someone, you need to own it. Stop dancing around the bullshit that you are feeding into your mind. In other words, stop making excuses for yourself. Then, fix what you have done; whatever it takes. For this is the ultimate repairer of *karma*.

Life is this weird/strange space. As we pass through our lives we each will encounter all kinds of things: some good, some bad. The sad thing of life is, most of these actions, particularly the negative ones, will be perpetrated by others – other unconscious people who do not care enough about you to stop caring about themselves.

Ultimately, this is the true test of spiritually. Who do you care more about: you or them?

# As Good As You Can Be

05/Apr/2014 08:09 PM

In western culture we are continually indoctrinated with the ideology, *"Be as good as you can be."* To most, this becomes a very self-centered process leading to achievement, yes, but it also leads to disappointment and depression if one does not rise to the top.

In the martial arts, many practitioners strive to be the best physical-practitioner that they can be – forgoing any internal or spiritual development. To the MMA fighter, they strive to be the best brawler. To the guitar player, they hope to develop the best licks. To those in the business world, they hope to climb to the top of the corporate ladder. And, the list goes on.

The question you have to ask yourself is, *"What is being as good as you can be?" "What does it mean to be the best?"*

In Sanskrit, one of the primary words used for the term, *"Good,"* is, *"Shubha."* When we look at the actual meaning of this word it is much more closely linked to the understanding of auspiciousness than with the commonly understood meaning of what is or isn't GOOD.

English too has its subtle understandings, but these are often lost by those who wish to ascend the ladder and rise to the top of whatever field they are in. Here lies one of the primary dilemmas with faltering human consciousness. People only care about the being, *"Good,"* in them. They only want themselves to, *"Be good."* It is only they, personally, that they want rise to the top. They only want them to be known as the best. They do not think about a higher self or the rising of universal consciousness. All they want to be is considered, *"The Best."*

Again, if we look to Sanskrit, the word, *"Purusaharshabha,"* may be assigned to personal best. But, at the source of this word is the understanding that being the best Individual Soul is also being a person who is consciously directing their Individual Self to rise to their Universal Self. And, when this occurs, the desires of the Individual Self are lost to Cosmic Understanding or *Samadhi.* Thus, all boundaries of the Individual Self are lost to Cosmic Consciousness.

Virtually all of us wish to do what we do well. There is nothing wrong with that. But, each of us has to decide, and this must be a very conscious decision, that we will work to leave behind the constraints of ego and the overpowering of others, while we are focused on reaching our desired end-goal.

If we are not mentally more. If we are not focused upon a higher consciousness and a greater good in all that we aspire to, than any accomplishment is lost, as it will simply become a personal achievement and these always fall by the wayside when someone else bests us or what we have done no longer holds a value to the people of this world.

Being your best is more than YOU focusing on raising YOU. As has been documented throughout human history, those who have remained in the mind's of the masses as the BEST or the great contributors are those who make a contribution to the ALL not just the SELF. Use this as your guidelines for a pathway to being the best.

# Like a Broken Record

05/Apr/2014 08:46 AM

There is the old saying, *"You sound like a broken record."* Meaning, that a person is saying the same things over and over again – focusing on the same subject, etc...

The fact of this life is, everybody sounds like a broken record. They say, speak about, and do the same things over and over and over again.

Some people live their entire life in this matter. They do not even think about what they are saying or what they are doing. They simply act out their life in the way they have become accustom to. They say the same things. Do the same things. And, nothing ever changes. The only time a person is ever forced from their broken record status is when something big occurs.

Life changes radically when someone is forced into a new reality. This can come about via all kinds of methods; i.e. love, sickness, the death of a loved one, violence, an accident, encountering new people: good or bad, finding religion, etc., etc., etc... Then, and only then, does the record a person is playing in their mind changed to any noticeable amount.

There are some people, however, who are constantly seeking the new. New experiences, new friends, the places, new love, new sex, new jobs – you name it... But, even people who are motivated by this desire commonly encounter any of the new from the same broken record perspective. The experience is new but they are the same. They are simply a person defined by seeking new experiences. Thus, their record is still broken.

In life, there is little escaping the broken record syndrome. We are human; we have evolved to be as we are. We are, by nature, sedentary, territorial creatures. Thus, on an innate level we desire all this life to have continuity – particularly our own space and our own thought process.

We can hide from this fact but we cannot escape it.

Do you want to accept that you area broken record or do you want to deny and fight it? Ultimately all you can be is what you are. What broken record is that? Who is that? Why is that? Your record, your choice.

**Unconsciousness**

04/Apr/2014 08:40 AM

We live in a time of interactive reality. All things are linked by so many means that the list can go on forever. This being understood, at the heart of ALL THIS is we humans. We the people... We are the source, the cause, and the conclusion of all this interactive reality. What we do with it is what we do with it. How we live out our Life-Time is what defines all things. As we, individually, are the sourcepoint for all things.

At the heart of all life is us. We individually live it, experience it, and react to it. What we do within the short time we have here in this Life-Space is not only how our life will be defined but what will set the course for the next available circumstances in motion – not only for the remainder of our life but for the next and the next and the next generations.

At the heart of this Life-Experience is our individual consciousness.

What is consciousness? Consciousness is who we are. Moreover, it is who we choose to be. It is what we create. It is how we react to, and interact with, the world around us.

With all this being understood, consciousness is the root of all our reality.

How do you choose to be? Do you put you first? Or, do you put this Life-Place and other people first?

If you put you first, (if you think about you first), *karma* is created. If you put you first, don't think or even care about others, or actually damage the lives and Life-Time of others, worse *karma* is created.

How you treat the world around you is the sourcepoint of Life-Reality – not only yours but everyone's. Moreover, how you treat the world around you is how others will treat you.

All life is based on you. It is how you act and react to this world. It is how you think about and treat other people, nature, and this earth.

You have a consciousness. You are you. But, after these prerequisite are established, it is the conscious, (or the unconscious you), that decides what to do in your Life-Space.

Being conscious is a choice. Choosing to be unconscious is also a choice. Not thinking about those around you, not caring about damaging the lives of others, hurting life, (at any level), knowingly damaging this planet, or anything else for that matter, is why each of us lives in a world defined by uncertainly, anger, aggression, and chaos. An unconscious person is the sourcepoint for all of that.

From the beginning of rising human consciousness forward, it has been understood that it is the individual who must become and remain the source of all of their reality. Each person projects a mindset that can and will influence the entire world. This is particularly the case with our current interactive reality. This is why you must question yourself constantly; is what I am doing hurting others or damaging this Life-Space? If it is, that is an unconscious action that makes all of life worse.

Think of other before you think of you. Think of this planet and the betterment of this earth, before you think of you. Help people before you consciously or unconsciously hurt them or damage their life.

Do you truly want to live better and make this Life-Place better? If so, choose to live consciously. Think before you act. Think before you do. Then, rethink what you have done; change it if necessary, and make all of life a conscious, tranquil, and better place.

# Trauma Equals...

03/Apr/2014 02:05 PM

I was speaking with a lady who operates a refugee center today. We were discussing the case of one woman who had a very traumatic experience that took place in, what she describes, as a space similar to a bathroom shower. As such, she cannot go into showers, shower rooms, and places like that. From this, cleaning herself has become an issue and the other residence of the facility have become offended by her odor.

Some people pass through life having encounter no traumatic experiences. That is great! Most of us, however, have encountered varying levels of trauma in our lives. Obviously, most of these occurrences do not rise to the level of the aforementioned woman. But, none-the-less, we understand that once these experiences have been lived, we are forever changed.

I have worked with refugee centers, both in the U.S. and in Asia, for many-many years. The one common element that a large majority of the people who arrive at these centers have encountered is, some level of trauma. Some of these traumatic experiences are extreme.

I have often wondered how some of these people continue living their lives after having gone through what they went through – after witnessing the most brutal and lowest level of humanity. Yet, somehow they continue. They are strong. They are more than the people who unleashed the trauma upon them. But, they have emerged damaged.

The question always remains, how can you help people who have encountered very specific levels of trauma? From this, there is a lot of physiological mumbo-jumbo that goes on.

...And, here arises one of my primary beefs with shrinks. They believe simply because they have studied the courses and earned the degrees, that the prescribed methods that they were taught in school actually will work in every circumstance. In reality, all that shrinks do is to process the limited amount of information that they are provided with by their client, (and everybody hides something), and then prescribe their opinion about what to do. And, that is all that it is, an opinion.

I'm not even going to go into the untrained professionals who do not even have a degree and think that they have what it takes to hand out advice – not just to trauma victims but to anybody. That is just ego. I have seen a lot of this type of person at refugee centers. Mostly, they are there to stroke their ego – some are even there trying to get laid by manipulating these people. That is just wrong!

These people need help. Not ego gratification or desire fulfillment on the part of those who are claiming to be there to help.

I will say that each case of trauma is such a uniquely framed composite of one person's reality, and that no one answer, answers everything. This is what makes these situations so complicated.

From a personal perspective, I think that each of us must step outside of ourselves and try to make a contribution to the over-all good of life. Most people spend their entire existence simply thinking about their own momentary reality: their job, their loves, their hates, how to make more money, how to get a better car, a better house, and so on. But, what does all that equal if you cannot help those who need help?

But, each of us must be careful with our motivation. There are those of us, similar to the ego-filled people that I just spoke of, who go to these centers thinking they have something to teach, trying to give lessons, trying to force their religion down these people's throat, trying to tell these people how to heal, trying to tell them where it is at. But, they do not truly understand anything because they do not actually listen to these people and learn from their reality. They are simply basing the information they are dishing out on some form of fabricated nonsense – something they heard somewhere or something that they believe because they believe. Commonly, this type of person only moves towards the individuals in the establishments who desire to be controlled. But, the trauma-filled do not deserve to be handed a load of ego-driven bullshit like this. They deserve simple answers that can cause them to begin to heal to some degree or at least become more functional.

To conclude, it would not be fair to go into details, but we did think of a way for this woman to get and stay physically clean. I do not believe that there is an instantaneous cure for the trauma she encountered but she is being helped in that direction with the hope to get her out-and-about and intermingle with society on a more interactive level.

This is life. There are some fucked up people in it who do not care who they hurt or traumatize. That is, until it happens to them.

Waiting for *karma* is never an answer. If you are a person of consciousness, if you hope to make any true contribution to this life-space, you really need to get off your ass, stop talking, stop thinking about yourself, and get out there and try to help the damaged, the broken, and the traumatized that exist in this world.

# The Holy Man Circuit

03/Apr/2014 08:30 AM

*"The 60s were great but they ain't ever comin' back."* I wish I had coined that phrase but that was actually done by the uncle of one of my friends. I have, however, used it in a couple of pieces of literature and have exclaimed it more than a few times.

Times change... The mind of popular culture changes. In one period people are drawn to the higher realms of consciousness, then in another they are drawn to Self.

The 60s and the 70s were a time when people looked beyond themselves and sought a deeper understanding, while striving for a better humanity. It was a great period of time. People let their hair grow long, didn't shave, (both men and women), played dress-up in pseudo yogi clothing, wore prayer beards, and the like. Some people miss that era. Me too. Some people try to hold onto it, but it is gone.

During this period, access to spirituality was abundant. Ram Dass traveled and gave lectures. Bhagavan Das did concerts. Baba Hari Dass had his Sunday morning satang in Santa Cruz. Krishnamurti led small gatherings in Ojai. Thích Thiên-Ân had his center in what later become known as Koreatown, here in L.A. Sant Kashavadas, Yogi Bahjan, Pir Vilayat Inayat Khan, and Swami Vishnudevananda frequently gave lectures, held gatherings, and lead retreats. Stephen Gaskin would come off of The Farm, give talks and have meet-and-greets, Tim Leary was always around, even Ken Kesey would come down from Oregon and give talks every now and then. (I wrote my experiences with these and others teachers down in a notebook, way back when. Maybe one day I will dig it out from where ever it is and put it out in book form.) Anyway... I, of course, traveled doing the sound for my teacher, Swami Satchidananda. By the end of the 1970s the Dalai Lama also came onto the holy man circuit. It was a great time for spirituality. But, times change...

People can argue, attempting to prescribe a definition to why things changed, but that is just Mind Stuff. The fact is, times did change. This doesn't mean that the spirituality of that era was any less real, it simply means that it was what it was – perfect in its own regard.

The truth be told, certainly not everyone was a spiritually based person in that timeframe. Most, held onto the focus of Self. It was simply that the possibility for an individual to expand their consciousness, from being more exposed to new realms of higher reality, was much more pronounced.

Occasionally, I met people who are really locked into that era. Though now they have become old. That's all good. That's who they are. But, holding on to what was, keeps a person from experiencing what the NOW has to offer.

My advice to these people has always been, if you want to lock yourself into that level of spirituality move to India. Though I must state, many falsely believe that all of India is some sort of spiritual *Shangri-La*. It is not. India is one of the most violent places I have even seen. And, it comes at you from out of nowhere. Too many rats in a cage, I guess. That being said, if you make your way to places like Haridwar or Rishikesh and live in an *ashram*, you should be fairly safe. Most of them are free. All they ask for is your devotion.

Ultimately, what all this teaches us is that spiritually must rise from the inside. It must be who we are. Yes, we may be guided towards it by external stimuli, but if it is NOT who we are, then it fades away like the passing trends in popular culture.

# Meditation

02/Apr/2014 08:27 AM

Meditation is an integral part of the spiritual path, particularly the eastern spiritual path. ...Not so much in the fundamental western traditions, however. I have heard many a Christian minster claim that meditation allows demons and the devil to enter your silenced mind. Whatever...

Meditation is commonly defined by silencing your mind. Various traditions have different methods to achieve this state. I have written extensively about these techniques in my various books so I won't go into here. But, the main goal of meditation is to not let your thinking mind run ramped and control you by allowing your thoughts to equal emotions to equal actions that may not be in your best interest.

Many people have tried to meditate. They have tried to stop their thoughts. But, it is not easy. Formal eastern spirituality tells the students to keep at it, keep trying – force your mind to stop thinking. Some people can achieve this, some people can't. And, still others say, *"Forget it,"* and don't want to do it at all.

It is important to note that this does not make a person who feels this way any less spiritual. Trying to stop your thoughts can be quite frustrating and it can, in fact, make the person who is attempting meditation to become quite frustrated with themselves. This is not what meditation should be about. It should not frustrate you.

As most everybody knows, I have been involved with the martial arts for virtually my entire life. Some claim that the movements of the martial arts lead to a state of meditation. I don't know... Yes, you become very focused. Yes, you become very concentrated on preforming the techniques in an exacting manner. Yes, you become very good at doing them in their prescribe manner. But, is that meditation or is that simply a very focused linking of the body and the mind. It is not so much thought-less; it is instead thought-full. So, meditation? I don't really think so.

I was very closed linked with *The Sufi Order* in my younger years – from my teens into my early twenties. In *The Sufi Order* there was *The Sufi Dances* that later became known as *The Dances of Universal Peace.* They are great. Every week I would look forward to Monday nights. We would meet and greet, dance in a prescribed manner, chant and sing in association with the dances, and be, *"Spiritual."* Are theses dances meditation? No, not really. Your thinking-mind is still there.

I use *The Dances of Universal Peace* as another example of how movement does not necessarily lead to meditation, though some may claim that it does.

You don't have to meditate to be spiritual. That is the main point here. If you can SIT and find your way to a silenced mind, great! Some people can. Some people can't.

I believe that the biggest downfall to meditation is that some people learn to lie to themselves. They may be able to SIT for the prescribed amount of time, doing this while their mind is still racing. Or, they may be sitting there beating themselves up, *"Why can't I silence my mind?"* If this is you, then meditation, (or attempting to), becomes only a waste of time. Find another method that makes you feel focused and spiritual.

Meditation... Try it and see if you like. See if it works for you. But, if you don't and it doesn't, do not force yourself.

# Listening

01/Apr/2014 12:23 PM

Have you ever had the experience of telling someone a story and then, some time later, they bring it up but remember it totally different from how you told it?

I used to think maybe I didn't explain myself correctly. So, in some cases, I would retell the tale. In a few of these instances the exact same thing would occur a week or a month later. So, what is it?

What it is, most people don't listen. Most people put their own spin on all of the reality they encounter. That take it in, they translate it in their brain, and then it is repeated based upon their own definition of suchness.

The fact of the matter is, few people truly listen to anything that is being said to them. They may hear the words that are being spoken but throughout any discourse, and certainly by the end of it, they have attached their own personal definition to what was said. They may love the words that were spoken. They may hate the words that were spoken. They may not believe the words that were spoken. But, no matter the definition they have assigned, it is uniquely their definition. It is not the essence of what was said.

You tell the same story to twenty different people and there will be at least nineteen different versions of it.

This is one of the defining factors of humanity, particularly modern humanity; each person had been born and has been indoctrinated to be a whole unique individual onto himself or herself. As such, most people never truly listen; they only hear what they want to hear and come to define the words as it applies to them. Good or bad, this is the way it is.

I could say it is best to truly hear what another person has to say before you draw your conclusions but I doubt that will happen. With each day and with each year of life, the mind of the average person closes more and more, ultimately only experiences life in the manner that they have deemed acceptable. From this, it is rare that new or different understandings are let in. Thus, nobody hears what is truly being said.

People may hear words spoken but before a sentence is even completed it has been translated into the individual's mind space. It has become theirs. Thus, it is never whole or true to itself again.

# Refining Your Desire

31/Mar/2014 08:06 AM

Most people want something that they do not currently have in life. For some, these are small things like a specific pair of shoes, a certain guitar, a new computer, or even a new car. For these things, a person can focus, save their money, and eventually hope to buy it. These things are definable and one can clearly focusing on getting them.

There is another element of desire, however, the BIG things. These are desires like money, success, fame, and even love. As these things are relatively indefinable, they are much more difficult to focus upon achieving.

Pretty much everyone wants more money. But, what is money? You can say it is paper, it is an energy source, it is this or it is that. And, that's just it! This is the reason that large amounts of money elude so many people, because it is nearly impossible to define. As such it is difficult to form a clear desire and a method to bring it into your life.

Hand-in-hand with the desire for money is the desire for success. Success... Again here is a hard to define realm of reality. What is success? Many feel it is climbing the ladder in their desired field of employment. Okay, but here comes one of the biggest deterrents to actualizing the desire for success and, in fact, other large desires in life. That deterrent is people. To succeed, to have success, you need the approval of other people.

What is the commonality of all people; desire. They each have their own set of desires. And, if their desire for you to not climb the ladder of success conflicts with your desire to succeed, there will be obstacles on your road to success.

In regard to success, many people desire fame; they want to become movie, rock, or rap stars. As someone who has been in the film-game for a long-long time I interact with this type of person all the time. Everybody tells me they are going to be a star. Okay, but what does that mean and how do you get there? Again, to achieve this phenomenal level of success you must pass through the realms of desire of a lot of other people and, in fact, you have to become their desire to actually become a star – an almost impossible feat to accomplish.

Love... Most people seek love. The people who I have witness existing in long-term relationships are the ones who are accepting and forgiving of their mate. They understand that you are most likely not going find the, *"Perfect,"* fantasy, like you held out for when you were a young teenager. What you may find is someone who you connect with and you can exist in the same space as.

There are many people I have know who as they got older and are not in a committed relationship would constantly be on the look-out for one. They may even do all kinds of things to meet new people. But, each time they would find someone who would be willing to be with them, they would sabotage the relationship. Maybe they were looking for someone just like their mother, maybe they were looking for the most beautiful woman in the world, whatever... But, what they were not willing to do was accept the limitations of their own character and realize that they were not all that perfect either. If you truly want to be in a relationship you have to accept imperfection.

In regard to relationship sabotage, I had one friend who raised snakes. Here he was a forty-something bachelor, constantly seeking love, and raising snakes in one of his bedrooms. Now as interesting as Herpetology may be to some people, it is a little weird okay... If you are doing something weird. If you are off on some weird tangent in life, let's face facts, finding a mate is not going to be easy. You have severely limited your options. So, if love is your goal, and if you haven't found it existing out on the outskirts or normality, become normal.

But to the point... If you desire small things, your desires can be met. Like I have long said, if you want something and you find it you are elated. But, what if you don't want anything, then you are free.

If you are going to have desires, refine them to the degree that they are obtainable. Then, set about on a path to achieving them. If you have to change you, do that. Because if there is something that you really want and you do not already have it in your life, then there is something wrong with you.

Mostly, do not lose your peace while having grandiose fantasies. Desire small things and they can be found.

# Sometimes You Have To Prep

30/Mar/2014 08:25 AM

In life, we all wish that we can walk into situations and have everything in place to get all that we hope to complete accomplished. We don't want to set up. We don't want to tear down. We don't want to learn how to use new equipment. We don't want to learn new complicated computer programs. We don't want to have to read the instruction manual. We just want to do what we want to do – create what we hope to create. Unfortunately, life isn't like that.

In fact, if life were, it would be pretty boring.

But, think about the pieces of computer hardware that you try and try to get to work but it will not link into your system. Think about the pieces of electronic musical or recording equipment that breaks your brain as you try to figure out how to make it make music. Think about the software program that you need to create whatever it is you hope to create and the learning curve is so steep that you think you will never master it. Think about these things and then think about similar obstacles you overcame in the past. Now, they are all a cakewalk. You've got 'em down.

This modern world is this complicated mess. Some people still run from it. Every now and then I meet someone who refuses to even try to play the game. Good for them! But, I also see that they are wasting so much talent not even trying to do anything.

Not trying equals not doing.

So, here is the name of the game... What is it that you want? What is it that you want to accomplish with your life?

If you want it, you have to prep. You have to learn what it takes to achieve it. You have to learn want you will have to do to make it happen. You have to learn what you have to learn, no matter how un-fun it is. Then, you have to go out there and do it.

It may be hard. It may be a complete clusterfuck. It may take you a long time. But, you want it, learn how to do it, and make it happen.

# Forgetting What Stories I Have Told

30/Mar/2014 08:17 AM

As an author, poet, blogger and/or whatever else you want to call the literary genres I dance around in, I have written a lot of stuff. As a writer, (at least my breed of), what I write abut is based upon personal experiences. I write in the first-person.

...When and what I read, I always like that better – getting into the head of the author(s).

But, as the years have gone on, and as I have written so much stuff, sometimes I forget what stories I have told. Sure-sure, some of them are very clear in my mind: the living and then the writing about. But, then there are others. ...As I start to put them down I forget, *"Did I already tell that one?"*

Some people re-tell stories intentionally. Like Marguerite Duras did in her seminal novel, *The Lover* and then, *The North China Lover.* Sometimes time gives us new perspective on the stories of our lives, how we interpret them, and how we think they should be told to the world.

I guess that is the thing about people like me... I am very open about pretty much everything. Who I am is who I am. What you see is what you get. Thus, I tell the story of me. And, though some people, as the years have gone on, have attempted to put their own spin on my life, my words, and me; that has always been done by the people who don't know me and/or have never even met. Thus, that is simply their folly. For who I am is out-there for the world to read. And, I am alive and here to meet for anyone who actually has the desire – that is as long as they aren't a psycho or have some stupid hidden agenda.

Anyway... What this all says is that life is about living. From my perspective, life is also about telling your stories. Because from that, other people may be able to avoid some of the pitfalls you have encountered and possibly even live similar moments of ecstasy.

That is if I don't retell the same story too often in too many different ways... :-)

# I Don't Want To Know!

30/Mar/2014 08:15 AM

Have you ever noticed how some people are loud and boisterous in their life and their actions, forcing you inside all of their inner details. Though you never wanted inside, though you never wanted to know; now you do and then they are upset that you know?

It is like when you are in a restaurant or walking down the street and a couple is arguing. I never understood why they take that life-stuff into public. In one or two of these incidences I have even been asked what my opinion was. This, from people I don't even know. I always pretend that I wasn't paying attention to what they were saying – though, in fact, it was pretty much impossible not to hear them. But, what I really want to scream is, *"I don't want to know!"*

Sometimes friends or family get into it when you are around. Have you ever had that happen? Then, again, what are you supposed to do? It is their business but you are dragged into it.

I was down in OC (Orange County) a few years back and the family I was visiting got majorly into a massive screaming match. Normally, I would have just got up and left but I wasn't the one who drove. It was one of the screaming family members. So me, I went outside and was leaning against the car, listening, (but trying not to), to all of the screaming in the distance. I guess the neighbors called the cops. They drove up; saw me, and asked what was going on. Just a family feud... They smiled and drove on.

Another time that I didn't drive, I was out in the valley with my friend at one of his friend's houses. The shit hit the fan between these friends. Massive screaming and what I thought may come to blows. I said, *"Fuck it."* I wasn't going to get in the middle of this. I left, called a taxi, and paid over a hundred dollars to get back to my car in Venice. The friend I went with called the next day. He had gotten plastered as the fight continued into the wee hours of the night and passed out there. I'm glad I left!

I've had husband and wife teams, who I was actually really close to both of them, get into it in my presence. Then what? I know and care about both of them? After the arguing has diminished then I am put in the middle as they try to make me take sides. Similar things have probably happened to you.

I have had noisy neighbors who have been way too loud and brought me into their life when I had no desire to know anything about them or it. Then, they get all-weird with me when it was their fault in the first place dragging me into their life. I don't want to know! Okay!

I have known Wickens who after they reveal too much of themselves to someone actually try to cast a spell to make that person forget. That kind of stuff is just wrong. Don't try to mess with Mother Nature to actualize your own desires when you are the one responsible for the all and the everything in the first place.

Everybody argues at one point or another: every couple, every family, most friends... Some people do it very loud.

Then, there are the people who want to get up in everybody's business. Even when that business is none of their own. They want to find out hidden secrets. They want to get in the middle of discussions and fights so that they can give their opinion. They want to pass out free advice. Not me.

Leave me alone. Leave me out of it. I don't want to know!

# Paying For Your Crime

29/Mar/2014 03:02 PM

Whenever somebody is sent to jail for doing something that has been deemed wrong by society, it is stated, *"They are paying for their crime."* Or, when they get out, people say, *"They paid for their crime."* But, whom did they pay?

When criminals set about on a path to steal something or harm someone they know exactly what they are doing. They are setting about on a course that has a desired end result and they do not care who they hurt in the process. In fact, they generally do not even think about the impact that their actions may have on other people. They are simply thinking about themselves; what they want, want they need, and how they want to feel.

In fact, many people who commit crimes do not even view their actions as criminal and deny their culpability to the bitter end. Or, they deny both publicly and internally that they did anything wrong and try to gather a following of people to support and proclaim their innocence.

If you ever watch the shows that chronicle the time before a criminal is sentenced or the time they are spending in prison, little thought is ever given to the victims of the crime. Even if the victim or the families of the victim are allowed to speak at their trail, this changes nothing. What was stolen is rarely returned and the physical and mental injuries that are incurred by the victim can never truly be repaired. Ask someone who has been victimized by a criminal if their life was ever the same and most certainly they will answer, *"No, it was not."*

Criminals do what they do motivated by whatever distorted logic they may possess. What is left after their actions is the damaged life of their victims.

Societies set up laws to deter criminals from committing crimes. Yet, this does not stop them. Courts hand out prison sentences that are felt applicable for specific crimes. Yet, that does not stop them. Religions allow people to find redemption for their crimes by confession their sin. That is just bullshit.

Like I have long said, if I was going to be a Christian I would definitely be a Catholic. In that branch of Christianity you simply go confess your sins to a priest, they give you a few *Hail Mary's* and *Our Fathers* to do and you are good with god. Sounds great but what about the victims? Again, I call, *"Bullshit."*

Have you ever been a victim of a crime? If you have then you know what I speak about. How has whatever happened to the perpetrator of the crime given you back the innocence you possessed before it happened to you? Yes, you may be glad they were sent to prison and are suffering while doing time but it does not give you back the you that you were before they did what they did to you.

It is the same scenario for people who damage our lives and cry out, *"I didn't know."* Yet, the damage still remains. So, that is no excuse.

There are some who claim, *"Let's go out and get an eye-for-an-eye."* I have known a few who have walked down that road, but then they too became criminals in the eyes of society. And, in a couple of those cases they ended doing jail time and encountering all of the bad things that are known to go on in those environments.

The answer? I don't have one. I wish people would stop doing bad things but they probably won't. I do know that all life begins with you and with me. Meaning, we must think of others before we do things that can knowingly or unknowingly hurt someone else or their life space. We must set an example of how people should behave by doing good things. But other than that, let's just please stop saying and believing, *"They paid for their crime."* Because they haven't paid for, replaced, or fixed anything; at least not to the person it matters most to, the victim.

# Personal Meditation

28/Mar/2014 08:46 AM

People commonly enter into the practice of meditation to calm and focus their mind. Most schools of meditation teach methods that cause the mind to let go of thoughts and enter into a space of emptiness. Though this is a great means of removing the Self from the chaotic nature of the modern world, meditation can also be employed to train the mind to lead the Conscious and Unconscious Self to a higher level of personal interaction with this Life-Place.

Each of us is defined by the psychological make-up we were born with. We are also each defined by the life occurrences that happened to us in our youth. Add to this the life experiences that happen to us a adults and we are often left with a scrambled egg mishmash of random thoughts and personality traits that do not lead us towards the greater good.

A personal program in meditation, (or *Personal Meditation* as I call it), can be used to refine our consciousness to the degree where we emerge as a more whole and a more complete human being no longer dominated by random, uncontrolled thoughts and emotions.

If we look to people who laid the foundations for modern psychology such as Sigmund Freud, a technique that he used to refine his very complex and some would say damaged personality was self-analysis. With this he would mentally investigate his thoughts, memories, ideas, and feelings. He was then able to draw conclusions about himself and human consciousness as a whole.

Though this is a commonly used form of personally orientated psychotherapy, those who are drawn to the spiritual mindset, particularly those drawn to eastern wisdom, may find this technique a bit self-involved – focusing on the, *"Personal I,"* instead of the, *"Universal I."* That being said, the, *"Personal I,"* is the basis for our transcendence to the, *"Universal I."* Therefore, if we do not have a highly refined and completely understood sense of the, "Personal I," it will be a, *Hard Road to Nirvana.* To this end, *Personal Meditation* is an ideal tool.

The question will then be raised, *"What is personal meditation?"* The answer is, for each of us it will be a little bit different. As we are each unique individuals, with our own set of defining factors: both good and bad. As such, we will each need to define our own start point.

Knowing who we are is not difficult. It is very evident, in fact. And, if we are honest with ourselves, we each know what we need to work on. This is the start point of *Personal Meditation.*

The first thing you must do to begin your practice of *Personal Meditation* is to enter into a comfortable positioning. Then, take a few deep breaths and simply watch where your thoughts race to.

In most forms of traditional meditation you sit and try to stop your thoughts. This is not the prescription of *Personal Meditation,* however. As what you are thinking about, where your mind wanders to, is YOU. This is the YOU that you must define. So, in the early stages of *Personal Meditation* simply watch your thoughts and very consciously begin to study what you think about. Once you have become comfortable with this process, the next step in *Personal Meditation* is to begin to observe how each of these thoughts makes you feel.

This is where you start to understand how YOU are YOU and how and why you feel the way you feel and how and why you react to life situations the way you do.

Remember life is lived predominately in your head. Your thoughts and your emotions are what guide you through this existence. Yes, what you think and how you feel may be instigated by occurrences in the outside world, but all of that Life-Stuff is actualized in your own mind.

Once you come to have a firm grasp of your thinking process; leading to an understanding of why you feel the way you feel, it is time to begin to take control of who and what you are. At this stage of *Personal Meditation* it is time to stop allowing thoughts, feelings, and emotions to dominate and control your actions and reactions. Again, as your mind is the basis of YOU, here is the place and the space that you begin to take control over how you feel, why you feel what you feel, and what is the physical outcome based upon your feelings and emotions.

Therefore, while in the meditative state, knowingly take control over the emotions you are feeling, that are guiding you to behave in a particular manner. From this, you become the true YOU and are not simply dominated by the hands of fate and the actions of other people.

Ultimately, what you want to achieve from *Personal Meditation* is you knowing you and thereby you consciously controlling you. What emerges is the best YOU that you can be.

# The Three D's of Self-Defense

27/Mar/2014 07:54 AM

Martial artists are forever seeking new methods to refine their personal science of self-defense. Once the physical and philosophic basics of a system are mastered, then comes the metal refinement that takes the student forward, moving them towards the level of martial arts mastery.

In order to raise the ever-evolving understanding of my martial arts students, I personally prescribe a method that I called, *"The Three D's of Self-Defense."* This method is provided to help define a precise course of action for each confrontation and to ultimately chart a pathway towards victory. *The Three D's* are:

1. Deflect
2. Deny
3. Defy

To briefly go into the basics for this three-part self-defense philosophy, we can view each element individually.

## Deflect

A physical confrontation is never to anyone's benefit. It is only the ego-driven martial artist that desires to go toe-to-toe with another person and emerge victorious. To this end, it takes the larger man (or woman) to walk away from a fight rather than to allow another person to drag them into a physical altercation. Therefore, the first means of deflection is to walk away from any confrontation.

Certainly, we all realize that walking away is not always an option. This is especially the case when a person either grabs you or strikes you and is not going to stop until they are disabled. To achieve self-defense in the most conscious manner possible, while keeping yourself free for personal injury, the true martial artist will always deflect an attack rather than encounter it directly.

Forcefully blocking an assault has been shown time-and-time again to lead to injuring the blocking component of your arm or actually breaking your blocking hand. Therefore, learning the science of opponent energy manipulation and deflection is the ideal first tool of effective self-defense that each martial artist should master.

**Deny**

When there is no way to exit a physical confrontation and stop it before it begins, and deflection has not halted an opponent's attack, the next step in conscious self-defense is to deny their ability to continue forward with their assault. The quickest and most debilitating way to engaged an oncoming opponent is to strike them before they have ability to strike you. For example, they are rapidly moving in towards you to attack. Before they have the chance to connect with a punch, kick, or grab, you deliver a powerful first-strike to a debilitating part of their body.

When encountering an enraged attacker, each situation is defined by its own set of circumstances. Therefore, there is no one strike that should always be used. But, a powerful straight punch to the face, a front kick to the groin, a hammer fist to the temple, a knife hand or fist to the throat are all viable first-strike weapons in an offensive defense.

**Defy**

A physical altercation is rarely won by simply delivering one strategically placed blow to an attacker. Though occasionally, if you deliver a powerful strike to debilitating location on your opponent's body, this may occur. But, you can never rely upon this. I have witnessed a number of incidences when a person was walking away from a confrontation, after having knocked their opponent to the ground, only to have the opponent jump up and charge after them. Therefore, you must defy their ability to come after you once the first round has been won.

No honorable martial artist would ever kick an opponent when they are down. That being said, you must be sure that you actually have the ability to completely leave the scene of the confrontation before you turn your back on your attacker. To this end, simply leaving your opponent with a bloody nose may not be enough. Unless they have formally conceded the fight, you must continue forward with your offensive defense until they are fully subdued.

Again, each confrontation is defined by its own set of parameters, so it will ultimately be up to you to know when you can safely leave. But, before you attempt to leave, be sure that your opponent's ability to come after you has been nullified or you may not emerge victorious during the second round of the confrontation.

**Three Together**

The elements of, *"The Three D's of Self-Defense,"* can also be tied together and used as one cohesive self-defense methodology. For example, an attacker races towards you. Before he can make impact, you deflect his initial attack. Immediately, you follow up with a powerful, well-placed, strike that stuns him. Finally, wasting no time, you follow thru with a debilitating second punch, kick, break, or throw that ends the entire confrontation. By defending yourself in this manner you allow your attacker no time to rethink or redirect his initial attack and you emerge victorious.

The martial arts are a refined science of physical and mental training designed to make the practitioner a more conscious and aware interactive participant of life. For this reason, the true martial artist never trains simply to learn how to fight. Instead, they train in order to gain new mental and physical understandings that will keep themselves and their loved ones safe. They achieve this by avoiding confrontations whenever possible and achieving physical victory only when absolutely necessary.

Strive to become the best, most conscious and competent martial artist that you can be.

# Problem vs. Problem

26/Mar/2014 08:12 AM

Have you ever noticed how some people come into your life or your life situation, create a problem for you and then when you let them know about the problem that they created they blame you for them creating it?

Most people exist based upon a very selfish level of consciousness. They consider themselves and their life space before they ever even begin to think about anyone else. And, here lies one of the primary problems with the concept of, *"Living in the now,"* which is commonly presented as one of the most sought after levels of consciousness on the spiritual path. Living in the now is based upon personal perception. It is based upon how, *"I,"* feel in this moment. It is not based upon taking ALL into consideration for then one would shift from the Self-Involved NOW to, what I believe is the greater-good of the All-Involved NOW.

All this being as it is, most people think about themselves first and, as such, any problem they may create in your Life-Space they immediately take it back to their central focus of, If you confront them about it, if they are alerted to it, if they are scolded about it, all they do is try to shift the focus of the conversation back to themselves, *"I didn't know. I don't care. Who cares?"* Or, *"It's not my fault."* In some extreme cases people even attempt to completely shift the conversation and state, "It's your fault." But, what people virtually never do is own it – accept what they have done, apologize for it, and set about on a path of fixing what they have broken.

In fact, some people are so unaware of anybody but themselves that they do not even realize that they have created a short-term or long-standing problem for another person. If they do not know, how can they care?

One would think, with the ever-expanding consciousness of this world, that people would be more conscious. They are not. The fact is, those who walk the path of refined consciousness are few and far between. Then, even of the few who are of conscious mind, they too are based in a selfish mindset. *"I am. Therefore I am. And, as such I am always right."* The spiritual path breeds this mindset as people walking it can become quite full of themselves and their own implied righteousness.

There are some people whose lives are based upon gaining an adrenaline fix whenever they can. Thus, they go around creating problems for themselves and others simply so that they can get that fix. I have known and interacted with a few people of this mind. But, this is a small breed. Most of those who create problems in your life are simply those you see everyday and who are too self-involved to actually care of the consequences they create in the life of another person.

The answer? Well, there really isn't one prescribed antidote. I used to believe that one must always keep their options opened. Meaning, have the resources to move away from any situation where you are confronted with negativity at any level. But, this doesn't always work. For one, this type of counterattack usually cost money. And, we don't always have enough of that to actualize our needed move away from the situation. Also, sometimes when we are presented with these problems, created by other people, we find ourselves in environments where moving away is not an easy option; i.e. school or a job. So, then what? I used to try playing nice with the person but I have realized that equals little because then they do not understand that there is a problem. And, Confrontation only equals confrontation. Hiding can work, but commonly crossing-paths will occur. Being passive/aggressive has worked for some people I know and that has become their prescribed method – meaning ignoring the person when you see them. Some believe doing onto them before they do onto you again is the answer – you do to them what they have done to you.

In the end, all this is the all this… Each situation where another individual has created a problem in your life is defined by its own set of parameters. Some people are simply negative, power tripping, unconscious assholes, and no matter what you do or say they will not care. Most people are not like that, however, they will change if you provide them with motivation. …Though they probably are not refined enough to say they're sorry.

Each life situation is defined by each life situation. How you handle it is chosen and defined by you. This is the complicated equation of life, deciding what to do for each situation you find yourself in and this is also what sets your next level of *karma* in motion. The main thing to keep in mind is to be more, not less, than the person who has created a problem in your life. From this, they may even learn from your example, but don't hold your breath awaiting this outcome.

    This is life. We all deal with the stuff of life.

# A Wave or a Flip Off

25/Mar/2014 01:49 PM

I was cruising down the street over in RB (Redondo Beach) today and I noticed that the guy in the car in front of me was making all these hand gesture out of his window. He was pointing this way and that and waving his hand around. He pulled up to a stop sign with his left turn signal on – all good. He then started pointing with his hand that he was going to turn left – strange... Anyway, as he turned I could see him in his side view mirror. He reminded me of Cheech Marin as he was Latin with a big bushy mustache like Cheech used to have back in the day. Anyway, in his mirror, I could also see that he was looking at me. Then, he boldly stated, *"What the fuck!"* Like I was doing something wrong. Weird...

Now, I don't know if he was trippin', psycho, or simply mad at life, but what he was doing and the way he was acting was not normal. And, this is the thing about the road, you never know what kind of person you are going to be forced to interact with.

Like the other day I was pulling into a gas station and there was a guy apparently waiting for a pump to become available. He was doing this as I was pulling into one of the open pumps. All of a sudden he starts to back up. If he had not stopped he would have hit my car. I honked at him. He stopped. When we made eye contact, he waved a gesture of, *"Sorry."* All good... But, the situation did make me think of times gone past when people would get angry at me for alerting them to their oncoming mistake. I mean, which is the better option: being notified of an oncoming collision with a little honk or being allowed to plow into a car?

A couple of months ago I was leaving the parking lot of one of my local *Starbucks*. As I was leaving the parking lot the guy in front of me was checking his phone or something and he had not realized his path forward was clear. I gave him a little honk on the horn just to let him know. From his truck, I could see him going off in the mirror, *"Fuck you! Fuck you!."* How strange I thought... He was fired soon after this. Obviously too angry to be involved with customer service.

But, the road is weird; like when somebody cuts you off or does something really bad that causes you to slam on your breaks or veer out of the way and you are planning to drive up next to them give them a hard look and flip them off. Then, just as you do, you realize that it is a really pretty girl driving the car. All anger is gone...

Like on the freeways, when you are driving a million miles an hour. Do you ever think about just how quickly your life could end if someone did something stupid at that speed? It wouldn't matter whose fault it was or was not because you would be dead or at least gravely injured.

Driving is a weird science. So, many weird things can happen or be set in motion at a moments notice.

This afternoon I was back up in PV and decided to stop and grab a latte' before I got back to the editing I am working on. As I drove down the street *Starbucks* is on, an old man waved his hand at me to slow down. I looked at my speedometer. I was driving thirty MPH, the speed limit. But, because the man was old, he saw me as driving too fast.

A wave it is better than a flip off. A wave makes you smile. A flip off makes you angry. Your choice. Your reaction.

*Just a few thoughts about life on the road...*

# Doing What We Do

25/Mar/2014 08:29 AM

Life is defined by doing. We do what we do. For most of us, what we do leads to the definition of our lives. We do what we do and that becomes who we are. But, what if what we are doing damages the lives of other people? That too then becomes the definition of our lives. And, a life defined in that manner is never a good one.

Most people do what they do instigated by their interests and gaining some form of emotional or financial reward for their actions. This then becomes their motivational factor.

We all need money to survive and we all hope to be praised for what we do. But, life is much more than that. Life is about creating the greater good, not simply the self-empowered person.

We all do things that are not good for life and the earth on the whole. For example, most of us drive cars. We drive, yet we know that driving a car, powered by a catalytic converter, is bad for the environment. Yet, we make excuses that we must get from here to there. Thankfully, (though it is probably already too late), new technological advances are being focused on making driving a less polluted venture. But, this is on the larger scale. Life and life definition begins at a much more refined level. It begins with YOU and how YOU interact with people and with the world.

As stated, people do what they do for emotional and financial reward. Sometimes people are simply elated and they do what they do because they are happy or what they are doing makes them happy. Whatever the cause or motivating factor, the conscious person always takes others into consideration while they are doing what they are doing because if they don't they have the potential of damaging others while doing what they do, no matter how enjoyable they may find it.

Do you care? This is an essential question that you must ask of yourself. Do you care more about that what you are doing? Or, do you care that what you are doing is damaging the life of another person?

A common claim that a person makes when they have hurt the life of another person, either by selfish actions or by being selfishly unaware is that, *"I didn't know."* But, when someone says that they are actually saying, *"I didn't care to know." "I didn't care enough about another person or this Life-Space to investigate the parameters before I took the action that damaged another person's life."* Yet, by the actions they took another person life was damaged. Now, this damage can be big, it can be small, but it damage none-the-less.

We all do things in life that are not right. Most people do not want to eat their ego and actually admit that they did something wrong. But, what makes us who we are, and how we are ultimately defined, is how we fix the damage we cause to another person's life.

Sure, fixing something that is broken is not easy. But, it can be done. The first thing to do is to stop putting yourself first. Think about other people before you act. Then, go about removing the damaged elements you created. Finally, get some glue and actually repair the damage you instigated.

That is the definition of a life lived well – fixing what you have broken.

# Some People Don't Want the Cure

25/Mar/2014 07:57 AM

Most of us when we are sick or injured we go to the doctor. Most of us if we have toothache we go to the dentist. Sure, going to the doctor isn't fun. They usually make us wait way too long in the waiting room before we get to see them. This, even though we had an appointment. Sure, going to the dentist isn't fun. In fact it is kind of weird...

I think back to when I was a kid. My dentist was this aging Chinese-American man and he used to sit around and smoke while he took care of my teeth. Times have definitely changed...

But, we go, get done what needs to be, get the meds, whatever, and then we are out of there, hopefully better.

There are some people who just don't want to be cured, however. I spoke to this one guy who claimed that his shoulder got damaged by a physical therapist. It was really painful so he said. The final cure was to have removed. What! Man, that weirded me out big time. Anybody who would even think of going to those lengths... It makes me cringe even now.

Then, there was this one guy I knew. Nice guy, a friend of a friend. But, he had big-time back issues. Sometimes he could hardly move. He went to the doctors, they could find nothing wrong. He wanted them to operate; they would not as they didn't know what to operate upon. All this pain, but he wouldn't go to a chiropractor or an acupuncturist. *"No, that's fake shit,"* he would exclaim. My conclusion he wanted the pain and the attention he got by feeling the pain.

Life is a projection of our own reality. And, I am certainly not diminishing the physical conditions of those who actually are experiencing them. But, life is mostly a mental projection. I am sure we have all witnessed times when we each have projected a whole mental mindset of what would, what should, and what could be. In some case, this focusing on the negative may have even made us sick. But, at the end of the day, nothing came to pass.

Most of us have felt pain or discomforted and prepared for the worse. But, when we go to the doctor it was simply a minor issue and we were cured with some antibiotics. Yet, we spent a lot of time in turmoil concerned it would be something catastrophic.

As we are locked into a physical body, there is illness, there is pain, and there is ultimately death. But, we are also a mental project of how we interact with reality. If you feel pain, you can mentally remove yourself from the pain and overcome it. This is something that monks and martial artists have been doing forever. As such, you can also be the source for mentally create the pain in your life.

Do you want to be cured or do you want to be defined by the lack of the cure? Most of us would instantly choose the first choice. But, there are others who choose the second. The fact is, in many of our lives, on subtle levels, we too choose the second; even if only for a moment.

There is a cure in life. We should forever choose it over the opposite.

# Lost in Translation

25/Mar/2014 07:47 AM

I believe we all have had the experience of talking to someone and we say something that really didn't come out the way we meant it to, leaving the conversation a bit uncomfortable. On the flipside, I am sure we each have been upset about what another person said. But, if we question them, they too exclaim that the statement they made wasn't really what they meant to say and the words came out wrong.

I am sure that we have all had a similar experience of communication when we were sending someone an email or in a chat.

In communications sent via email there is seemingly the time to think about what you are writing and the words you are using. But, when the person you send the email to reads it, they may misinterpret your intensions and get riled up or angry with you. I am sure you also have become annoyed at the words somebody emailed to you even though you later find out they did not mean it the way it was read. Something was lost in the translation.

I remember in the early days of the internet, (way back, in the way back when), I used to believe I was required to answer all sincere emails. Which I did. But, even then, ideas, thoughts, and ideologies got misinterpreted. Thus, things went awry.

Even in recent times, when I have reached out to communicate with people, in some cases, it has just gotten weird. The person read what they wanted to read into my email and responded in a completely inappropriate manner.

I believe this is the problem with communications via instantaneous sources such as the internet – people define what is sent to them by the mindset they possess in the moments they are reading it and respond accordingly. Additionally, once you send somebody something they can then take your words, misrepresent your intentions, and broadcast those misrepresented words to other people. It has happened to me...

All of this leads to the realm of, Not Good.

Though we are certainly never going to move away from the world of instantaneous messaging, at least until something better comes along, we have to either live with the consequences or adapt our approach to this style of communication according.

Me, even to this day, sometimes I am so sorry I either struck up a conversation or answered the questions present in one. But, this is life. This is the New World. And, no matter where you find yourself in it, you are going to have to deal with its ramifications.

Personally, I have learned my lesson. I now only communicate with people I actually know. That way, if some of the words or the interpretations go awry, I can fix it face-to-face. Or, if I must, I answer in the briefest, most concise manner possible. Mostly, I just tell people I do not know if I receive an email or a message from them, (if I tell them anything at all), *"Sorry, but too much gets lost in translation..."*

**Everybody Has a Reason**

24/Mar/2014 08:24 AM

Everybody has a reason for doing what they do. You may not like it. You may not understand it. It may even totally mess up your life, but they believe they are doing what they are doing for a set of logical principals that they have defined in their own mind.

Most people take other people into consideration before they do what they do. They question how their actions are going to affect those around them. They weigh out the variables, *"If I do this, that will happen."* Then, they decide on their next step taking all people, all life, and all possible impacts of their action(s) into account.

There are other people who do not care. They do what they do based on a very selfish mindset and they do not even consider the ramifications of what their actions may have on the life or the livelihood of other people who may be affected by what they have chosen to do.

There is also the third type of personality, those who consciously attempt to damage the lives of others. They do what they do, and they actually hope to hurt other people or mess with their life by the actions they have set in motion.

In all of these three personality cases, there is one common denominator; each person has a reason for doing what they do. They have made a conscious choice to do what they do.

In life, no matter how much we try to shield ourselves we are probably going to be forced into interaction with each of these personality types. From this, in some cases our lives may be made better, in other cases our lives and our life-evolution may be truly damaged.

For this reason, each of us who walks the path of consciousness and conscious living must truly investigate, first-and-foremost, who we are and then we must come to a definition of how we interact with all those around us. Finally, before we take any action, we must very consciously define our reason for doing what we do.

If we are walking the path of consciousness, consciously, there is no excuse for either damaging others –

either by not being conscious enough to have considered the ramifications of our actions or to set out on a path of deliberately hurting others.

In all things in life, you are the center-point. You are the source of the universe. You are the source of where all things begin and end. Thus, you must choose to remain conscious enough to not have a reason to hurt anyone or damage his or her life in any manner. Instead, you must strive to make this Life-Place and the lives of all those you interact with better.

Be better.

# Age

23/Mar/2014 08:28 AM

I had kind of a funny experience last night. I was watching the evening news and they were speaking about how three people had gotten injured at the San Juan Capistrano Return of the Swallows Parade. One had a spooked horse fall on them, one fell off of a cart pulled by a horse, and one had a hearth attack. The ages of these people were fifty-one, fifty-five, and fifty-seven. My initial thought was, *"Those people were old."* My next thought was, *"I'm fifty-five!"* I laughed at my thought process and myself.

Age... It is a funny thing. I was speaking with one of my barista friends at *Starbucks* about a week ago and he detailed how one of the new girls at the shop makes him feel so old due to the fact that everything he references, from music and culture, she has never heard of. He is about thirty and she is eighteen. I said that happens to me all the time, *"I'm fifty-five."* He began to intensely study my face. *"I never thought you were that old,"* he exclaimed.

That happens to me a lot. And, I guess it is not a bad thing. People, if they don't know, think I am younger than I am. My doctor, who is my age, exclaims the fact every time I go to see him.

This is probably due to the fact that I have not gone grey. Which is a good thing, I guess, as I am not one of those people who would dye their hair. But this whole thing also causes me to ponder why I have held onto a relatively youthful appearance, as I have partied hard and lived a pretty intense life. I truly never anticipated I would live this long. In any case, this is who I am. And, by all standards, even my own, I am old.

I have actor friends who knock five years off of their age. This is the common number and the thing to do in Hollywood. So, if you look at some of your favorite stars and you want to know their real age, add five years to what they claim.

In modern culture youth is the thing everyone seeks. It is somehow, some kind of Holy Grail. People do all kinds of things to maintain the look of youth. When I was growing up, however, I always put my stock in the aged and the knowers, as they were the ones who had lived and, as such, understood the truths of reality. In many cultures, not of the West, this is also the case. Here, we hate the old. No one wants them around. They are just a burden. If something happens to them at a parade you think, *"That happened because they're old."* Me too... I initially thought the same thing.

No matter how young we look, no matter how young we feel; age catches up with us all. Get ready for it. Here it comes and there is nothing that will stop it...

# Nobody Really Cares

22/Mar/2014 08:31 AM

People claim they care about things. They say they care about global warming, saving the whales, freeing Tibet, immigration reform, art, music, cinema, but they do absolutely nothing about anything. They simply dance through their life, living whatever momentary reality they are living, and that is that. They may even get into long discussion about what they believe to be right or wrong, write some comments on some webpages, but still they do nothing – as talking is not doing.

There are certain instances in life when people congregate. There was this big immigration rally; focused on providing citizenship to illegal immigrants held here in L.A. several years ago and it drew large crowds of Latinos. Sure, Latinos make up most of the illegal immigrants here in the U.S... There were even signs at drive-thru restaurants like *El Polo Loco* during this rally stating that you may have to wait a long time because several of their staff members went to the rally. Some places even closed.

I won't go into the logistics or the right or wrong political ramifications of what this rally was or was not. But, I will discuss, what came from it – nothing. Sure a large group of people congregated, speeches were given, they marched, it gave the newscasters something to talk about, some police got in trouble for doing things against policy, but whatever... Mostly, it was a large street party, now forgotten. Same with occupy, New York, L.A., Oakland, etc.

People congregate to get their adrenaline agitated. It is the same as going to a nightclub. But, then they go home and fall back into mundane existence.

People care until they care no longer – though for a moment in their mind they believe that they do. In your mind is not in your life.

When you actually find somebody caring and getting out there and actually doing something to actualize a desired end goal, virtually always it is based upon something that will benefit them personally – even if they may falsely claim it is for the good of all.

There are places in the world where you have to care or die. It is not like that in the West. Here, caring is, at best, about something that makes the individual feel better, more empowered, or in a position of authority and control for caring about what they care about.

Think about when you were young, you probably really liked a singer or a musical group. Their posters were on your wall. Maybe you really liked an actor. You discussed them all the time with your friends; had fantasies about them. But, then you grew up. Do you still have posters of your favorite band on your wall? Probably not.

I have witnessed people get into arguments and fights over one person believing in one thing and the other person believing the opposite. They believed, sure. They argued, they fought, okay. But, then what? Neither one of them did anything to make anything happened. All they did was believe, which lead to meaningless violence.

This happens in religion and in politics all the time.

On the artistic level this is no different. People like what they like, don't like what they don't like based upon whatever momentary reality they are basing the existence upon. They feel this is a basis for caring. But, do they really care?

I receive questions all the time about what I do and why. Most people are cool but there are even some people who take the time to attack what I do. Okay, but why? How does that change anything? Why do you care? I am me, you are you. I do what I do based upon a philosophic premise. Why do you do what you do? And, how does attacking me or anybody else equal anything? Art is such a ridiculous medium to instigate controversy over.

Life is about doing, not undoing. And, if your caring is based on hurting, damaging, or negativity you are really caring about the wrong thing.

It was like when Donald G. Jackson passed away. I cannot tell you how many people kept asking me, *"Who was he? What was he like? Please make a documentary about him!"* Some people he knew actually contacted me and wanted me to give them the footage I was in possession of so they could make a documentary. Like I was going to do that! ...For I have long ago realized that though people have great intentions, nobody ever does anything. Anyway, I did do a documentary, more than one, in fact. Nobody has seen them. Except for a few very hardcore people who actually truly did possess an interest in Don, how his mind worked, and our filmmaking process – very few people ever viewed the film(s). They may have thought that they cared. They may have believed for a moment that they cared. But, they did not care.

This is an ideal example of life and the life of caring. In your mind you may believe that you care. But, in your life you can't really be bothered unless something is handed to you on a silver platter.

People care when they can care from home. People care when they are discussing things with their friends of like-mind. People care when it doesn't cost them any money. People care when it doesn't cost them any time. People care when they don't have to do anything but believe they are right and you are wrong. People care when they receive personal empowerment by caring. People care when what they care about benefits them. People care when they can go to a street party, get adrenalized while being surround by people who are screaming the same slogan. People care... Wait, people only care about themselves.

Nobody really cares...

**Defining Who You Are**

21/Mar/2014 04:22 PM

Every now and then I meet people who still smoke. This, even though we all know how bad smoking can be for your health and the health of those around you. Generally, these people too know the pitfalls.

Though there is a part of me that questions why anyone would smoke when everybody knows the heath problems is can cause – not to mention how much it costs to smoke. But, when you look at a person who is still smoking it is clear to see that smoking has come to define them as a person. It is who they are. And, giving up who you are is never easy.

From a personal perspective, both my father and my mother smoked. That was a part of their generation. It's important to keep in mind, my father died at forty-six. I'm sure smoking had a big part to play in that.

My father-in-law died from lung cancer. He had smoked his whole adult life. Believe me when I tell you, that is a horrible way to die. Yet, most smokers never believe it will happen to them.

When I was growing up a lot of my friends smoked. I never did. In fact, one of my longtime friends began smoking at age thirty-five. I never understood that one.

You know, I am aware that there is the whole rebellious, *"I am cool,"* and, *"I am an adult,"* thing about smoking when you are young. But, the problem is, smoking is physically addictive. Quitting is never easy.

Today when you speak to smokers, many of them say I am going to change over to *Vapes*. But, this is simply an extension of their addiction and they too are not healthy.

The whole point of this is, smoking is an ideal illustration of how you set the course for your life in progress at a very young age. Me, I was into yoga and the martial arts, so I was not drawn to the smoking lifestyle. Though I must state, literally every one of my martial art instructors was a smoker.

Some people are drawn to smoking; other people are drawn towards other things. But, wherever you find yourself in your life, you need to take a long look at what defines who you are. You need to examine if what you set in motion in your youth is still who you are today and will it lead you towards what you want to be tomorrow. If it will, great. If not, change.

# How You Deal

21/Mar/2014 12:44 PM

We all have things that make us mad, angry, unhappy, frustrated, and all of those kind of emotions. For each of us we deal with those emotions the way we deal with them. For most people, they never think about how they deal. They simply do what they do. Thus, it is not so much a focused expression of how they feel but they are simply feeling something so they react.

For example, in the Punk days back when what we did was called *Slam Dancing* or *Slamming*, before it became known as *Moshing*, my friend would go jump into the pit with one intention and that was to get into a fight. Unfortunately, he was not a very good fighter. He would always get beat up unless myself or one of our other friends would jump in and help him out. This behavior was his reaction to the undefined way in which he was feeling dissatisfaction with his life. Many people behave in a similar manner.

I had this one acquaintance that said whenever he encountered a situation that he did not like or if he was mistreated by someone or something he would take that experience and turn it into a part of one of the scripts he would write. That is perhaps a better way to deal with the unhappy moments we all encounter in life.

In each of these cases, the people dealt with what they felt in the most appropriate method they felt they had at their disposal. One was obviously more refined than the other.

The thing to think about is that we all encounter these emotions. Emotions that push negative feelings in us to the surface. Even for those of us who try to understand why we feel the way we feel, we are not immune to being drawn into the chaotic and angry thoughts that go hand-in-hand with feeling this way.

When we encounter these situations we need to claim victory over these life-events and control them as opposed to letting them control us. For if we allow them to control us, then we are dominated by them which can lead us down the road to doing bad things which can equal further badness in our life.

One of the best ways to defend against the onset and possible life-control of negative emotions is to choose to refocus the energy and do something creative and positive based on the understanding that we each are the ones who controls all of the I-Stuff in our life. By doing this, instead of allowing negative emotions to be in control of you, you control them. Thus, no further negativity is born from whatever caused you to feel that way in the first place. From this, any negative feelings instigate by events in your life are nullified, and you emerge that much more in control of yourselves and your Life-Time.

# The Possible Outcome

21/Mar/2014 12:33 PM

I believe that each of us has encountered periods in our life when we are confronted with something OUT THERE that we believe if it happens it will negatively effect our life and possible change our entire existence forever.

In each of our lives these threats are different but we understand that if they actually occur, everything is going to change. They may be physical threats, emotional threats, financial threats, employment threats, and the list goes on. But, the threat is there. We know it may happen but we don't know when, or even if, it will. But, something has clued us that it may be oncoming. It is a very scary space to be in.

From this, our mind is set into obsession and we wonder, question, and run the various scenarios through our brain attempting to predict the possible outcomes. We try to decide what we will say, what we will do if, in fact, what we believe may happen actually does come to pass. It can become quite maddening.

Life is defined by the chaotic force(s) of other people who love, hate, or do not even know you. Each of these entities has their own agenda for transversing this Life-Place. As such, they want what they want and they do not care what you want. Or, they may even want to take away what you have.

Generally, when we are presented with these possible life changing crises, it is brought about by someone who wants to do us harm. The plan they have hatched can be large or it can be small but it is, no doubt, based upon a vindictive mindset.

Most people could care less about raising their human consciousness. Most could care less about the *karma* that they may incur by doing wrong things to other people. They are simply motived by an animalistic mindset that they want to hurt and/or damage you. Many times this may be based in the fact that they think you did something wrong to them. Whether that is true or not is irrelevant. But, that is their motivating factor and they are on a path to damage your life.

Perhaps it is based upon the perception that they don't like you and they want to GET you. Whatever their motivation, what has occurred in these situations is that you have heard about the ongoing plan and you are left in the paranoid state of questioning, *"What will come next?"* And, *"What will it do to my life?"*

For centuries people have retreaded to places like monasteries simply so that they will not have to deal with this level of Mind Stuff. They go away, so they can free themselves from the nonsense of humanity. And, humanity is based upon a lot of nonsense. But, most of us are not of that mindset. Most of us do not want to spend our years living in quiet, peaceful, meditation. As such, these moments of the unknown on-comings will most likely occur. Then what?

It is easy to say, *"Don't worry about it. It won't be as bad as you think."* Or, *"Just see what happens and then decide on your next move."* Good advice, but how can you stop your thinking-mind when possible disaster is eminent?

From a perspective of the martial arts, if you know you are going to be attacked, and there is no way around it, the best thing to do is land the first punch. This may end the fight altogether. Strike them before they can strike you.

This ideology may work in your circumstance. It may not.

Also, from the martial arts we learn the concept of deflecting the attack. A punch or a kick is launched. Instead of taking the impact of that blow or blocking it forcefully, you redirect the energy of that attack. Step out its path and redirect the energy of the assault.

In regards to this type of Life-Situation what this means is that you perhaps leave the battleground, thus you cannot be attack. Or, if you already know the direction from where the attack will be launched, you prepare yourself to cause it to move away from you by preparing your Life-Documents to substantiate your right-ness and the attacker's wrong-ness as they instigated the situation.

Finally, from the martial arts we learn that if we are struck we must immediately counterattack to keep from encountering additional injury. Though never the best defense, through training the martial artist learns how best to counterstrike against each type of attack.

In your life, you too should learn the sensitive and weak points of the person who is instigating any assault against you. Then, go after them. And, strike hard.

We all want life to be easy. We all want life to be free and happy. We never want to encounter situations that take us from our peace or divert us from our chosen path. As such, we should never attempt to hurt or damage other people. If an undefined assault comes our way, however, the only mind calming medicine is to make it go away. Thus, do not sit in paranoia. Instead, directly encounter it. From this, you may still lose the battle but you will have at least fought the good fight.

# Nobody Remembers Their Name

21/Mar/2014 12:23 PM

  I often jokingly tell stories about some of the calamities I have encountered while casting a movie. Nobody ever believes me until they try to do it themselves. There have been so many times I have discussed this subject with students in my classes or at a seminar and there is always someone who is dismissive if not downright argumentative about the realities of casting an indie movie. Then, they try to bring-up a film and I always hear back from them telling me, *"You were right!"*

  Hollywood is a strange beast. And, I use the term, *"Hollywood,"* to describe the film business in general. But here, in actual Hollywood, people come to be stars. They come to be stars on the big screen. And, they expect to have it happen overnight with no effort. They feel they have a look or talent and that should be enough. From my experience, I can tell, you it is not.

  In any case, I have discussed some of the situations that have occurred while attempting to cast in a film in many other places. There is extensive discussions of the subject in my books: *Zen Filmmaking* and *Independent Filmmaking: Secrets of the Craft.* But, one of the ideal examples that comes to mind is when Don Jackson and I were originally going to film *Lingerie Kickboxer.* We planned to shoot it on 35mm and do it in a twenty-four hour period just to show the world that it could be done. We had shows like *Entertainment Tonight* and reporters from industry magazines like *The Hollywood Reporter* scheduled to meet us throughout the shooting day at various locations. At 4:00 AM, the night before the shoot, I receive a phone call from the actress who was to play the lead role in the film, she told me she couldn't do it because she had to go to a family reunion with her boyfriend. Thus, the production came to screeching halt.

  There have been numerous other times where I offered actors and actresses the lead or a supporting role in a film and they either didn't show up for the production or called me the night before saying they decided not to do it or their agent told them not to do it.

  I won't even go into the bullshit-ness of agent here…

So, there went their roll. One of the more amusing phone calls I received was from one actress who called me up and rudely stated, *"I'm not going to be in a film just so you can have somebody make-out with me!"* What? She sure had a high opinion of her self. In any case, I had offered her the female lead in a film where all she had to do was kiss a guy to establish they were in a relationship. Not too much to ask for a starring role. And, this chick was a stripper by trade and had never been an actual film – even though her resume said she had.

Remember the number one rule of filmmaking, *"Everybody lies."* Anyway...

Aside from not showing up or not showing up on the next day of a shoot to complete their role, some people have left my set before they were even filmed due to the fact that they arrived and discovered that we were not a major Hollywood production. Though I certainly never claim to be.

Just a side note here: This is one of the problems that occurs from people being an extra in a movie or on a T.V. show. In those situations, the productions are BIG. Thus, the novice actor or actress comes to believe that all productions should be that big. From this, what happens is that their minds have been mislead into believing that the BIGS are the only real productions. They are not.

All this being said, let me get to the point, because I could go on for hours upon hours about this subject... I have worked with a lot of very talented actors and actress since I enter the film industry many years ago. The majority of them are nice, professional, and came to do their job and did it with excellence. At the end of the day, they were in a movie. In fact, some have used this on-camera experience to springboard their careers. Others did not move up the ladder, but at least they have one film that they were in to show their family and friends.

I had a realization while I was driving this afternoon... It was, all of those people who turned down the opportunity to be in one of my films, (for whatever reason), I do even remember their name. And, nobody else does either.

You really need to accept opportunities when opportunities are offered to you in your life.

# 16mm Cameras Are Noisy

21/Mar/2014 07:43 AM

I finally got the chance to see the entire Dave Grohl documentary, *Sound City* the other night. I had seen bits and pieces of it here and there but it was nice to sit down and actually watch it from start to finish. It's a nice piece; especially for someone like me who actually recorded at Sound City way back in the way back when. For others, it may be a little too inside as it really focuses on an era gone past, with interviews with the founders, the staff, and the rock stars who recorded there.

One of the large focuses of the film is how technology changed everything for the studio and the recording industry as a whole. In one segment Grohl speaks with Neil Young who, like some crotchety old man bent on some conspiracy theory, states in essence, *"That they made a mistake in an algorithm when they designed CD technology."* He believes this is why music sounds better recorded analog. This made me smile. You know Neil, if they had made a mistake back when they were developing the technology they would have fixed it by now. Anyway...

The movie culminates with Grohl bringing many of the rock stars that recorded at Sound City together and recording a project on audiotape, produced by Butch Vig, using the original board, the *Neve 8028 Console*, from the studio.

Sure, music recorded on tape, through a great console, sounds better. But damn, it is an expensive and time-consuming process. As someone who actually knows how to operate one of those boards, I can tell you it is first about understanding what does what and then it is about instinct and inspiration – making the right choice to get what you desire. But, it is not easy, not cheap, and it can be very frustrating. Think about having to move exact elements of audio tracks tape-to-tape or to have to precisely cut, match, and tape pieces of audiotape together when you want to mix a song. It is scary complicated and not easy.

As someone who has strived to be at the cutting edge of technology the moment I can afford to get my hands on it. ...Me, I love the ease of the digital age. Sure, it sounds different. But, you just have to accept things for what they are. The truth be told, most people don't have the ears to hear the difference between analog and digital anyway.

It is like in the film industry when we used to use 16mm cameras. Damn, those things were noisy. You had to have your camera housed in what was called a, *"Blimp,"* to mask the sound of the camera's motor if you did not want it to bleed over onto the dialogue. More than once though the sound of the camera was heard on our audio tracks. As such, I had to create a soundtrack that would hide this fact. Video cameras changed all this. They are silent. And also, just like what occurred when digital hit the recording industry, this brought the price of everything way-way down. Now, everybody can afford to be a filmmaker or a music creator. Good or bad, that's the way it is.

Just like recording on audiotape sounds better than recording digitally, (if you have the ears for it), the aesthetic of a movie shot on film is much better than digital, (if you have the eyes for it). But, this is the new world, everything changes all the time. Just like in life, we can each hold on and remember the way back when, as far as we go way back when. But, anything more than that is simply paying a lot for nostalgia. Oh wait; Dave Grohl has plenty of money so he can do just that. Nevermind…

Great movie, Dave!

# The Price of Enlightenment

20/Mar/2014 07:20 AM

It forever perplexes me why people turn to modern spiritual teachers who claim to be conduits of spiritual knowledge when all they do is reiterate the words that have been said a thousand times before. Sure, many people are seekers of truth, knowledge, and a better life, but all these false profits do is to capitalize upon this seeking and this desire for a more enlightened and spiritual life to make a living and gain ego gratification for themselves.

Oftentimes, these people speak of, *"Energy,"* how and why an individual should live a certain way and how by doing so All-Things will be better for them and for the world. But, they do not speak about this subject from a space of pure knowledge. They speak from the place of ego, or *"I am teaching and you are learning."* Mostly, they speak to people who will pay to hear them speak.

This is not true spirituality! If a person is not an ideal conduit of what they are saying, they are a false profit. Investigate whom you are listening to.

Let's examine this a bit further…

About a month ago I was asked to speak at a symposium. As I took the stage the announcer said, *"Here's Scott Shaw the author of many best-selling books and a spiritual teacher."* I immediately interrupted him, *"I am not a spiritual teacher, I am just a guy you asked to come here and speak."* He was a bit taken back. The crowd all laughed. The lecture went on.

You can call me a martial arts instructor. I have the certifications. You can call me a professor. I have the degrees and I teach at the universities. But, I never refer to myself as a, *"Spiritual teacher."* Anyone who does is false unless they are truly living the life.

For example, when I was Swami Satchidananda's soundman, I would travel with him and at every venue he spoke there would be hundreds of people in attendance. Sometimes thousands. He lived what he taught and people understood that. That's why he was so sought after as a speaker.

Now, I am not saying he was perfect. I have discussed him in other writings. But, I will say, he was who he was and he did not pretend to be anything else.

A funny story relating to this occurred at the Los Angeles Integral Yoga Institute. A few of the Swamis were complaining about one of the disciples preparing and drinking coffee in the morning. They asked *Gurudev* about this. He joking answered, *"No coffee in the ashrams. That's why I don't live in the ashram because I like to drink coffee."*

That is truth. That is honesty. That is true spirituality.

He was not some fake, pretending to hold knowledge that he did not possess, while attempting to lure people under his spell to make money, live high on the hog, and make a name for himself teaching regurgitated words. He was who he was: whole and honest.

Here we arrive at one of the biggest problems of modern spirituality and those who teach it – the people who are doing it, and doing it wrongly, operate themselves and what they teach like a business. Spiritual truth and enlightenment are not a business. It should not be run like one. Yet, these so-called teachers run a publicity and marketing campaign like one would put in place for a business. They knowingly try to lure in more clients.

That is simply wrong. If you speak the truth, truth seekers will find their way to you. You do not need to say or do anything to get them to listen.

This is my problem, (and it should be yours), with modern spiritual teachers. If someone is charging you for the knowledge they have to offer, there is something wrong in the equation. Knowledge, truth, and enlightenment are free. You should not have to extend any of your money, (or anything else), in order to receive spiritual teachings.

So why do these so-called teachers charge for their services? Because they are simply selling you their ego.

As mentioned earlier, many of these fakes turn to the subject of, *"Energy."* Energy has been one of the common focal points of spirituality since the New Age arrived. They will state, *"Your energy is this. Your energy is that. You need to change your energy. You need to focus your energy."* But, what is energy? It is one of those nondescript things that anyone can call up and put their own unique definition upon. As it is not defined, it is one of the biggest factors of deception on the spiritual path. If someone is talking about your energy or cosmic energy they are simply using long spoken of false tactics to guide you in the direction they want you to go. And, moreover, energy is one of those things that they can blame when a person does not achieve what they had hoped, *"You didn't put enough energy into it."* Or, *"Your energy was not pure and focused enough."* Nonsense!

Let's look at this process from a bit of a different perspective…

If you want to look to a successful teacher of this modern era and veer away from specifically eastern knowledge for a moment, Anthony Robbins is an ideal personage. He came from a relatively middle-class background and now owns mansions, islands, and all the trapping of pure success. He accomplished this by studying human consciousness and then packaging his studies into a highly defined method that could actual help people move forward and rise up in their life.

I must state, I am not a fan of him or his teaching, but he does provide an ideal example of a success story based upon helping to raise human consciousness and what can be achieved.

There are people like myself who knowingly attempt to live a humble life in a reserved manner. Then, there are people like Tony Robbins who exist on a grand scale. The problem is, there are a plethora of false teachers who claim knowledge, yet they cannot even focus this knowledge to the degree to live at that higher financial level embraced by people like Tony Robbins or Deepak Chopra, yet they aspire to it. Therefore, what does that say about what a modern teacher has to offer you if it isn't even precise enough to cause such a financial income that they can live on the large scale they desire? What it says is that they are trying to use hype and your desire to know more to get you to pay for what they have to offer so they can climb the ladder. But, that style of teaching and the foundational elements that go into it are just not right. Thus, they will never succeed in their aspiration but may damage the lives of a lot of people while they try.

If a teacher is not an ideal expression of what they are teaching, if a teacher is repeating words that can be heard everywhere else, if a teacher is not a true embodiment of the energy they guide their students to embrace, they are a false profit.

Don't follow false profits.

## Why Are You Feeling What You Are Feeling?
18/Mar/2014 12:28 PM

If you are happy, you are happy. If you are angry, you are angry. If you are sad, you are sad. Okay... But, why?

What makes one person happy makes another person angry. Why is that? It is the complete opposite of emotions yet it is brought about by the same causation factor.

People feel what they feel. For each of us there are things that make us happy, mad, sad, glad, and all of the emotions in-between. But, how much time do you spend analyzing why you feel what you feel? How much time do you spend questioning how you will act or react to an emotion before you do something based upon that emotion?

Most people never bother. They feel what they feel which causes them to do what they do. They simply are guided by their emotions and never take the time to wonder, *"Why am I feeling this way?"*

This is the reason that so much of life is dominated by emotions and why so many bad things are accomplished dominated by emotions. ...People never take the time to look deeply within themselves and gain a true definition of whom they are and why they are the way they are. In fact, most people don't care. They dismiss any question of, *"Why?"* They simply move through life guided by a desire to feel a particular way. If that emotion is accomplished, great! If not, look out; they are going to be horrible to be around.

Anger is an uncontrolled emotion. Therefore it is a negative emotion. Feelings of happiness, love, joy, and fulfillment are controlled emotions. Thus, they are seemingly positive emotions. But, love can turn to hate very quickly if another person emotionally hurts someone else – if one person does not behave in the manner the other person wishes that they behave. As such, all emotions, even seemingly positive ones, can become negative emotions very quickly.

If you do not take the time to gain a true definition of self, of whom you truly are, and why you feel the way you feel, you will forever be dominated by emotion; which may not only make you feel terrible but may guide you down the road to hurting other people.

Take the time to know you. And realize, emotions are temporary things – stop doing anything that hurts another person based upon them. Let go of a mindset of control and dominance. Let people be who they are and do what they do. No longer let emotions be the dominant defining factor for you doing what you do. The world will be a better place.

**Is That Who You Are?**

18/Mar/2014 12:12 PM

A few years ago I was sitting around having lunch with a friend of mine and he asked, *"Is that who you are? ...A cult filmmaker."*

For the record, I never considered myself a *Cult Filmmaker*. A *Zen Filmmaker,* yes. But, a *Cult Filmmaker,* no.

What I do is to make something out of nothing. I use available sets, urban and rural locations that I find visually interesting, create and guide the actor's dialogue on the spot, and make a film out of what occurs from this process.

Yes, my mind is a bit abstract, so I commonly, (but not always), explore abstract realms of reality in my films, but that does not make them cult. They simply are what they are.

As I am frequently questioned about this fact... The difference between the *Zen Films* that I have made and the ones that I made in association with Donald G. Jackson is that I am acutely organized and time orientated. I bring people on the set so they can work, get their part done, and then go home. Like I always say, *"Give me a few hours of your life and I will make you a star."* Don, on the other hand, was complete chaos. His idea was that we would congregate as many people as we could get, drive to far off locations in multiple cars, and then (maybe) the people who we cast would get a part in the film. But, many times they did not. Few, ever got the part they thought that they would get. He did this, while spending all kinds of money, buying people all kinds of food and stuff like that.

A side note: (and I have mentioned this in other writings), Don was the biggest waster of money I have ever met. If he did not spend money on everybody and everything, he would have been quite rich. But, because he always paid for breakfast, lunch, and dinner for everybody, paid for the concerts, the clubs, the movies, the strip clubs, and everything else, paid for his various girlfriend's rent, and paid for more boob jobs than I can even count, he was most often broke. He did this, and no one ever appreciated what he was doing for them.

I learned from him though. I learned what not to do. It's just not fair to make people believe that they are going to get a part in a film, travel to a location, and then nothing – zero. And, it certainly is a waste of energy to spend all your money on people who do not appreciate it.

This is also why more films that involved Don Jackson came out after his death than while he was alive. We would film stuff, he would lose interest, then he would hide the footage away somewhere in his house. Nearing his death, he gave all the footage to me. Thus, all the movies we did could finally be constructed and completed. In fact, more than a decade after his life, I still have a few more to put together.

To me, this is the filmmaker I am. I get it done.

Anyway, that's just to answer or re-answer many of the questions I receive about what went on between Don Jackson and myself and how we were the same and/or different...

To the point... Like my friend, I understand that many people consider me a *Cult Filmmaker.* But, here lies one of the key factors of life: people see you, the way they see you. They define you, the way they define you. That does not make their definition correct, however, that simply makes it their definition.

Who you are, is who you are, defined by what you do. If what you do causes people to have an incorrect opinion of you, you have two options. One, you can fight to make them understand. But, the reality of life is most people never step out of their own head long enough to truly understand anyone or anything. They see something, conceive their definition, and that is that. Your second option is the one I choose to employee – just be who you are. By encountering life in this manner, the people who are open and understanding enough will come to you and let you be who you actually are without attempting to define you by some incorrect definition.

Don't get caught up in seeking definitions, it makes life far too inaccurate.

### "I'm still young."

18/Mar/2014 08:14 AM

I forever think that it is strange when you are talking to different people, discussing different situations, and these differing people make the same statement about completely different subjects. This recently happen to me when a few people I was speaking with all made the statement, *"I'm still young."*

Youth is great. For people to realize that they are young and define themselves by it is even better. Me, I never felt young. I grew up fast, had little, if any, parental supervision. The fact is, where and how I grew up, I didn't want any. But, that's just me...

Youth is really something people should hold onto because it is gone so quickly. Old people are old, right?

I remember the first time I realized this. It was when I was a young boy and my grandmother took me to the beauty parlor with her. There I was with all of these elderly ladies who were getting the same hairdo. You know the look: short, curly, white hair with a tint of blue due to whatever it is that the beautician is putting into their hair. All the old ladies rock that look.

I have long noticed that for some strange reason many women gravitate towards that hairstyle. With each year of age, they cut their hair shorter and shorter. Many do this even before they have gone grey. Why is that? Why do people want to be old? Why can't they keep their hair longer? It really looks so much better when they do.

I believe this is all based on something I long ago realized... When people are in their late teens and early twenties, everything is about style – whatever it is they deem their style to be. Then, as they get older, conformity sets it. They merge with the masses and project themselves as what is deemed appropriate by the dominant culture. I think this is very sad... Sad, how few people hold onto their own unique style. Sadder still, that so few people embrace youth and instead choose conformity and age.

Now, I am not saying people should be like those eighty year old women who wear miniskirts, are all inked-up, have their hair dyed blonde, and believe that nobody notices how old they really are. I am saying embrace the youth in the space of your life you find yourself in.

We all get old. Old is brought about by many varying circumstances. Sure, there is biological age – but in many ways that is very relative. But, I believe more definitive things happen in people's lives that kicks in, *"The old."*

For example, I have this elderly lady who is my neighbor. She was always so full of energy and spunk. Then, maybe six months ago her kids took her car away.

Believe me, I can understand the reason why – there are way too many old people out there on the road who just should no longer be behind the wheel. Yet, they are. But, this lady wasn't like that. She was very astute and conscious.

In any case, I bumped into her the other day and we made small talk, as we tend to do. Man, the age has hit her hard. It came overnight. Obviously based upon the fact that she no longer has a way to get around. And, the area we live in is far from everything. So, without a car you are really stuck.

The kids took her car; she got old. That was her motivating factor. Other people have their own. But, I believe you really need to fight, *"The old,"* as long as you can. Do what you can. Live in a space of doing the things you can to keep, *"The Young,"* alive.

There is no absolute cure. We are all dominated by two of the primary factors of life. They are: if we live long enough, we all get old, and we all die. But, choosing to live youth is a far better alternative than accepting age and being dominated by who and what you are expected to be by a certain age in the short space of time we call our lifetime.

Age is relative. Do not let is slip away. Embrace youth.

# Hollywood: The Impossible Game

17/Mar/2014 08:40 AM

People come to Hollywood everyday hoping to become stars. Once here, they pay hundreds of dollars to get headshots, pay thousands of dollars to take acting classes from teacher who, themselves, have never appeared in film, T.V., or commercials to any substantial degree, if at all. Then, if the person is lucky enough to get an agent, they will buy clothing for auditions that they have no hope of getting, believe that they are actually appearing in something when they are only an extra in a film or on a television show, (FYI it is very easy to get extra work), buy video cameras to practice in front of, and this list goes on and on.

As someone who was born in Hollywood, I have a bit of unique perspective. In fact, I used to walk to Hollywood High School down the boulevard of the stars everyday until I got a car and then I drove down Hollywood Blvd. to get to school. I lived between Hollywood and Sunset Blvd. So, I saw all of it, the whole Hollywood game from a very inside perspective. This is what caused me to never want to be involved in the film industry. But, I too fell prey to many of the drawbacks once I gave into the curse when I thirty-two years old. In other words, I know what it's like. The stories I could tell you...

All this is also why I go out of my way to help young actors and filmmakers wherever I can – because I know that most who come here will never achieve anything except maybe an overextended credit card bill.

Like I always tell young actors and actresses who delve into the indie film market, ninety-nine percent of the people who hope to make a film will never complete it because they do not have the focus, the finances, or the dedication to do it, so be careful. This same premise is why I developed *Zen Filmmaking.* To help those young filmmakers get past some of the hurdles and actually make their dreams become a reality.

But, let's face facts; Hollywood is an impossible game. Sure, some people do come from nowhere and actually make-it. Good for them! But, what is the truth behind their success? We will probably never know.

And, think about this, how many actors who had a T.V. series that you really liked or where in a movie that you remember, disappeared and were never heard from again. They had success for a second and then they were gone. Where did they go?

That is the truth about Hollywood; many people come here, most leave with only broken dreams. The others may have a moment of success and then they are gone. The few who make it, by talent, luck, *karma*, whatever, are the blessed ones. But, the main thing is, if you come here; never fall under the illusion that anyone or anything – that any about success will make you more than you already are.

Success is internal. Everything else can be taken away from you or it can simply fade away.

Hollywood, it is an impossible game. Fortunately, or perhaps more than likely, unfortunately; it is where I am from.

Like the line I fed one of my actor's in the *Zen Film, Samurai Vampire Bikers from Hell,* "Hollywood? Hollywood's just a state of mind."

## What Do You Do When It All Goes Away?
16/Mar/2014 08:30 AM

*"What do you do when it all goes away?"* This is a question that few people ask themselves. And, a question that most people never want to confront. But, it is something that each person should consider as it can happen in a moment and everything can change overnight.

I, personality, have had it happen to my life more than once, and I can tell you, it is very scary.

Everything going away can come about by any number of means: a loved one's death, sickness, an act of god like an earthquake, tornado, hurricane, or tsunami, a car accident, being cheated by another person, being robbed, getting fired, and so on. In most of these cases, it happens in an instant and then life as you know it is gone – it has changed forever and there is nothing that you can do to alter the cards you were dealt.

In these cases, some people turn to family, friends, or their savings account for assistance. But, this is the modern world, few people have substantial saving accounts anymore, few people have friends that will really stand behind them the moment the going gets tough for more than a moment or two, and many people do not have families they can turn to for help. In fact, when most people encounter a time of crisis, other people who are not going through the same trauma commonly shun them or make them feel guilty or stupid for not being MORE.

This is why you must question, *"What will I do when it all goes away?"* Because when it is gone that means it is gone.

Now, family is great support network. But, some people, including myself, have no remaining blood relatives and others are estranged from their family. So, when there is no one to turn to, where do you turn?

When you are young, it is a common practice to draw from the sustenance of your family. But, I have known people that have lived in their parent's home way longer than they should have simply to keep from forcing themselves to go out there, become an adult, and make a life and a living for themselves. These people make all kinds of excuses for this behavior, but at the end of the day they are setting themselves up for a hard fall, as they have not established any true self-created existence for themselves.

In fact, in a few of these cases, these people lived in this environment waiting for their parents to pass away in order to gain possessions like the family home, family monies, and so on. But, in each of these cases, I have watched these people squander whatever their parents had amassed, as they did not understand what it truly meant to forge a living for themselves, and then they were totally destitute when it was all gone.

Friends too. ...They are what appear to be a great support network. They are always there to give you advice, to hate the person you hate, and to hang out when times are good. Let times go bad, however, and will they give you a place to live for free forever? Probably not. Couch surfing gets pretty old, pretty quick. And, friendships can go by the wayside quite quickly when you are the person in need.

Have you even known someone who has gone through a major crisis in his or her life that was not a blood relative? Did you help them? How long did you stand by them?

Many people rely on their jobs and believe them to be their pathway to the future. In these modern days, however, we have seen so many companies going out of business that it is not even funny. From this, many people have been robbed of their livelihoods and even their pensions. And, with so many people being forced from their jobs that there are not enough jobs to fill the employment needs. Then what?

People also get fired from their job. This can happen for all kinds of reasons. It can be downsizing, personality conflict, it can even be the individual's own fault, but whatever the case, in an instant, life, as they knew it, is over.

I'm not even going to go into massive climatic, geological, or nuclear disaster here as we have all seen the results of that on T.V. But, then what?

The, *"Then what,"* is an abstract question. Hopefully it will never happen to you. But, for those of us it has happened to – for those of us who had people die – for those of us who believed in people and were turned away – for those of us who took massive financial hits at the hands of others – for those of us who had our lives changed by the unthinking actions of others, we know what is out there. We understand what can happen. Then what?

Now, I could list a number of personal examples that have happened to me, but I will save you from that. I will simply state, that I know what I am talking about when it comes to this question and how it feel when there is no one reaching out a hand of help. I could also provide you with a long list of people I have seen this happen to and there was nothing I could do to change their reality. From this, a few I have known have chosen to leave this Life-Place. As such, *"Then what,"* becomes the ultimate question of life and they chose to answer the question with death. They believed that was their only option. Death was their choice – their ultimate Life-Choice.

What do you do when it all goes away?

What do you do if it all goes away? Think about it.

# What Happened to the Sword?

15/Mar/2014 07:44 AM

I have recently been receiving a bunch of questions about what happened to the samurai sword I used in *The Roller Blade Seven* and do I still have it? In fact, one person offered to buy it from me for quite a substantial amount of money.

Actually, I used that same sword in a few samurai based movies I did back in the early 1990s: *Samurai Vampire Bikers from Hell,* (a minor shot in) *Samurai Johnny Frankenstein,* and in *Samurai Ballet.* Then, I put it to rest for a long-long time. I used a different sword in *Max Hell Frog Warrior* and *Guns of El Chupacaba.*

By my nature, I am not a collector of THINGS. In fact, I frequently do a house cleaning, getting rid of all kinds of stuff that most people would probably keep forever and other people may have been interested in possessing as collector's items. This includes other film-based items I have been questioned about including the sunglasses and the suit I wore in *Roller Blade Seven,* my rollerblades from the film, the frog masks from *Max Hell,* (that were also used in *Hell Comes to Frogtown),* the chupcabra costume (that cost like thirty-grand to have made), and so on. In fact, I can't even tell you when I tossed most of that stuff. For me, the clearing out of stuff is a very freeing, cathartic experience. ...Getting rid of the old energy and allowing the new to come in.

The sword I actually kept for quite awhile. In fact, it is the sword I used in the climatic scene in *Vampire Abstracta* AKA *Vampire Sunrise.* Just prior to filming that movie I found it hiding in storage and I decided to give it one more appearance on the silver screen.

The fact of the matter is, by then, (actually by way back when), the sword was pretty trashed and falling apart. Though it was an interesting piece in my cinematic history, I knew it was time to let it rest. So after filming *Vampire Abstracta,* I took it apart, said a few mystical prayers over it, thanked it, and I said my goodbyes. Then, I sent it to sword heaven in the never-never-land of the *Zen Films* forever. So, to the potential buyer,

*"Sorry, it is no more. Though believe me, if I still had it, I would have happily sold it to you for the amount you offered."*

In any case, life moves on. I try not to be bound by THINGS. If you are, then you are always worried about those items getting damaged or stolen. I try to live my life a bit freer than that.

# Three Butterflies

14/Mar/2014 08:41 AM

Today, when I was driving around listening to KCRW I looked to the sky while I was at a stoplight and I saw a really pretty yellow butterfly fly by. I pointed it out to my lady, which caused us to reminisce how a week or so ago, when we were walking, returning from a local park, we saw this really large black, fuzzy caterpillar, on the sidewalk. She tried to remember what color butterfly a black caterpillar turns into, and me, I hoped no one would step on it, as we really need new butterflies.

You know, when I was a kid I saw butterflies all the time. Then, in the late 1980s, the powers-that-be decided it was a good idea to spray the insecticide Malathion across So-Cal to kill off whatever invasive insect was encroaching on the region. Helicopters would fly over late at night or in the early morning hours spraying the poison and BAM they were gone. Also gone, however, were the butterflies. Their populations have never recovered. So, now it is very rare to see them.

A bit later in the day I had parked in a parking lot and I saw another butterfly fly by, a bright orange one. Then, a bit later we saw a third large butterfly flying by – through the urban skyline. What a great sight! When you see butterflies fly... It just makes life so much better.

But sadly, this is L.A., and Butterflies have become so rare. ...So rare that you really take notice when you see them in the sky.

Something has really been lost, I believe. Lost, by the hands of man and lost to this modern age. Lost... And, the only thing that has been gained is a world where butterfly are no longer in abundance. We really need to do something about that.

# Radio Show

13/Mar/2014 08:31 AM

I was being interviewed at a radio station a couple of weeks ago and out of nowhere the DJ asked, *"What do you think is the best rock song ever?"* Wow... What a question.

My answer was, *"I believe there are three: The Doors, Light My Fire, Jimi Hendrix's version of, All Along the Watchtower, and Neil Young's, Like a Hurricane."*

The DJ continued, *"But, what if you had to choose just one?"* *"I can't..."* He then questioned, *"All right then, what do you believe is the best rock album ever?"* I answered, *"The Doors."*

You know, there are people and there are bands out there that change everything. Then, there are people who really make what is, the best it can be. Hendrix changed the way the electric guitar was played forever. And, there have been people, like *The Doors,* and Neil Young who have come be ideal illustrations of a genre.

Rock has evolved. Punk changed everything. Bands like *The Ramones* and the *Sex Pistols* changed the perception of everybody. Then, there are the early proponents of Punk like *The Weirdos* and *Black Flag* who laid the foundations for the exaggeration of the movement.

There are also the overlooked. People like Junior Brown and his Guit-Steel. Though based primarily in the Country-Western genre, he is one of the most amazing stringed instrument players ever. Yet, few have ever even heard of him.

Rap or Hip Hop came through to the public initially via people like *Kurtis Blow* and groups like *The Sugar Hill Gang.* Again, a genre took form and it changed the evolution of human consciousness.

The DJ's question got me to thinking that the sad fact is, though music has continued to evolve and there have been some great proponents who have come and gone over the years, there has been no revolution changing the minds and temperaments of humanity rising from the music industry in a long-long time.

By the way, the interview that was scheduled and the radio show I was on was supposed to be about living in the now and how one should do just that. So much for format and scheduling...

# Through the Walls

12/Mar/2014 08:28 AM

I spent the last few days in Yosemite and I had an interesting experience. Well actually, I had a couple of interesting experiences on this recent trip but I will speak about one of them now.

I was staying at the *Yosemite Lodge.* In recent years they have been doing a lot of upgrading on both the *Yosemite Lodge* and the *Ahwahnee Hotel;* the two hotels in the Yosemite Valley. I bounce between the two of them on my excursion to the valley. A lot of upgrades... But, the one issue they have not addressed, at either of the hotels, is the fact that the walls are paper-thin and you can hear pretty much anything your next-door neighbor says or does.

Okay, that's the backstory...

On the night in question, we had an elderly lady saying in the room next to us. She was very rude, unthinking, and unconscious about the fact that there was someone in the room next to here. Her T.V. volume was on high, she spoke loudly on the phone, and so on. My lady friend and I even commented that she was actually much louder than the Korean family, with a couple of kids, we had staying next to us the night before. But, what can you do? This is just the way the Yosemite Lodge is. So, you shut up and deal with it.

Anyway, we were sitting around in the evening enjoying a nice bottle of the grape from the Toscana region of Italy, (my favorite), and quietly discussing: life, love, god, and things in general. We hear her T.V. turn off. *"Great,"* I thought. A few moments later, I hear her get on the phone, call the front desk, and ask them to contact the room next to her as we were being loud and this is, as she put it, *"Quite hour."* What!

What she was really saying is that, *"Now, that I am done being rude, unconscious, uncaring, and unthinking about how my actions are affecting anybody else, I want everyone else to be silent so I can go to sleep."* This was a first for me, being complained upon. ...Because I always try to be conscious of other people's space, even in a situation like this.

There was a part of me that wanted to scream through the wall, *"Are you fucking kidding me!"* But, I chilled and said nothing. A bit later we hear the footsteps of the security guard, (or whomever), walking on the wooden planks outside our room – obviously checking out the woman's story. I could hear him walk away as we were obviously doing nothing out of the appropriate. Had he knocked, I would have had a few choice words for everyone involved. Luckily, he did.

But, what did occur from the actions of this woman was that our evening was ruined. Not only had she been rude prior to her phone call with all the noise she was making, but then she made that selfish phone call. My lady decided it was best to just go to bed and to go to sleep. So, I poured the rest of the wine down the sink and climbed in between the sheets.

The moral of this story is, most people do what they do based upon a completely selfish mindset. They never step outside of themselves long enough to study or even care about the affect they are having on others – even their next-door neighbor. Over the past year or so I have encountered this, *"Through the walls,"* life-fucking experience a few times at the hands of other people. There is always the initial desire to scream, *"Shut up,"* but if you do this then you are the one who becomes the villain because the person next to you is obviously living in space of enhanced unconsciousness.

The thing about this whole matter of unconscious existence is that it permeates this Life-Place. Most people are bound by it and could less about the affect they having on other – no matter where they are. That is, until it happens to them.

The fact of the matter is, even if you bring a person's rude behavior to their attention, most people are so dominated by lack of self-awareness or lack of caring about anyone else that they do not even express an apology, they simply carry on with their own life, as they believe themselves to be the center of the universe. So, aside from being deaf, what can you do? I don't know… This is just life.

From my perspective, I always try to extend my consciousness to include others in hopes that I may keep people in my surroundings from paying for my realm(s) of life. I always study where I find myself and try to keep the effect of ME from affecting others. But, that's just me…

Ultimately, you can do what you can do to make this Life-Space better. You can do it the best way you can do it. But, the reality is, at the end of the day, your life my still be altered by the unconscious actions of others. That's not right, but this is life.

# I Don't Like Looking At Bad Things

08/Mar/2014 09:00 AM

Don't you hate it when you click to a webpage and you really hate the images and you try to click away but for whatever reason you are held there for a moment that seems like hours?

Don't you hate it when you are watching TV and there is a really violent scene or something really bad, ugly, or disturbing taking place and you try to change the channel but your remote or box freezes up and it takes what seems like an eternity for the channel to change?

Then, these images are locked in your brain. There, but you don't want them to be there. There, but you never wanted to see them in the first place. But, it is you who is stuck with them in your brain. Sometimes these images are remember forever...

Some people like horror movies. Now, I'm not talking about old-school horror movies; those weren't that scary. They were, in fact, kind of fun. But, modern horror movies – with all the expanding technology, from the 1970s forward, man those can be pretty gory.

Me, I don't like them. I don't want those images in my brain.

Some people like to watch violent movies, where people are injured, hurt, and/or killed in a very bad way. I've even known some filmmakers who make movies like that.

Me, I am not about that. I don't like it. Watching violence; even simulated violence, is just not fun and/or nice. Plus, it leaves horrible images in your mind about the potential, (or lack there of), within humanity.

Bad is always bad. Violence is always violence. Depicting horror within humanity and the bad things that people can do only cast these horrible actions to eternity. Sadly, our world has embellished the bad, honored the violent criminals for so long, that bad is emulated, honored, and projected all around us. This, when many of us, including myself, never want to see it.

Let the bad dissipate.

# Beauty in the Abstract

07/Mar/2014 01:22 PM

    I was over in the LBC (Long Beach) today. I was driving down the street and came up to a stoplight. There were two guys standing on the corner waiting for the light to change. They both had skateboards in their hands and one was also holding up a bicycle. The light changed. The two guys tossed down their skateboards and kicked off. The one guy, with the bike, pushed the bike next to him as the pair crossed the street and faded off into the distance while riding their skateboards. Interesting…

    You know, all the questions ran through my mind as to why the guy would push the bike and ride the skateboard, and all those kinds of thoughts. But ultimately, I realized it didn't matter. Art is art. Beauty is beauty. And, there is beauty in the art of abstraction when life does not follow its common-course and you get to witness new and different things that cause your mind to shift its patterns of the commonality of everyday thought. Very Zen…

    There is beauty and there is art everywhere. In some places, however, you are simply more apt to see it. I suggest everyone live in a place where there is an abundance of unexpected street art.

# Venting

07/Mar/2014 07:31 AM

Have you ever noticed that you meet some people and you can just feel their anger and dissatisfaction at life? It is revealed in the subtleties of their words and in the way they speak and the way they interact with you and with other people. Commonly, this energy can be felt long before you even really get to know the person.

The thing about this is, witnessing this obviousness in a person's character is only a precursor to what is to come. An angry person is an angry person and they do and say things that alter the balance of life.

We all get angry. We get angry at how people behave towards us, what people do to us, and our situation in life. This, and a million more things causes anger to grow in each of us. Most people, however, feel whatever anger they feel, for whatever amount of time they feel it, and then they let it go. Others, however, become defined by their anger. This causes all kinds of problems in the life of that person and the lives of others that this person has the ability to interact with.

Anger causes people to explode. It causes them to vent. Meaning, they may yell, scream, throw things, punch a wall, beat up someone, and/or do whatever it is they have to do to express their anger in a physical manner. But, all of these actions only lead to one thing, destruction.

On one of journeys to India I spent time with the spiritual teacher, Bhagwan Shree Rajneesh, who latter became known as Osho. He developed a meditation technique where people would go through a cathartic episode: jump, yell, scream, and supposedly release all of their tension. Though in theory, this all sounds good. But, expressing of anger or frustration in this matter does not get to its source and cure it. Even yelling at the person or persons who makes you angry does not heal any hurt. All it does is amplify the anger and perhaps lead to new problems that may cause additional anger. Or, it may cause the anger you feel to be reciprocated towards you, which them becomes a never-ending circle.

People express anger and frustration in many ways in this modern age. This is due to the fact that no longer are relationships based solely upon a one-on-one dynamic. Relationships span the globe and human consciousness via the internet. Many people believe they are actually friends with people they have never even met. But, if you ever watch shows like, Catfish, (the MTV series), it can easily be seen that oftentimes people on the other end of the internet are not who or what they seem.

People also express their anger or dissatisfaction with life on the internet. In some cases this become quite amusing. You can find them attacking other people that they do not even know. Sometimes they use multiple screen names but by their grammatical style you can conclude it is one person. All this and more, people do crazy things to express their anger.

But, you must remember, the anger any person feels is based in Them-Self. If you are angry, it is only you who is angry.

Think about this, *"Who is angry?"* You are. Is the person next to you, who you do not know, angry? No, they are not.

They are they. You are you. They feel what they feel. You feel what you feel. What this means is that there is no commonality to anger.

Sure, there is mob mentality, where a small or large group of people congregates and feed off of each other's anger and dissatisfaction, causing it to grow. But, that is not the sourcepoint of anger. You are the sourcepoint of any anger you feel. And, only you are in control of you.

If you are a conscious person, if you are on the path of consciousness, anytime you feel anger, you must question, *"Why am I angry?"* You must do this before you take any action. Because action based in anger only cause the natural balance of life to shift and become unbalanced. From this, anger only escalates because people become angry at you for your reaction to being angry at whatever it is you are angry at.

Anger perpetuates anger. All this leads to is a lack of disharmony.

Venting or expressing anger in a physical manner does not make the anger go away. Just as Rajneesh's meditation techniques did not free anyone from anything, it only gave them something to do for a little while.

Anger begins with you. It must end with you. The less you do based upon an angry mindset, the less you will have to make up for in the future.

See the truth, your anger is simply based in your dissatisfaction with your desires not being met. Go to your inner source any time you feel anger, define the root cause for why you feel what you feel, and then become more than your anger. Control it as opposed to it controlling you.

If you do this, believe me, the world will be a better place.

# Internet Piracy Is Not a Victimless Crime

06/Mar/2014 08:08 AM

I was flipping through channels last night and I came upon the *Arsenio Hall Show.* Prince was on.

At first glance, this show was kind of interesting in that this same show could have taken place twenty years ago when Arsenio's first late show was on the air. But, there they were, Arsenio and Prince both looking quite good for their age.

I was never a really big fan of Prince back in the day. Though me, being who I am, I do own all his vinyl and most of his CDs. It was later that I came to appreciate his music and his contribution to popular music in general. This, though I do have an abstract connection to Prince in that my high school friend, Lisa Coleman, was his keyboard player for a number of years in the Purple Rain era and an actor, Kevin Thompson, who I have used in a number of my films was a Prince impersonator until that era dried up. In any case, it was an interesting show to watch.

When Arsenio was talking to Prince they discussed his love and hate relationship with the internet and how music gets out-there for free which really impacts an artist's bankbook. Though Prince made his own contribution to the changing evolution of music by being one of the first artists to break away from a major record label, what he said made me think back to the time when the whole Napster thing took place and there were a lot of musicians out there rallying against people getting their music for free. I remember when they spoke to Dave Grohl, *(Nirvana, Foo Fighters, etc.),* and he said, *"Why should I care, I'm already rich."* I believe that is an important, and oftentimes overlooked statement to keep in mind when one views this subject.

There is a certain group of people who now expect to get everything for free on the internet – whether it is music, movies, books, or whatever. But, by taking those items for free you are really causing the person who created those things to not earn money for their creation. As money is one of the most essential elements to life, it is what we must have to survive. And, by taking these creations for free, you are really creating *karma* for yourself.

It is one of the most instrumental laws of understood spirituality; do not take things for free or steal things because then *karma* is created. One should always extend a payment for whatever they receive, as then *karma* remains clean.

But to view this subject in a little bit more in-depth manner; first of all, do you think the websites who host these downloads are doing it for free? No, they are not. They are earning money by being in existence or they would not be there.

From a more philosophic standpoint, (if you want to make excuses for yourself), downloading movies and music financed by major studios or corporation can be viewed as, *"Sticking it to the man,"* if you want to view life from an anarchistic point of view. But, for people like myself or on a much higher scale, someone like Prince, who finances all we do out of our own pockets, it becomes a very different ballgame. For me, I can't make the same claim as Dave Grohl. So, every dime taken out of my pocket really changes my reality.

The other side of the issue is that there is nothing I can do about it. My books, music, and movies are out there on this offshore websites being offered for free. Do the people or corporations who run those websites care about what affect they are having on me and the other creative people in my predicament? Probably not. Why? Because they are generating money to support their lifestyle based on the creations of others.

There is just something wrong in that equitation.

This is what people really need to think about when they do what they do, whether it be downloading things for free, without thinking about what effect it has on the creator of the work, or simply not taking the time to think about the impact they are having on this world by their various actions.

What you choose to do and how you choose to do it affects everything in this world. How you choose to live your life affects the next evolution of this Life-Place. So, if you are doing things that negatively impact other people, don't cry when *karma* comes calling. Because you are the one who set it in motion.

Internet piracy is not a victimless crime. And, the victim may end up being you.

## Why Do You Believe?

06/Mar/2014 07:23 AM

Whenever I teach a course on filmmaking I always begin by explaining the number one rule of filmmaking to the students. The number one rule of filmmaking is, *"Everybody lies."* Meaning, that in the film game everybody lies about everything. They lie about their credits, their abilities, their training, their film's cast, crew, equipment, budget, EVERYTHING.

It is pretty easy for the students to understand this concept when I detail this fact. But, let's think about life. How different is it? Not much…

People lie. It is a simple fact of life. They lie for an untold number of reasons. But, the fact of the matter is, they do lie.

The problem that arises here is that the average person is schooled to believe what a person says is, in fact, the truth. Unless an individual is caught in an outright lie, what they speak is believed to be true. In fact, most people want to believe what another person says. But, people lie… They distort the truth to use it to their own ends. They lie to gain power, control, self-worth, wealth, fame, whatever, in order to gain whatever it is they hope to gain by altering the boundaries of the truth.

This lying goes on everywhere in life. Whether it is a small white-lie or a massive deception; lying is one of the dominant factors of life. It exists in person-to-person relationships, certainly it is abundant on the internet, and it also flourishes within religious and spiritual communities, even though most would hope and think this is not the case.

All lying begins with one sourcepoint. It begins with you.

Ask yourself, *"How many times have you lied?"* Also, question yourself, *"Why did you distort the truth? What did you hope to gain?"*

To each person there will be a somewhat differing answer. But, the root action is the same, a lie was told.

Let's think about this for a moment, *"What happens when you lie?"* The answer is, another person makes a choice, based upon a false set of facts. From this, though you may gain what you had hoped for, the other person's life is altered forever.

Let's also question, *"What is the consequence of your lies."* If you are not caught, most people feel they got away with it. They gained whatever it is they hoped for. Thus, they won.

If you are caught in a lie, however, most people lie to get out of their original lie. But, it all ends up in the same place. People's lives are altered due to your falsehood and in many cases these people are left to progress through the rest of their life less than they would have been had you not lied.

And, I use the term, *"You,"* meaning everyone…

Some will say, *"Everyone lies. So, what's the difference?"* True, but all life begins with you. And, all life ends with you.

While you are here, in human form, you are an instrumental element in all the reality that surrounds you. As such, what you do affects EVERTHING. Thus, it is your choice how you want to create not only your world but also the world around you.

It is very simple; if you lie you hurt people. If they lie to you, they hurt you. The circle needs to be broken. Tell the truth.

**The Road You're On**

05/Mar/2014 08:16 AM

I used to have a couple of rules: no weddings and no funerals. But, then life comes along. You must do what you must do – obligations and responsibilities to meet. And, you can't stay an outcast forever. So, I sometime have to attend events I really have no desire of attending.

Yesterday, I had to attend a funeral. The funeral of a young man. He was only twenty years old. Done in by drugs.

Now, I wrote about this young man a year or so back in the *Scott Shaw Blog 2.0.* If you are interested you can find the passage in the book, *The Chronicles: Zen Ramblings from the Internet.* In any case, as detailed then, he was one of those kids with all kinds of promise. …Really smart and what looked to be a good future ahead of him. But, then things went array. His father, one of those guys from a high-end family, who never could quite find his path here in America. He lived off of the money of his parents who were based in South Korea. Once they died, his finances dried up and, in a fit of rage, he popped himself in the brain with a bullet, with his kid in the next room. The mother, a working stiff, tried to make things work, but the damage had been done.

The last time I saw the kid, he was recovering from stroking out on drugs. The stroke was so bad that when he returned home from the hospitable he couldn't even remember how to climb into his own bed. But, with physical therapy he recovered; more or less. But, he was still lost in the game. At family events he would be flashing gang signs in the family photos and so on…

*"Drugs are bad, okay…"* I am saying that like the *South Park* character, Mr. Garrison stated in an episode of the T.V. series. But, it is true, they are. They can really mess you up and kill you, like they did with this young man.

For the record, I am no stranger to drugs. I have known several people who have ended up in the hospitable due to drugs, a couple of people that have died from them. I, myself, wrote about an OD experience I had in the book, *Last Will and Testament According to the Divine Rites of the Drug Cocaine.* So,

I am not speaking from some self-righteous pedestal. But, from experience.

Not only can drugs kill you but they can also mess up your life and the lives of your family and the people around you. But, drugs are out there and people are going to do them – as did the aforementioned young man.

This is where the paradox begins. Like I said in one of my books, *"If drugs are so bad, why do they make you feel so good?"* But, when you look at the end-results, like I did yesterday, the conclusion you reach should be pretty obvious as to your reaction to the taking of drugs.

I have been embedded in Korean and Korean-American culture for all of my adult life and much of my youth. As such, there are certain protocols that are observed at the funeral of a Korean-American. Namely, an open casket. Though I try never to do the walk-by, as is common in funerals, as I was speaking to the young man's mother and grandmother yesterday I did see his face. Though I am sure they did all they could to prepare the body for viewing, you could tell this boy had died many hours before they found him. It was almost like a horror movie, the color of his skin.

Now, I am not trying to gross you out here. But, this is just a reminder of what death is; the end – disintegration of the body. But, this is the road this young man chose to walk. He took drugs. He ingested the type of drugs that commonly lead to death.

This is what you have to think about as you are living your life – as you are traveling down the road you are on. Where is it going to lead? What is the effect of what you are doing? And, how will it affect you and the others around you?

Life is short. All we have is what we do and how we live in this minuscule amount of time. As such, everybody needs to question, "What road am I on?"

# The Hoo Do

04/Mar/2014 07:30 AM

There is an energy that permeates this Life-Space. It is called many things by many people. Some base their entire life around attempting to control this energy. But, there is one that that is for sure; it is out there.

As someone who has spent their entire life walking in the realms of the mystical. Or, maybe better put, someone who has spent their entire life observing how the mystical interacts with life; I have witnessed many unusual things. And, I have met people who hold access to unique elements of this Life-Space and some who even hold control over certain elements of this aforementioned abstract energy.

Some people pray that they are not impacted by the control another person has on this energy: be it good or bad. Others claim that it does not exist. And, still others know that it is there but run from the fact that this energy is out there altogether. But, all one has to do is look at the facts of life and it is easily understood that there is energy out there and some people control it better than others.

Now, here is where it gets sticky. Sure, there are people out there who work with abstract universal energy and its control. But, these people are few and far between. Thus, if you stay out their energy sphere you have little to fear. The real problem comes from those who do not know what they are doing but yet in moments of anger, passion, jealousy, or whatever, control this universal energy and unleash it upon another. And, this happens in very subtle ways.

In some cases someone you know, deep-down-inside, does not want a positive change to happen for you. And, thus, out of nowhere, your chance to move forward is forever gone. They don't want you to change or to go so their unspoken prayers keep you locked where you are.

This is a complicated element of life. As such, it is also the basis for a lot of paranoia on the part of some people. It is also the subject that many a Christian sermon has been based up. Their answer is to pray for the protection of the lord. But, they too, (the ministers), want to hold you within their flock, so the question(s) must be asked, *"What is their motivation?"* and *"Who is exercising energy control over you now?"*

Mostly, the people who speak on this subject know little about the subtitles of energy, energy manipulation, and the conscious or unconscious energy-effect people have upon one another. This being said, the energy is still out there and it may affect you. What to do?

The best defense is to study who you associate with.

The fact of the matter is; certainly, in this modern life we all interact with people who we may not really like or we may dislike, *"Their energy."* Then, there are those who we like. But, just because we like someone does not mean that they do not have the potential to interrupt our lives or cause an outcome to our Life-Path that we do not desire.

This being said, look for the subtitles in all the people you meet and even those you already know. The truth of a person's being is very easy to see if you take the time to truly view it. All you have to do is to step back, turn off your thinking mind, and it is easily seen.

Watch life. Observe people. And, be silent in your hopes and desires – do not speak of them to others. From this, you will understand the energy of this Life-Place and you may be able to protect yourself from the misguided energy of another.

# Sometimes You Have To Try

03/Mar/2014 03:26 PM

In each of our lives opportunities are presented to us. We meet people, we receive offers, we have ideas, inspired by life-situations, and so on. But, it is us that must move on these opportunities if we hope to take the next step forward in our life.

This is the primary problem of why and how people get stuck in their Life-Space. ...They do not take the appropriate steps to move forward.

There is any number of for reason for this. Mostly, this type of action, (or perhaps better-put inaction), is brought about by trepidation and/or the fear of the NEXT.

Now, this is not everybody. Some people are extremely forward and push and push and push and push at all level of life. They see something or someone they want and they go after it. But, this is not the average person. Most of us are not like that and are cautious in the steps we take, the people we contact, and the actions we make in order to move forward on any new set of presented opportunities. That's not bad or good, that is simply life…

But, this is where we each have to study and analyze Life-Opportunities when they are presented to us. We have to think about where we are, in comparison to where we want to be. If where we are is not perfect and we wish to be somewhere else on either the physical or emotional platform of life, then we need to take the steps to get to that desired end-goal when opportunities present themselves.

If you get a phone number, make the phone call. If the person doesn't answer, leave a message. If you are invited to an event, go to that event – see if it offers you what you want. If you are invited to a one-on-one or a one-on-one-thousand meeting, go to that a meeting. If you don't like it, you can always leave. But, if you do not step up to these opportunities then you will never know what the next step in you life could have been. From this, you will always wonder, *"What if…"*

Now, I am not saying if you want someone or something, be a stalker. There is too much of that nonsense going on in this world and nobodies needs to add to that level of weirdness. What I am saying is that, I can tell you from personal experience, each new step – each new evolution of life comes with a bit of unsureness. But, if you don't take the step forward to explore what that opportunity could mean, you will never know and, thus, your life may never progress in the direction you had hoped.

Take the chance, even if you are a bit nervous about taking it. Find out what life has to offer.

**The Neighbor's Wife**

03/Mar/2014 03:24 PM

As anyone who knows me knows... I love music on vinyl. Well, the fact of the matter is, I love music however it arrives. But... There is just something very special about music on vinyl. Not only in its sound but also in its presentation.

When I have time I scour the flea markets, swap meets, and thrift stores for various pieces of cultural memorabilia. That includes vinyl. Vinyl I never owned, vinyl I already own, and vinyl I once owned and gave or threw away. That was the case with one of the LPs I found today: *Shakti* with John McLaughlin. It was really a very revolutionary piece of orchestration in its time and it is still a great listen.

The copy I found had a bit of expected age to the cover and the inner sleeve. But, the vinyl was virtually unplayed. I guess it was a little too esoteric for the original owner. That's good for me!!!

When I got home, I, of course, put it on. Great-great music.

It made me think back to a time, many-many years ago, when it was first released. I was living in a small apartment near the college I was attending. Having returned from India, after having spent the better part of my teenage years deeply involved with eastern mysticism, I was still deeply engulfed in the mindset and wearing pseudo yogi clothing – meaning, hip/modern yogi clothing, circa the 1970s. My friends in the building called me, *"Swami,"* (due to the fact that I had been initiated in *sanyass)*. And, as such, I still held onto the title, though I virtually never used my Sanskrit name, except in a few close circles of friends.

...And, I was, of course, an active musician.

I remember one of my downstairs neighbors... He too was a musician. He was laying carpet during the day and dreaming of playing music at night. One evening I was over at his apartment, when his wife invited herself up to my apartment to play the *Wurlitzer* electric piano I owned. It was a pretty rare commodity back then – pretty rare among us rock n' roll types. In any case, I happily obliged. Upstairs, in my apartment, it soon became very clear that she want more than simply to play my piano, she wanted to, (dare I say), play with me. Now, you have to keep in mind that that this was a different time in history. A time when love was free. Or, at least, freer. So, I put on the *Shakti* LP and we did what we did. Though I do admit, the worry of her husband coming to see what she was up to did partially haunt the experience.

    The moral of this story is, a particular piece of music oftentimes steps beyond its boundaries of sound and comes to define a moment in our lives. Once that has happened, no matter what else is going on, when we hear that music, we are brought back to that time and to that space. Thus, music is, no doubt, one of the most definitive elements of this modern life. In a way that is sad, because once a particular piece of music is etched so deeply into our brain in association with a particular experience, then it is never truly free, to be free, again.

# Shut the Fuck Up!

03/Mar/2014 03:11 PM

There are some people who, for whatever reason, just love to hear themselves talk. They talk and talk and talk, pretending to know some deep rooted truth about life but their lack of true understand is so self-evident that you just want to scream, *"Shut the fuck up!"*

If you don't like a book you are reading, you can close the cover, and throw it away. If you don't like a website you are on, you can click the mouse and move onto another site. If you don't like what is being said on the radio or TV, you can change the channel. But, if you are around someone who is talking, and you hate what they are saying, what are you supposed to do? It's a free country, right?

I mean, you can tell them to, *"Shut up,"* and if they don't, you can kick their ass. But, then that gets all legal. And, that is never to anyone's best interest.

No doubt, we have all encountered life situations when we are stuck somewhere and are forced to listen to some rude, unconscious individual who talks and talks, trying to make themselves seem all-knowing, trying to publicize themselves or their accomplishments, trying to impress others, or whatever... But, no matter their cause or motivation, they just will not shut up.

Sometimes we are in a space where we can get up and move away. That's the best way to remedy one of these situations. But, this is not always possible.

I remembering having lunch with a friend one day on an outdoor patio at a restaurant on the *Santa Monica Promenade* and one of the street musicians located himself right in front of us and began to play horrible music. Plus, he played it very loudly. The friend I was with asked the restaurant staff if they could do something about the musician. But, as it was a public place they could not. So, we were forced to listen to this man's playing throughout lunch. We finished and then we were gone. But, our lunch had been ruined by the hands of the musician who felt he had something worth contributing to the ethos.

In another space of my life I have been forced into a worse situation than the one previously described. A neighbor of mine is some sort of *New Age Guru* and like some *bad-karma* from some past life, I have been forced to listen to him telling people in person, over the phone, and via what I guess are webinars, how people should live their lives. He does this over and over and over again. And, he does it loudly, which is why I am forced to listen to him. I mean, it is really unbearable. One would think that a truly conscious person, a true teacher of spirituality, would keep their teachings refined and pass their knowledge along quietly. But no, this individual wants to spread his words out the window onto the neighboring neighbors who do not desire to hear any of it. All this, while he frequently screams the mantra, *"Fuck me,"* over and over and over again, whenever he is upset. So, he is obviously a truly spiritual person, I facetiously say... Yet, his disciples never hear this side of his personality. But we, his neighbors do.

The reason I tell this story is this is the perfect example of why no one should claim to be spiritual – no one should claim to have knowledge – no one should claim to be a teacher – no one should attempt to impart whatever it is they feel they have to give the world: be it music, words, or enlightenment, unless all participants; all those within hear-shot, have asked for it. Because those who don't want to hear it, don't want to hear it!

I mean come-on, just the other day, here in L.A., the Catholic Church has again had to pay out millions of dollars due to a priest molesting several young children. A priest... One who is supposed to be holy. One who has been schooled and deemed worthy to speak about and teach what the Church calls, *"Truth,"* to the masses. Holy, while ruining a child's life forever. ...There is never any getting better after encountering that type of situation in a young child's life.

And, the Church pays out money... But, where did that money come from? It came from the collection plates – money given to the Church by the believers. Believers in what? Priests who molest children? I am sure that is not what they intended that their donation to be used for.

Yet, as has been proven time-and-time again in this modern era, the priest skipped town, (in this case the country), and has continued to talk while doing who knows what else to unsuspecting innocent children.

This is the perfect example of why all the talkers should just shut up. If an educated person, who is held in reverence, cannot be trusted to speak the truth and live a holy life, why should anyone else have the right to spread their nonsense to the unwilling masses?

All of this comes back to the point of who and what we are. If we are true to ourselves, we never attempt to tell anyone how he or she should live. We never attempt to impress anyone with our knowledge. We also do not force our way into the existence of others. We never broadcast ourselves to the ears of people who do not want to hear us – because all that does is create negative *karma,* (like the previously two described situations). For that style of life behavior not only disturbs but, in some cases, ruins the lives and life-time of others.

Silence, is the ultimate contribution.

Not knowing, is true knowledge.

Being without BEING, is the ultimate understanding.

**Ray Manzarek**

03/Mar/2014 03:10 PM

I was in *Amoeba Music* yesterday and I came upon a copy of the *Butts Band* LP. *The Butts Band* was an offshoot of the *The Doors,* featuring Robbie Krieger and John Densmore. I purchased a copy of this album when it was released in '73 but I don't even know what happened to it. I must have given it away or something??? But, I did pick up the copy I saw yesterday. It was good to hear that music again after all these years.

Purchasing that record sent me to thinking about Ray Manzarek who sadly passed away recently.

*The Doors* were obviously one of the seminal bands hailing from the 1960s and were a true influence on my life. The lyrics and poetry of Jim Morrison obviously guided me as a young poet and their music was a theme for much of my adolescence.

Growing up in and around Hollywood, California I did have a certain connection to Ray Manzarek and *The Doors.* I remember when *The Doors* had gotten rid of all their amplifiers in the early 1970s and *Guitar Center* (at its original location across the street from where it is today), had them all for sale. It was quite a site for someone like me to see all of these Acoustic Amplifiers with, *"The Doors, Hollywood, California,"* spray painted on them.

Though I was already a musician, (which is why I was at *Guitar Center)*, I was still pretty young and didn't have much money or I am sure I would have purchased at least one of them. When I did generate enough cash, a year or so later in my life, due to *The Doors* use of *Acoustic Amplification,* the first high-powered amplifier I did purchase was made by *Acoustic.*

On the more subliminal levels, my *Hollywood High School* friends and I used walk past Ray's house on our way to *Bronson Canyon* where we would hike, get high, and sometimes even catch poison oak.

The first time I ever faked my ID was to see Ray Manzarek at *The Starwood,* (which was one of the premier and most cutting-edge nightclubs in L.A. at the time).

Through Ray's album, *"The Whole Thing Started With Rock & Roll Now It's Out of Control,"* I was introduced to Patti Smith whose poetry and music also came to be an important influence to my early life.

I was lucky enough to meet and interact with Ray a few times. One of the most ironic, I believe, was on the day the Oliver Stone film, *"The Doors,"* was released. I was at the second showing of the film at a theatre in Westwood. I was standing in line when Ray walks past. As the story goes, he and Stone didn't agree upon the direction of the film, so he was cut out as a consultant.

There he was, Ray Manzarek with his wife, paying and standing in line to see a movie that was largely about him. *"Hey Ray, what're you doing?" "Just coming to see the movie, Scott."*

I always believed that was very strange and sad. The other sad thing was, most of the people standing in line or in the theatre didn't even know who he was!

After the film I spoke with him. *"A lot of those things didn't happen,"* he said. *"And a lot of other things in the film didn't happen that way..."*

So is the life of being famous... And, so is the reality of cinema...

As someone who has had a biopic made about them I can kind of understand. A group of young filmmakers at a Midwestern university made a *Zen Filmmaking* multi-part feature about me back in 2007. Though it is an obviously very slanted view about myself and my filmmaking style, I think it's very funny. You can get to it by searching *Zen Filmmaking* on *Youtube.* But, that's me... I'm not Ray Manzarek. And, Oliver Stone didn't make a multi-million dollar film about me. At least not yet, anyway. :-)

In any case, Ray was always a cutting edge musician who shaped the musical minds from the 1960s forward. His energy, his insight, and his talent will be missed.

# Better Than I Will Ever Be

03/Mar/2014 03:09 PM

In each of our lives we all hope to become somebody/something. We have a vision for where we will end up. We know someday (soon) we will be there. Then comes life. Then comes the bills we have to pay. Then comes age. And, we all pay the price. Few of us ever end up where we hoped we would be.

Though there is a certain commonality based upon the time we live in, for each of us what we hope to become is different. We all have our own individualized desire for where we will end up. Most of us, (myself included), never make it to living the life of our dreams.

I had the opportunity to watch the documentary made about the Detroit based musician Rodriguez, *"Searching for Sugar Man,"* last night. In brief, his story is, he recorded a couple of albums in the very early 1970s. They didn't do very well in the States but somehow they made their way to South Africa, where everyone listened. In fact, his music became an anthem for the overthrow of *Apartheid*. But Rodriguez never knew this. He lived his life as a working-poor home demolition worker in Detroit. He helped to change the world for the better and he didn't even know it.

I had heard about the documentary and the man for the past year on so. ...On the news and so on. But, to watch it, to listen to his music – the music he created was, and still is, simply awesome. More than I could ever hope to create.

For me, I always joking state that when I was young I hoped that I would grow up to be Neil Young. And, that joking statement is, in fact, pretty much the truth. I hoped to be a singer, songwriter, and guitar player of his caliber. Then came the spirituality. It overtook me. And, still does. So, I studied with the gurus, went to India – did all that... Prior to actually arriving, however, I thought I would go to India and live there forever – live the life of a *sadhu*. But, I went, I saw through the illusion, and I came back. Then, what was I suppose to do??? As the sourcepoint of eastern spirituality had never left me, what could I do but do what I do? Speak of it as I understood it. But, people like Alan Watts and Ram Dass beat me to the punch. I was left adrift.

And, this is the reality of life. Even as was, (and is), the case of the great musician Sixto Rodriguez, we try to create our reality based upon our talents, our desires, our dreams, and what we have available to us. But, few of us ever get to live it as we have dreamed it.

We each have our faults. These faults, (and I use the term, *"Fault,"* for lack of better word), come to define us and, in many cases, they halt us from actualizing our dreams.

Our faults are who we are, how we envision reality, where and with whom we find ourselves in life, and what *karma* we have created based upon what we have done to others motivated by our individualizes desires.

For me, it is the abstract. I see the world in an abstract reality that most people cannot accept. It is kind of like the atonal music that is created by East Indian musicians like Ravi Shankar. To them, that atonal, varied rhythmic structure is an accepted reality. But, move that away from a sitar based composition and most people will not accept or even understand that type of musical structure. But, me, that's my life…

For you, more than likely, it is something completely different. That being said, there is a set of life-realities that you have been dealt and then there are those that you choose that will probably keep you from fulfilling all of your dreams. That's just life…

For Sixto Rodriguez, though he was finally tracked down by a couple of ingenious journalists in 1998, he still lives in the same house he lived in for forty years. And, though he did get to live his dream of being a rock star, especially on his first visit to South Africa, he found it necessary to continue working as a demolition worker and playing gigs in small clubs when he could. With the release of the documentary, hopefully things will change for this great talent. But, he is seventy-one years old now. Much of his life is gone.

The thing is… When you are young you believe that there is always tomorrow. …That you will have another day and a second chance. Though this is an accepted system of belief, it is not reality.

Personally, it was a thought process that I never fell prey to. Maybe my mindset came from seeing so much death early in my life. But, for whatever reason, I always knew that tomorrow was never a promise, so I worked and worked and worked for today.

Each day passes and we get older. Each day passes and we become farther removed from living our dreams. It is for this reason that we must strive to do the best we can with the life cards that we are dealt.

All this being said, there are so many people who are more than I (or you) will ever be. Like Sixto Rodriguez. I could never be the singer/songwriter that he is. And, this is the barometer for all of our lives. We can dream. We can work towards our goals. But, no matter how good we get, there will always be those people who embody the essences of perfection that remind us that we will never be what we truly hope to achieve. But, at least they are out there. Those perfect vehicles for the perfect embodiment of art, science, spirituality, and reality.

# Friendemy

03/Mar/2014 03:09 PM

The term, *"Friendemy,"* has come into use in modern consciousness. Basically what it means is that it is a person you love to hate or someone you associate with but do not really like. In life, this type of relationship is very common. There are people you may go to school or work with and though you must be in their company you wish that it were different.

The *Friendemy* ideology goes much deeper than this, however. It travels to a much more subtle level.

Think about this, how many people have you once liked but now you despise? You associated with them, wasted all kinds of time with them, and they turned out to be someone you really hate. Maybe this was due to the fact that they were a backstabber, maybe they lied to you, cheated you, or perhaps they did something that really messed with the evolution of your life. And, as such, you lost a lot of Life-Time due to your interaction with that person.

Personally, I have known so many people who were all-about hanging out with a specific individual that they did not observe the signs. The signs being, studying the way other people think about a person. Are they disliked by others and why? Or, listening to their discourses as they talk about past-relationship and how they ended badly. If they speak of fallen friends of the past that fell away for ridiculous reasons, you can pretty much expect you will be next. You can pretty much anticipate that person is going to mess with your life.

It has happened to me too...

This is the thing about life; people are who people are. Whatever has brought them to this current space. Whatever has brought them to interact with you is caused by whatever it is. There's a million desire based causation factors. But, once you start the interaction it will be you who decides whether to continue the relationship or not. The problem is, and the question must be, what is going to be the cost to your life for interacting with a specific person?

Some people believe in people. I am one of those. Some people believe that people are essentially good. I am one of those too. Some people believe that if you interact with a person on a nice/conscious level, they will not do anything to harm you. That's me, as well. But, sadly, there have been times and there have been people who have taken advantage of my hope for humanity and really messed with my life. Many of you out there may have had a similar experience.

People want to be with you. That is simply a human condition; people want interaction. Once they are with you, they want to absorb what you have to give. They may even want to influence you. This may be on a small or very expansive level. But, the reality is, at the end of the day, there are many people out there who gain pleasure by messing with people's life. The sad part of this reality equitation is that they may not even consciously think or care about what they are doing. They are simply doing what they are doing based upon a very unconscious, animalistic level of human consciousness. None-the-less, the outcome is the same, your Life-Time has been spent and the next step in your evolution may have been damaged.

*Friendemy...* As a person who attempts to see the good in all people – not being trusting is a hard pill for me to swallow. It may be for you, as well. But, people have their own agendas, you really must be careful whom you talk to, communicate with, and allow into your life. Because the damage they may leave behind may be massive.

# Stirring the Pot

03/Mar/2014 03:09 PM

There are some people who like to create controversy and disharmony. I believe that we have all met people like this. The say things and do things that are either distorted or not true simply to get people to believe things about life-situations or other people in order to cause them to become angry at that situation or that person. Some call this practice backstabbing but it is actually much deeper than this.

The reason that people commonly behave in this matter is that they hold a low sense of self-worth. Where this comes from can be anybody's guess. But, early in life they have discovered that they can gain a false sense of control over others by guiding them with misinformation and/or lies. The result of this type of behavior causes all kinds of interpersonal disharmonies that can lead to confrontations, arguments, fights, and on a larger scale, wars.

The problem with people who behave in this manner is that the people they are telling their stories to commonly are not aware that they are being lied to and strung along in order for the person to gain a sense of control and self-worth. In other words, people believe the lies.

I believe that most of us want to trust people and believe the things that we are told are true and valid. It is human nature to believe that others are the same as us – speaking the facts, as we know them. It is only after encountering people of the aforementioned type that we then begin to become less trusting and are forced to begin to critically analyze the words of others before we move forward with what we have heard.

From a person perspective, my friend and *Zen Filmmaking* associate, Donald G. Jackson, was notorious for this type of behavior. He would tell people all kinds of things about other people, simply to get a rise out of them. He would, in fact, totally break apart film production teams simply to satisfy his need to gain misguided control. There was several times when I was associated with him that people I considered friends would either shun me or accost me due to false words that Jackson had spoken. It was very strange.

For me, I saw through this character flaw early on and, as such, took his words with a grain of salt. I heard them but I did not allow them to influence me as to my judgment of a person's actual personality. Sadly, other people were not so astute and, as such, he caused our relationships to fall apart.

The causation factor for this type of behavior is rooted in a person's desire for power, dominance, and control. You can commonly see this type of behavior in the workplace when something has gone awry and higher management challenges middle management as to their actual management skills. From this challenge, the person in middle management begins to take out their lack of control on their underlings. They shift the blame, they blame others, they may even make up lies about their coworkers in order to shift responsibility, but the outcome of this style of human interaction is all the same – they have created disharmony due to the fact that they are not whole, confident, responsible for their actions, and complete onto themselves. Thus, they create havoc in order to shift the focus from their own inabilities to manage towards someone else. This type of behavior is commonly titled, *"Saving their own ass."*

Ultimately, (and perhaps sadly), we are all going to be forced to interact with this type of person as we pass through life. There is no way around it. In fact, in the workplace environment, this type of person may actually have a certain amount of control over us. But... We do not have to let this type of person control who we are, how we feel about ourselves, and how we make our life decisions about others.

We must each listen to all that we hear and then make our own choices about the truth and/or validity about what is spoken to us. Then, we must move forward, without judging, and make our own decision about people and this life-place free from the domination and control imparted by the words spoken by others.

Life is full of many people who embrace low human consciousness. In fact, we are more likely to encounter that type of person than one who actually embraces refined higher consciousness. This is life and that's the dilemma. But, by being whole and true onto ourselves, we can exist in a space of peace, knowing that we embrace the truth and are not dominated by the psychological inadequacies of others.

    Be silent. Don't try to control or alter the consciousness and understandings of others. Don't desire control or admiration. And, this world becomes such a better place.

# Getting it Right. Getting it Wrong.

03/Mar/2014 03:08 PM

When you create something, it is always curiously interesting to find out how other people view it. When you create something with art as a basis; be it a painting, a piece of literature, a photograph, or a movie, mostly people describe how they feel about it – if they like it or if they do not.

As we all come at art from our own preconceived notions and personal tastes, I always find it curious how other people come to define my work. Sometimes they get it right. They understand what I was doing. Other times they get it totally wrong.

I guess that is the basis of art, at the sourcepoint the creator understands what they are doing and why they are doing it. And, in most cases, the creator likes what they have created. Someone who was not involved in the creation – someone who has no vested interest in the work, may not understand the creative source-process and they may not like it. That's just life. That's just art and the interpretation thereof.

As I have written in various places in the past, and even in an article I wrote, *"Film Reviews: Fact or Fiction,"* as many of my films have been reviewed in magazines, books, and on the Internet over the years, I find it very interesting when the reviewer gets things right and more particularly when a reviewer get things wrong but presents their words as facts.

Now, I'm not speaking about when people hate my films and totally rip them. That's fine with me. If you don't like it, you don't like it. Whatever... I'm speaking more of when someone does not possess all of the facts, but writes as if they do, and presents the overall process incorrectly.

Recently someone sent me a copy of a book where the author mentions a couple of my films and one film made, (at least in part), by my *Zen Filmmaking* friend, Donald G. Jackson (RIP). The book was pretty good. My stuff got discussed in the, *"Honorable (and Dishonorable) Mention,"* chapter. That was fun and amusing. But, the author got a few things wrong. Let me explain...

In one chapter, he discussed Don's film, *Pocket Ninjas.* I believe he got his source information from the Internet, because he states that Don and the executive producer were trying to make *The Roller Blade Seven* for kids. This is not true. This was not at all the basis for that film – though I have seen it detailed as such on the Internet. Don was simply obsessed with roller skates and later roller blades from the 1970s forward. He came up in the era of pretty girls on skates. So, he would integrate that into his films whenever possible. Plus, though he never personally trained, he loved the martial arts. As such, he would also feature the martial arts in his movies wherever possible. Thus, was the basis of *Pocket Ninjas.*

The author also attempts to detail the relationship between the executive producer and Don in the book. Again, I guess he got the information from the Internet because it mirrors what I have seen but it is essentially wrong. The executive producer did not come to Don; Don had our friend Mark Williams (RIP) write a script based on an idea he had. He then took the script to the executive producer.

I had previously worked with the executive producer and he is a very nice guy. Don had also known him for years.

The executive producer was a formalized filmmaker; he had no intention of making a *Zen Film. Pocket Ninjas* was in no way a *Zen Film.* Bad, yes. But, not bad because it was a *Zen Film.*

In the book, the author details Don's removal from the film. But, he gets it wrong. The reason for the relationship collapse and Don being pulled was that the executive producer felt Don was letting production fall behind. Don, on the other hand, blamed the producer, who became the credited director. It was one of those common Hollywood dilemmas. Nothing new here... But, we all still remained friends.

That's the story. I hope the world will finally get it right.

The author also discusses, *The Roller Blade Seven* and *Max Hell Frog Warrior,* explaining that they are two of the best-known *Zen Films.* Maybe...

*Roller Blade Seven* is certainly, without a doubt, the most well known *Zen Film,* as it was released theatrically, on T.V., and by other methods around the world. Actually, Max Hell is somewhat lowered down the list. Here in the U.S. there has been a certain amount of talk about the film. They even mentioned it on the HBO T.V. show, *The Newsroom.* Thanks!

But, the fact is, other *Zen Films* such as: *Samurai Vampire Bikers from Hell, Guns of El Chupacabra, Undercover X, Hitman City, Vampire Blvd., Vampire Noir,* and *Super Hero Central* have all been much more widely distributed. But, that fact would be impossible to know unless someone asked me. ...Which no one did.

The author also makes an attempting at describing *Zen Filmmaking.* Certainly, I realize that is a bit of a complicated matter. :-)

And, the problem is, most people who talk about it, don't really get it. But, this author provides a fairly good overview. Good job!

In his description of *Zen Filmmaking,* however, the author details that in *Zen Filmmaking* shots are often repeated. The fact is, to date, this is only true in the two films he mentions. It is not a common trait of *Zen Filmmaking.* The basis for this technique being used in the two discussed films is, *Roller Blade Seven* was the first *Zen Film.* We set up that film-style in that movie which we created in 1991 and 1992. Don and I did not make another film together until 1996 when we created *Toad Warrior,* which later became *Max Hell Frog Warrior.*

When we reconvened as filmmakers, we decided we wanted to capture some of the essence and energy of *Roller Blade Seven,* which is why I wore basically the same outfit and we again employed that editing style. But, no other *Zen Film* that Don and I made as a team or that I have made employs that editing technique.

This is one of the things that those who watch a *Zen Film* commonly misunderstand – particularly the two films that were detailed in the book; *Zen Filmmaking* is constantly evolving, it is never a stagnant art form. Each film brings with it its own unique sense of creativity and artistic expression. And, the two discussed films are very different from every other *Zen Film* ever made. Ultimately, that is the essence of *Zen Filmmaking, embracing* the moment and allowing the creative environment of each film to guide you down the road to cinematic enlightenment.

But, as was embraced by P.T. Barnum and Andy Warhol, *"You may have gotten a few things wrong but thanks for the publicity Mr. Author."*

# Is Scott Shaw a Nihilist?

03/Mar/2014 03:05 PM

I was cruising down the coast between Santa Barbara and L.A. a couple of weeks ago with this sweet young lady. She was looking at her twitter feed and she noticed that somebody had quoted me.

It is pretty common that people quote my books, *Zen O'clock, About Peace,* and *Nirvana in a Nutshell* on twitter, because they are made up of short spiritual aphorisms.

Anyway, she noticed that somebody had commented on the original tweet, *"That sounds pretty nihilistic."*

She turned and asked me, *"What does nihilistic mean?"*

Her question made me smile due to the fact that she didn't know what nihilism was.

I gave her the basic off-the-cuff definition... *Someone who is nihilistic believes that life has no absolute meaning and that religions and philosophies hold no absolute truth.*

*"Are you nihilistic,"* she asked. Again, I smiled.

Do I believe that life holds an absolute meaning? No.

Do I believe that religion possesses an absolute truth? No.

Do I believe in a specific religion or philosophy? No.

Does that make me a nihilist? Maybe... But, I think it is a bit more complicated than that. By nature, I am extremely optimistic. I believe in people. I believe in goodness. I believe that people will make the right choices and do the right things – even though I have been proven wrong time and time again. But, I still believe!

So, is Scott Shaw a nihilist? Maybe. But, as a nihilist that would mean that I also don't believe in absolute definitions. So, the whole question possesses no merit.

Ultimately, if Scott Shaw is a nihilist, he is an optimistic one. :-)

# The Scott Shaw Blog 3.5

03/Mar/2014 03:00 PM

I have been writing a blog on and off for a few years now. For me, blogging has been both a blessing and a curse. A blessing because writing is one of the most essential elements of my life and a blog is a great way to get my thoughts and ideas out there as I refine them for future writings. A curse for a couple of reasons... One, is that it takes time to write these little ditties. And, as you can imagine, I am a pretty busy person with a lot of stuff going on. So, writing this, takes away from doing that. And, sometimes, writing this, becomes an excuse for not doing that.

*The Second Curse,* (wow, that's a good title for something), is that I have encountered a few negative experiences due to blogging. Now, I have talked about this at length in the couple of books that have been published based on my blogging, *Scribble on the Restroom Wall* and *The Chronicles; Zen Ramblings from the Internet,* so I won't discuss that here. But, let's just say, there are some weird people out there, who, for whatever reason, want to focus on the writings of someone else, instead of living their own life. And, this has lead to some life-weirdness both online and off.

But... All this being said, there are a lot of people out there who contact me whenever I stop blogging and ask me to recommence. I'm glad they enjoy the read!!!

So, here we go again. *The Scott Shaw Blog* recommences.

To begin with, I'm going to put up a few of the recent pieces I've written as a primer and I will, of course, continue to put new stuff up as it becomes available. Plus, there is all kinds of my other writings out there in the bookstore(s) or on the internet, if you really want to read other Scott Shaw stuff.

Also, please... If I don't blog for awhile, please don't think anything bad has happened to me; I'm probably just making a movie, working on an album, writing a book, or just living life.

And, as stated in the *Scott Shaw Blogs* of the past, all of my blogging is spur of the moment and off the cuff, so you may see some typos and stuff. But please, don't contact me about this. As long as the information is out there, I really don't care if there are misspellings and punctuation errors.

Okay, that's about it. *The Scott Shaw Blog* has recommenced.

Be happy. And, as always, Be Positive !!!

www.ingramcontent.com/pod-product-compliance
Lightning Source LLC
Chambersburg PA
CBHW081829170426
43199CB00017B/2685